THE WEST LESS TRAVELED

West

THE WEST LESS TRAVELED

The Best and Lesser Known Parks, Monuments, and Natural Areas

JAN BANNAN

Fulcrum Publishing
Golden, Colorado

Maps included in this book are for general reference only. For more de-tailed maps and additional information, contact the agencies or specific sites.

Library of Congress Cataloging-in-Publication Data

Bannan, Jan Gumprecht.
    The West less traveled : the best and lesser known parks,
monuments and natural areas / Jan Bannan.
            p.   cm.
    Includes bibliographical references and index.
    ISBN 1-55591-261-3 (paperback)
    1. West (U.S.)—Guidebooks. 2. Parks—West (U.S.)—Guidebooks.
3. Monuments—West (U.S.)—Guidebooks. 4. Natural areas—West
(U.S.)—Guidebooks. I. Title.
F590.3.B36   1996
917.804'33—dc20   96-26374
                                                     CIP

Printed in the United States of America
0 9 8 7 6 5 4 3 2 1

Fulcrum Publishing
350 Indiana Street, Suite 350
Golden, Colorado 80401-5093
(800) 992-2908 • (303) 277-1623

CONTENTS

West

ACKNOWLEDGMENTS

One of the joys of being a travel writer is contacts with so many helpful people. Park rangers gave gladly of their time and knowledge in helping me research this project, and I thank them all. Some took time from their busy work schedules to accompany me to discoveries, others sent valuable information to me, and a vast number manned visitor centers and answered my many questions.

In particular, I thank Adele Todd for reams of information sheets on the Upper Rogue River. Tim Smith, at Coral Pink Sand Dunes State Park, led me into the dunes to show me a threatened species of milkweed and filled me in on the seasonal aspects of these dunes. Libby Landreth answered my request for more details about Great Sand Dunes National Monument. At Oklahoma's Great Salt Plains, Gordon McDowell showed me how to have fun digging for selenite crystals. Bill Hanschumaker, educator at the public wing of the Hatfield Marine Science Center, filled me in on what the renovated public wing would offer visitors. Steve Gobat helped me with details concerning the newly created tidepools at Yaquina Head. Sherry Beagley was responsible for my fascinating tour of Alabaster Caverns State Park. Thanks to all these people, and the unnamed others.

Many of my research trips were camping trips using my small pickup truck and pretty much "roughing it," so it was quite a treat to use a new pickup camper that Jayco, Inc. loaned me from their press fleet. My sincere thanks go to a colleague from Outdoor Writers Association of America, Inc., Thayne Smith, for setting this up for me. It was great to have room to work on the project away from the often windy weather.

Special thanks go to Oklahoma Tourism and Recreation Department for introducing me to some enchanting places in Oklahoma. Jolie Lipson and

Sandy Pantlik were super escorts for a tour through the Cherokee Strip area, which included the Great Salt Plains and Alabaster Cave.

Camping on my research trips also provided an excellent opportunity to meet people and share their insights into these landscapes. It was Rod and Suzanne at the Rio Grande Village Store in Big Bend National Park who introduced me to my float guide for Mariscal Canyon. A fellow camper named Bill introduced me to the trail to the hot springs along the Rio Grande in Big Bend, and who taught me new facts for my stargazing. Thanks to all of the friendly people along the way.

But the publication of this book was possible because senior editor Carmel A. Huestis at Fulcrum Publishing believed my project was worthwhile. My greatest thanks go to her, but also to another editor, Sara Hanson, who expertly managed my book through the production process. Thanks also to marketing manager, Donna Hamilton, and to all the staff at Fulcrum for their valued assistance.

INTRODUCTION

West

After spending the first half of my estimated lifetime in the Midwest and the East, I moved west to more easily see what living and travel experiences it had to offer. And it has been wonderful. The many memories etched into my neurocircuitry include the mountain bluebird in the midst of the steaming Porcelain Basin in Yellowstone, the bison sitting in a hot spring, the serendipity of finding pristine white sand dunes when looking for gray whales, the cougar met on a forest trail, and the cave in Valley of Fire State Park where I felt a kinship with Basketmaker people from another time. It is so often the unexpected that thrills the soul in the outdoors.

Now, after almost twenty years of extensive exploring as an outdoor writer, I am intensely aware of how the diversity and magnificence of western landscapes make them national treasures. Their scenic beauty, along with their natural ecosystems, have great importance in our lives.

We are a pyramidal component of a tangled interconnecting web of life-forms that is so complex we sometimes forget that this foundation supports us, as well as populating this planet with exciting variety. For many people, the outdoors offers an emotional support system that reminds us of our natural roots. For those like me, it is essential to explore and, while doing so, enjoy the beauty and educational stimulation that these varied environs and ecosystems provide. It so happens that landscapes and their life-forms are valuable to humans both for individual and community reasons.

Many travelers are responding to the recent buzzword—"ecotourism"—by taking tours to see tropical rain forests and other possibly endangered foreign landscapes. The argument is that this "clean" industry puts money into local economies, jobs are created, and conservation efforts are encouraged. Yet, citizens of the United States have their own temperate rain forests and landscapes that cry out for preservation against future development. For example, monies from river rafting go toward keeping wild rivers flowing without the construction of new dams.

It is easy to embark on your own ecotourism tour to see unique western landscapes in the United States. Besides being a dazzling and fun nature experience, the acquired firsthand knowledge and intimacy with the land might induce the traveler to participate in decision making that could preserve these wondrous landscapes for future generations. Think of the years 2001, 2010, and onward, in terms of what the West will look like in those years, rather than in terms of space travel.

The natural history of landscapes is something one should discover on one's own, to actually be part of it. Television nature shows certainly impart a great deal of information with wonderful photography, but they give us a produced, distorted view of the world—a string of highlights clipped and run together. They cannot compete with what one finds along a quiet walk when something unexpected happens, such as the hollow breathing of offshore whales, or a brown pelican's dive that results in a fish, or a saguaro cactus blooming in the desert, ... and you're there. The resulting emotion is self-discovered, not scooped out onto the plate of your mind already processed by someone else. Life should bear the stamp of the individual response.

Consider that 90 percent of federally managed lands in the contiguous United States are located in the West. It is no wonder that this area is the major beneficiary of our outdoor love affair. The U.S. Travel Data Center reported, in 1991, that hiking was the most popular vacation activity, with camping rated second. The Department of the Interior reports that 108 million adults in the United States participated in recreation related to fish and wildlife in 1991, with $59 billion spent. Ecotours will not only satisfy these preferences, they will invoke all your senses.

Choosing from some of the most dramatic western landscapes, I invite you to use this book as a complete guide in planning your own trip without causing ecological damage. Information is given on geology, plants, wildlife, facilities, access, special sites, and recreational choices—including hiking, backpacking, canoeing, horseback riding, bicycling, and river running—for these destinations. Maps and photos of these landscapes are also included. General ecological and safety concerns are mentioned in this introduction, with other more specific suggestions in individual write-ups. Most of these eco-jaunts will be to less-traveled areas rather than to crowded national parks, though mention will be made of a few particularly significant landscapes found within such parks.

Pack this book and head for your first unique western landscape where the primary resource is wildness. Enjoy!

Earth-Friendly Guidelines

Destination Choices

When to Visit

Since some three million people already visit such parks as Yosemite and Yellowstone annually, try to plan your trips to popular destinations during weekdays and preferably in the off-season. Spring and autumn visits are quite lovely, less crowded, and more enjoyable.

Where to Visit

Consider trips to the less well-known landscapes, many of which are not only free but offer a quality experience. After your first visits to the featured landscapes—and each of you will have your own favorites—drive the back roads and make your own discoveries. For example, try one of the many backcountry byways off Utah Scenic Byway 12 to see unique red rock landscapes. Or study Wendell Wood's book (see Bibliography) to scout out seldom-visited ancient forests.

How to Visit

Imagine a better system for much-visited parks in which private vehicles do not inundate the landscapes and fill the parking lots to capacity. On a recent visit to Jenny Lake in the Grand Tetons, I couldn't find a parking space and left quite frustrated, though I do have good memories of the place. Instead of continually financing more road construction, why not develop a transportation system—using monorails, trains, shuttles, or other creative ideas—to move people through the more popular parks, with frequent exit stops? A little of that has been initiated already in a couple of parks, but more is needed. Until that happens, consider doubling up in private cars, and using what public transportation is available for getting there.

If you use a tour, check out how they operate, whether they have earth-friendly guidelines, and if they support conservation efforts. Does your credit card company contribute to conservation groups?

Do not rush through one park and head immediately for another; plan to stay awhile and leave the next park for another year. (This also helps conserve oil resources.) While you are there, use foot, horse, or bicycle power to get around whenever possible. On trails, the smaller the group, the less the disturbance to both the environment and the wildlife.

The Ecotraveler

Leave No Trace

One would think that by now we'd all know not to litter, but the truth is that some people are still doing it—even cigarettes in a dry forest—in these wonderful landscapes. *Please don't litter, and pick up any you find.* And remember to recycle; every three months, we throw away enough reusable material to rebuild our commercial air fleet.

When hiking, fit your shoes to the terrain, using lug soles only when necessary. Walk single file in the center of the trail and do not shortcut or cut new trails so as to minimize erosion and damage to the natural habitat. Stay on the trail in fragile terrains and avoid muddy trails, if possible, to reduce erosion damage. Riparian areas are sensitive; do not trample banks where beaver, otter, and mink live.

Mountain bikers should not skid or ride on rain-soaked ground; stick to established trails, and do not speed. Never drive or mountain bike cross-country.

Choose a picnic spot along a hike where you will not disturb the vegetation. Leave no food remains, including banana or orange skins, do not even bury them. Use air-lock plastic bags to carry in food and pack out what's left. Carry out all you carry in—including fishing line, hooks, and lures.

Respect all natural features and do not collect, trample, or deface them. Flowers can be photographed and trees can be touched, even hugged, but leave no graffiti on trees or rocks, nor blackened rocks or burnt logs from your fires. Never leave a campfire unattended.

Know all the rules for visiting wilderness areas. Be sure you have a permit if required. Camp only in established or previously used sites. Check for specific regulations concerning campfires, camping, and sanitary disposal. Do not contaminate the ecosystem with soap or, if you must, use only environmentally friendly products. Carry clean-burning stoves rather than collecting wood or boughs for a fire. The only wheeled devices allowed in wilderness areas are wheelchairs—no bicycles. Maximum group size is limited to 12 people and 12 head of stock.

If you travel using horses, train them before you go into fragile environments. Carry only "processed" feeds packaged in nose bags to stock to prevent seeding the landscape and overgrazing.

River runners and canyon trekkers must never bury human waste; pack it out. Boaters must use a river runner's toilet. The thin strip of canyon habitat is easily impacted.

Must I mention fireworks? Certainly, these are always incompatible with the outdoor experience.

"Leave nothing but footsteps" cannot be said too often it seems, and these should not be tearing jogging injuries upon the Earth. If you jog, do so in developed areas. For more details on the Leave No Trace program, contact the National Outdoor Leadership School (see Appendix).

Exploring Manners

Hikers, bikers, horseback riders, and any nonmotorized trail users should show courtesy when meeting other trail travelers. Yield to equestrians.

Mountain bikers, in particular, can wreak havoc with both hikers and horse-back riders, as can pets. Unless they are well trained and well controlled, it is best to leave pets at home.

Courtesy should extend to eliminating radios both on the trail or else-where in scenic environments. I cannot count the number of times my camp-ground experiences have been marred by loud, blaring music that interfered with the solitude and quiet that I had sought. Respect the enjoyment of others.

Do not trespass or camp on private property without permission.

Wildlife Encounters

It is not a good idea to wear perfumes, and your clothing should be of muted colors to avoid alerting wildlife to your presence, although I do like my photography models to wear something red as they hike the trail.

Learn more about the lives of the indigenous animals for the best view-ing; read up on their behavior and go to natural history museums. Usually the best wildlife viewing times are early morning or late afternoon; birding is best during spring and fall migrations.

In some parks, wildlife is more acclimated to humans, yet their lives are disturbed by approaching them too closely, so do keep your distance, espe-cially from nests and dens. A raised head and pointed ears, skittish move-ment, or alarm calls mean you are causing distress. Never feed, chase, or try to capture animals or even pet that friendly deer; it causes them to lose their ability to live wild and safe. Where will you be in the midst of winter when they must rely on their own resources?

If you fish, think of the future and practice catch-and-release techniques. Avoid walking or running boats through gravel bars as these are often spawning areas for fish. If you gather clams, crabs, mussels, mushrooms, or other edibles, be sure it is legal in that area and you collect only the limit.

To some extent, binoculars and spotting scopes have replaced hunting equipment, and the camera is now an excellent technique for identifying plants, birds, and butterflies—good conservation tools.

Wildlife consists of all living animals, not just the charismatic ones, even that scary rattlesnake has its place in the ecosystem. Learn about nontoxic ways to fight insects—citronella and other herbs, for example—or if you use deets, use less than a 30-percent solution for your own sake.

Archaeological and Historic Sites

An increasing number of travelers is a threat to treasures from the past that are so informative and interesting, even if the impact is unintentional, so think before you visit.

Look and photograph rock art but do not chalk or chisel it, repaint it, wet it, make molds, trace it, shoot bullets in it—yes, people have—or even touch it, as the oil on hands attracts dirt and hastens its destruction.

At ruin sites, know about *middens*, old trash piles, and do not walk through them. Stay on the trails and do not climb on roofs or walls. Camp and cook away from these areas.

Rather, learn from these ancient cultures and visit ruins with respect. The Archaeological Resources Act of 1979 imposes stiff penalties concerning the desecration of these treasures, as well as a reward for information leading to a conviction. Contact a ranger, federal land management authorities, or the local sheriff if you discover any illegal activity.

Caves

Before exploring wild caves, contact the National Speleological Society (see Appendix) for guidelines on protecting the cave and on safety for the explorer. Do not remove any rock formations or organisms from caves.

Safety Concerns

Boating and Water Sports

Do not swim alone, during an electrical storm, or dive in shallow water or where there are underwater rocks. Know your limits and ability.

Be knowledgeable about area boating regulations and never operate a boat when under the influence of alcohol or drugs. Boaters and water-skiers should wear Coast Guard–approved personal flotation devices (PFD), and observe safe recreation rules.

With all water sports, an emergency situation requires calm, constructive thinking, not panic. Exhausted swimmers can still float—even with a cramp—and swim if necessary.

Trails and the Backcountry

For a hike of any length or difficulty, be prepared for the unexpected, whether it is a change in weather, getting lost, or whatever. Take along drinking water, map, walking stick, suntan lotion, sweater, insect repellent, compass, sunglasses and/or sun hat, dry matches, compass, pocket knife, flashlight, a snack (add an extra high-energy bar just in case), and mini-first-aid kit (including forceps for tick removal, insect repellents, bandages, and aspirin). Carry these items, with hands free, in a knapsack. I like to include a bag lunch to enjoy in the solitude of some special found place.

Mountain bikers should wear a protective helmet. Be sure your bicycle is in good operating condition, carry a tire pump and patch kit, be a defensive rider, and follow the rules of the road.

Some trails in red rock country use *cairns,* stacks of tiny rocks, to mark trail routes. When you find one, sight the next one and head for it. Do not go too far without finding these route markers. In sandy terrain, footprints are good markers for the return trip, so know the track of your shoe soles.

If you suspect hypothermia from wind, cold, and wet conditions, it is imperative to get the victim dry and warm and have him/her drink warm liquids.

Unless you know the water is potable, do not drink it without first boiling, filtering, or treating with chemicals. The days of trusting that cool mountain stream are gone.

Risks are always a factor in outdoor expeditions, though a little knowledge certainly helps to lessen their probability. Parks with grizzly bears offer good handouts on what to do, and one needs to be alert for rattlesnakes and other poisonous creatures. Some cacti can be pretty painful if you get impaled. Check for ticks after hiking. I've found, however, that more problems arise from drastic weather conditions, steep hazardous cliffs, and accidental falls than from wildlife encounters. Life cannot be lived fully without some calculated risk taking.

I'm not going to tell you to never hike alone. If I abided by that rule, my experiences would be very diminished. Be prepared to accept what happens, the good and the bad, if you do go alone. There are both pluses and minuses to hiking by yourself.

At the Beach

Beachcombing, wave watching, whale watching, and exploring tidepools are wonderful recreation choices and are often so hypnotic that people can forget the possible dangers. The energy of the surf can pick up logs and roll them around like toothpicks; watch out that they do not land on you and that children do not play on them. Keep your eyes on the ocean in case an unusually large wave sweeps ashore. Know the tide schedule so that you are not stranded on an offshore rock or rounding a headland when the tide comes in. Every year, someone falls from an unstable coastal cliff, an unnecessary accident.

When legally harvesting shellfish, check whether a "red tide" warning exists, which can cause Paralytic Shellfish Poisoning (PSP)—a serious and even fatal disease for humans. Domoic acid in shellfish is another serious neurotoxin.

Map of Parks, Monuments, and Natural Areas in the West

LEGEND

1. Lake Louise
2. Manning Provincial Park
3. Olympic National Park
4. Dungeness National Wildlife Refuge
5. Nisqually National Wildlife Refuge
6. Mount Rainier National Park
7. Mount St. Helens National Volcanic Monument
8. National Bison Range
9. Lewis & Clark Caverns State Park
10. Oswald West State Park
11. Devil's Punch Bowl State Park
12. Yaquina Head Outstanding Natural Area
13. Oregon Dunes National Recreation Area
14. South Slough National Estuarine Reserve
15. Humbug Mountain State Park
16. Yaquina Bay Estuary
17. Willamette River Greenway
18. John Day Fossil Beds National Monument
19. Green Lakes
20. Crater Lake National Park
21. Upper Rogue River
22. Lower Klamath and Tule Lake National Wildlife Refuges
23. Snake River Birds of Prey National Conservation Area
24. Craters of the Moon National Monument
25. Yellowstone National Park
26. Grand Tetons National Park
27. Hot Springs State Park
28. Badlands National Park
29. Redwood National Park
30. Westport Union Landing State Beach and MacKerricher State Park
31. Mono Lake Tufa State Reserve
32. Anza–Borrego Desert State Park
33. Baja Sonoran Desert
34. Baja White Dunes
35. Valley of Fire State Park
36. Great Salt Lake Area
37. Mirror Lake State Beach
38. Harpers Corner
39. Snow Canyon State Park
40. Coral Pink Sand Dunes State Park
41. Kodachrome Basin State Park
42. Escalante State Park
43. Calf Creek Recreation Area
44. Dead Horse Point State Park
45. Great Sand Dunes National Monument
46. Alabaster Caverns State Park
47. Great Salt Plains
48. Organ Pipe Cactus National Monument
49. Picacho Peak State Park
50. Saguaro West National Park
51. Canyon de Chelly National Monument
52. Petrified Forest National Park
53. White Sands National Monument
54. Big Bend National Park
55. Tour of Lava Landscapes
56. Lower Rio Grande

Key to Maps of Specific Areas

The following key applies to the maps of the parks, monuments, and natural areas that appear throughout the text.

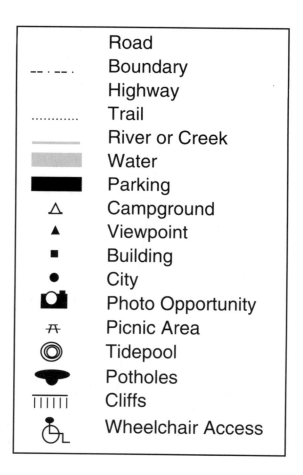

	Road
-- . -- .	Boundary
	Highway
....	Trail
————	River or Creek
▬	Water
▬	Parking
△	Campground
▲	Viewpoint
■	Building
●	City
📷	Photo Opportunity
禾	Picnic Area
◎	Tidepool
⏺	Potholes
ⅢⅢⅢ	Cliffs
♿	Wheelchair Access

1

RIVER CANYONS

West

Rivers of the West have a way of hiding in deep canyons, challenging explorers to join their rugged meandering journeys to feel the pulse of their beating hearts. These rivers uncover stories of the past, daring viewers to interpret the ancient geological happenings of the earth as revealed in the exposed, sometimes convoluted, layers of rock that soar above the water; in the stone sculptures and textures that bespeak a changing parade of weathering artists.

Rivers nourish the edging terrain where egrets, coyotes, and even cougar come for water and food among the green that has sunk its roots in the wetness. Often flowing through arid deserts in the West, these rivers are a coalescing force for communities of wild life-forms.

River runners get close to the interconnections of these waterways and can stop to explore along the way. Other visitors can also find ways to understand the mysteries of river canyons from a different perspective: Throughout the West are views located above a multitude of such canyons that are awesome in their scope. Hiking trails urge some to walk for closer interactions.

The power and energy of these rivers and their sediments have shaped many of today's western landscapes, through eras of violent uplift and subsequent intensified erosion, when water and weathering were constantly at work on the land. Often the question arises: Was the course of the rivers on flatter terrain maintained after uplift, or did the rivers take easier routes during and after the land rose? One theory suggests that a combination of these two possibilities may be the best answer to this geomorphic question.

Pilots of small planes can view these gashes in the earth from the air, following the water's journey amongst rocky landscapes that are difficult to maneuver on foot, and often unreachable by motorized vehicles.

On your explorations, be alert for the unexpected and open to sensory experiences. My trips to river canyons are now a collage of memories that include scampering squirrels, canyon wrens with their cascading song, the taste of wild strawberries, blooming cacti, light shows on colored rocks, and the sound of a flute heard from the depths of the Grand Canyon. May your own memories be as cherished.

Upper Rogue River
OREGON

Rogue River National Forest
Prospect Ranger District
Prospect, OR 97536
(541) 560-3623

Attractions: Hiking trails, geology, photography, nature study, fishing
Hours/Season: Overnight; June through October
Fees: Only for some campgrounds
Picnicking: Woodruff Picnic Area, Union Creek Picnic Area
Camping: From Prospect south to north along the river; forest camps are River Bridge (no fee), Natural Bridge (no fee), Union Creek, Farewell Bend (flush toilets), and Hamaker.
Access: From along OR 62 and OR 230; the Upper Rogue River Trail is accessed from River Bridge Campground, Woodruff Picnic Area, Natural Bridge Campground, Hamaker Campground, and Crater Rim Viewpoint.

Mention the Rogue River Trail in the Pacific Northwest and it usually means the 40-mile hike along the "Wild and Scenic" river section, where many river runners apply for permits to float the exciting rapids of a famed canyon. Less known is the 12.2-mile Lower Rogue River Trail that traverses an old transportation route through riparian coastal forest west from Agness. And few people know that the 45.5-mile Upper Rogue River Trail follows a section of the "river of flowing lava" through a region of water too wild for a rafter, with its log jams and narrow gorges. This is a trail for solitude where extraordinary lava formations can be seen along the waterway. From the headwaters of the river in Crater Lake National Park, the Rogue is 210 miles of downhill magic.

Geology

When the present Cascade Mountains were being up-lifted by fluid basalt lava, the ancestral Rogue River was forced to cut a channel through basalt rocks. From south to north along the trail, watch for these spectacular geological features.

The Takelma Gorge

This unusual narrow, deep channel in basalt follows a series of rapids and a sharp turning arm of molten lava. A meadow of hanging grass and wildflowers reaches from the forest to the brink of the gorge.

Natural Bridge

Much of the river's water is diverted into an underground maze of lava tubes and then violently released where the tubes collapsed. This is best seen in late summer when high water no longer covers the bridge.

The Rogue River Gorge

Like a newly caged lion, water roars through a narrow chute formed by a collapsed lava tube.

Takelma Gorge on the Upper Rogue River Trail.

Winding River Canyon

The Rogue River has cut through once burning pumice created by a Mount Mazama eruption (where Crater Lake exists today), leaving 250-foot vertical cliffs of compacted pumice.

Upper River Chasm

A dramatic view of compacted pumice cliffs.

Plants and Wildlife

Old-growth forest, huge sugar pines, yew, white fir, western white pine, alder, vine maple, cow parsnip, ferns, evergreen huckleberry, mosses, wetland plants, purple asters, twinberries, columbia windflowers, bunchberry, Pacific sedum, wild rose, vanilla leaf, skunk cabbage, Oregon grape, pinemat manzanita, and squaw carpet are a few of the native plant species.

Chipmunks, deer, rainbow and cutthroat trout, butterflies, and a wealth of other forest animals live in the vicinity of the river.

Activities

Anglers should bring their gear to fish in this stocked river; a license is required. A stroll along the river south from the Farewell Bend Campground provides an excellent opportunity for viewing wildflowers and wild strawberries growing in lava rock cracks. Look for potholes made by swirling rocks in the swift-flowing water.

Upper Rogue River Trail

This 45.5-mile trail can be hiked in sections that vary from 2 to 10 miles. Besides the noted geological highlights, the sights, sounds, and scents include quiet pools, plunging waterfalls, river rapids, wildflowers, lush forest, marshes, and wildlife.

Ecotouring and Safety Concerns

If you hike the final 2 miles to the mossy spring headwaters of the Rogue, remember to respect this fragile area. Use extreme caution at Natural Bridge and the Rogue River Gorge. This trail is open to hikers only.

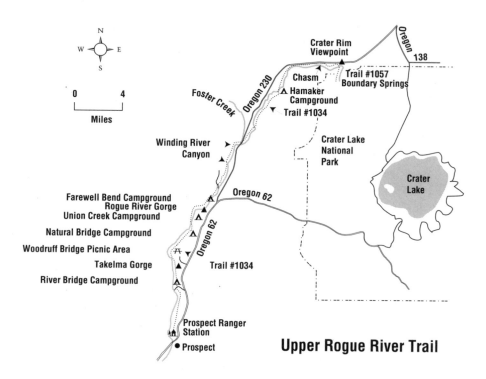

Upper Rogue River Trail

Grand Canyon of the Yellowstone River
WYOMING

Yellowstone National Park
WY 82190
(307) 344-7381

Attractions: Hiking trails, backpacking, nature study, geology, photography, wildlife viewing

Hours/Season: Overnight; except for the road between North Entrance and Cooke City, Montana; most park roads are closed from about November 1 to April 30. Snowmobiles may use unplowed, groomed park roads from mid-December to mid-March.

Fees: Entry fee per vehicle; additional for campground

Visitor Center at Canyon Village: Information, exhibits, and publications; open 9:00 A.M. to 5:00 P.M. through June 5; 8 A.M. to 7 P.M. from June 6 to Labor Day; check locally for autumn hours

Picnicking: Picnic area is located at east end of Chittenden Bridge, but many spots at viewpoints and along trails are good places for a snack.

Camping: Campsites (no hookups) are located at nearby Canyon Village (7,734-foot elevation) and available first-come, first-served with restrooms, showers, and laundry facilities. Firewood is available for sale. Open June 10 through early September, weather permitting.

Access: East entrance to Yellowstone National Park is 53 miles west of Cody, Wyoming, via US 14-16-20. South entrance is 64 miles north of Jackson, Wyoming, via US 89-91-287. West entrance is just east of West Yellowstone, Montana via US 20. North entrance is just south of Gardiner, Montana via US 89. The Grand Canyon of the Yellowstone River is in the north central area of the park.

Not far from its headwaters in the Rocky Mountains, the Yellowstone River (the last major river of the West that is free-flowing) runs through a magnificent gash in a volcanic plateau. Called the Grand Canyon of the Yellowstone River and encompassing two spectacular waterfalls, this landscape was one of the primary reasons for preserving this area as the first national park in the United States.

A painting of this canyon by Thomas Moran, who was with the Hayden survey party in 1871, helped implant the concept that grand landscapes are a powerful motive for conservation. Moran's painting was hung in the lobby of the U.S. Senate. Early photographs of the canyon by William H. Jackson shared this influence for preserving unique places. This national park is also an International Biosphere Reserve and World Heritage Site.

A walk along the rim reveals incredible examples of the canyon's geology and its colors. The river zigzags in deep, narrow gorges and conifers seem to sprout from rocks. The Yellowstone River's name was not based of the yellow colors found on the walls of the canyon. Rather, the Minnetaree Indians named the river after the yellow banks found at the downstream confluence of the river with the Missouri River, with words that French trappers translated as *rocke jaune*, or yellow stone.

Geology

Catastrophic volcanic eruptions occurred in the Yellowstone area 2 million, 1.2 million, and 600,000 years ago. Volcanic debris spewed out during the last of these episodes quickly covered thousands of square miles and caused the roof of the magma chamber to collapse, leaving a smoldering caldera that measured 28 by 47 miles, and several thousand feet deep. This basin, over time, filled with lava.

One of the lava flows, the Canyon Rhyolite flow, came from the east and stopped just west of the present canyon, creating a thermal basin that altered and weakened the rhyolite lava. Today, a sharp eye might spot steam still in the canyon.

Lakes were created by lava flows while glacier floods eroded, carved and deepened the canyon, sweeping it clean of small sediments but leaving large rocks.

The rhyolite lavas have been boiled and baked for millenniums to transform the original brown and gray rhyolite rocks physically and chemically into the soft yellow, pink, fiery rose, and reddish-brown hues of the canyon walls that we see today. Less altered, more resistant rhyolites rocks form the brinks of the waterfalls.

The Yellowstone River eventually flowed out from the north side of the water-filled caldera and cut through the canyon. The canyon is approximately 800 to 1,200 feet deep, 1,500 to 4,000 feet wide, and 20 miles long.

Plants and Wildlife

Among the park's many unique attractions is scattered forest growth that is predominantly lodgepole pine and includes alpine and Douglas fir, Engelmann spruce, and juniper. And, periodically, the mountain wildflowers near Mount Washburn offer splendid color displays. Particularly noteworthy is the "park flower," the fringed gentian, which blooms from June to September. The varied vegetation includes near-desert species near the north entrance.

The incredible spectacle of wildlife is reason enough for visiting Yellowstone National Park. In this protected preserve, the animals move with ease and seem to ignore the people. Bison graze in campgrounds, cross roads with little concern for traffic, and soak in the hot springs. Elk, coyote, mule deer, moose, black bear, pronghorn antelope, and even the frightening grizzly are at home in the park. It is not impossible to spot a wolf, though report such an unexpected sighting to park personnel. Bighorn sheep are at high elevations. Uinta squirrels and yellow-bellied marmots are numerous as are a native species of cutthroat trout and a native whitefish. Bird species include the magnificent trumpeter swan, white pelican, lesser scaup, osprey, and green-winged teal. Waterfowl is often spotted near the Yellowstone River.

Activities

Scenic Drive

A 2.5-mile-loop road near the North Rim leads to a spur road to Inspiration Point where the view extends 1,000 feet into the canyon. At Grandview Point, a distant view of the 308-foot Lower Falls is available. Lookout Point provides a vista of the Lower Falls with a steep trail leading to an even closer viewpoint. A drive along the South Rim leads to Artist Point.

Horseback Riding

Horseback riders can rent mounts in Canyon Village. Check the guide

Lower Falls of the Grand Canyon of the Yellowstone River seen from Artist Point.

brochure to the canyon area for longer hikes that are also good riding trails.

North Rim Trail

From Chittenden Bridge, a 2.9-mile trail follows the north rim of the canyon near the river until it reaches 109-foot Upper Falls. The trail then continues west of the nearby parking area past Cascade Falls, Lookout Point, Grandview Point until it finally reaches Inspiration Point.

South Rim Trail

A 3.25-mile trail from Crittenden Bridge accesses the steep Uncle Tom's Trail to the base of the 308-foot Lower Falls, with the main trail continuing on to Artist Point (a wonderful place) in 2 miles and ending at Sublime Point, offering great views of both the falls and the canyon along the walk.

A Loop Trail

For a wilderness look at flora and fauna, and a view of the canyon area, park at Uncle Tom's parking lot and walk across South Rim Drive. Take the 1-mile trail to Clear Lake through rolling meadows and forests and watch for bison, elk, squirrels, and be alert for bear by making some noise (whistle, sing, or wear a bell). Continue another 0.5 mile to Lily Pad Lake, go north at the intersection with the Ribbon Lake Trail, and then west on the South Rim Trail for another 0.75 mile to Artist Point. Return via the South Rim Trail to Uncle Tom's parking area in slightly more than a mile.

Ecotouring and Safety Concerns

The wildlife seem so at ease in the park that visitors have a tendency to approach them as if they are part of a Walt Disney movie. Do not do that! They are unpredictable and potentially dangerous. Either use long telephoto lenses for photos or be satisfied with a distant, habitat-type shot. The animals do not deserve to be stressed, and they are protected in the park. Feeding park animals is unlawful.

No bicycles or vehicles are allowed on trails. Never leave food unattended. Be alert for grizzly bears while hiking; do not run if you encounter a bear; if threatened, play dead!

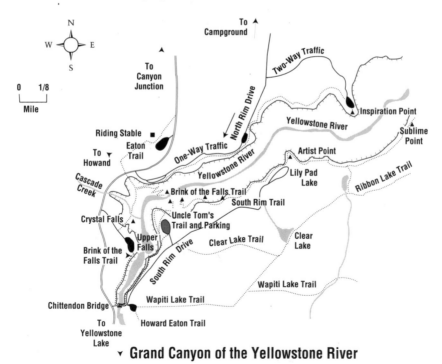

▾ **Grand Canyon of the Yellowstone River**

Dead Horse Point State Park
UTAH

Dead Horse Point State Park
P.O. Box 609
Moab, UT 84532-0609
(801) 259-2614

Attractions: Hiking trails, spectacular viewpoint, photography, nature study, geology, potholes, wildlife viewing, summer evening programs
Hours/Season: Overnight; year-round
Fees: Charge for day use and for camping
Visitor Center: Information, exhibits, publications, souvenirs, snacks
Picnicking: Scattered facilities near Dead Horse Point Overlook
Camping: Popular campsites at Kayenta Campground (April through October) have electrical hook-ups, no showers, and are available first-come, first-served. Primitive winter camping is allowed at the point.
Access: 11 miles northwest of Moab on US 191 and then 23 miles southwest on UT 313 to the end of the highway

As your feet stand on Kayenta sandstone at Dead Horse Point, the view is awesome as the Colorado River twists and turns 2,000 feet below on its way through the Colorado River Gorge. The river then turns through the Gooseneck so sharply that the river almost goes backwards. Yet it does continue to send its hoard of drainage water in a generally southwest direction and intersects the Green River as it flows from the northwest in a narrow, winding gorge. Wedged between the two rivers is the Island in the Sky of Canyonlands National Park.

The name of the park originated out of past cowboy history, when wild mustangs were corralled by fencing the natural narrow neck of the promontory. Though the story goes that the gate was left open, one time a band of unwanted culls, or "broomtails," remained on the point and died of thirst.

The winter season is short here with little snow. Although nights are cold, this season has pleasant daytime temperatures. At 6,000 feet, the area receives an average of ten inches of rainfall annually—an arid desert landscape of stark and magnificent geological beauty.

Geology

The excellent overlook at this park illustrates the result of 150 million years of erosion by the wild Colorado River. During the period of uplift, which accelerated river erosion and canyon carving, even small tributaries left their cutting patterns as squiggles seen upon the distant rocky landscape. Beneath the Colorado River is the 300-million-year-old Paradox Formation. Just above that, level with the river, lies the Honaker Trail Formation. Stacked above are the layers of sedimentary rock slashed through by the rivers—Cutler, White Rim, Moenkopi, Chinle, Wingate—until finally, the Kayenta sandstone that you stand on, surrounded by patches of Navajo sandstone that still remain from the level above.

Plants and Wildlife

Enjoying the view from Dead Horse Point Overlook.

Desert nature study is possible along the trails. Watch for deer tracks, skittish chipmunks, and jack rabbits, which are small and friendly. Lichens color many of the rocks and spring finds yellow and red wildflowers blooming. Two special habitats are worth exploring. One comprises the potholes seen along trails. These are depressions in slickrock that fill with water during the infrequent rains and become temporary homes for tadpoles and fairy shrimp.

The second fascinating habitat consists of the microbiotic crusts. These are rich composites of cyanobacteria and other small life-forms that dare to meet the desert's challenge by cooperative association. Watch for these dark, crusty patches scattered atop the desert soil. They are rich in nutrients, store water, and provide benefits for vascular plants.

Activities

Trails

An easy trail from the visitor center follows the edge of the promontory and reaches the main overlook in 1.5 miles. A somewhat longer and rougher trail (with some cairns among the slickrock to mark the route) continues from the day-use area at the point along the other side of the promontory, where the outcrop-pings of rock are varied and there are views of buttes, pinnacles, and benchlands in this bedrock vista. Several spur trails lead to varied rim overlooks, with one leading to potholes. The main trail eventually branches off to connect to the campground, where a spur loops back to the visitor center. Another trail heads northeast of the visitor center to good potholes; this path is being extended to the park entrance.

Ecotouring and Safety Concerns

Potholes form in depressions in slickrock and support tiny organisms.

When exploring, watch for microbiotic crusts and try to avoid stepping on them. Use caution along the promontory edges. As you view the Colorado River and its steep-walled canyons that hide many of the exciting rapids that river runners have the courage to experience—usually with commercial expeditions—keep in mind that money channeled into local areas helps to protect against dam building.

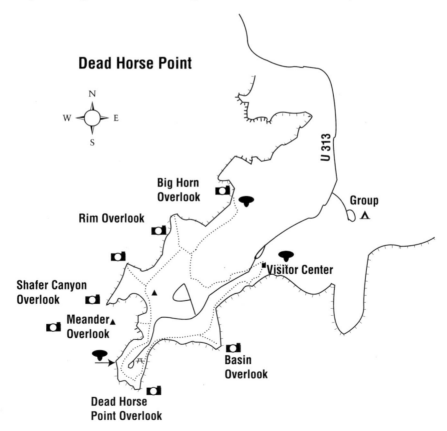

11

Harpers Corner, Dinosaur National Monument

COLORADO

Dinosaur National Monument
Superintendent, Box 210
Dinosaur, CO 81610
(970) 374-2216

Attractions: Scenic drive, hiking trails, backpacking, geology, photography, nature study
Hours/Season: Day use; entry road normally open (clear from snow) from April through October
Fees: None; fee for quarry area of monument
Visitor Center: Information, exhibits, and slide program at monument headquarters at beginning of scenic drive
Picnicking: Plug Hat, Canyon Overlook, and Echo Park Overlook picnic areas on scenic drive
Camping: Improved campsites are available in quarry area of monument, north of Jensen, Utah.
Access: Harpers Corner Scenic Drive begins at Monument Headquarters, 2 miles east of Dinosaur on US 40.

So many visitors to Dinosaur National Monument miss the truly smashing Harpers Corner Scenic Drive and the trail that meanders on a high finger of land to an outstanding canyon viewpoint of the Green and Yampa Rivers. This dazzling canyon country section of the monument occupies 326 square miles of wilderness added to the original 80-acre quarry site in 1938. The monument has hot daytime temperatures with cool nights, summer thunderstorms, and snow in winter.

Geology

While hiking the trail, note the evidence showing that this area was once covered by ancient seas: rocks with embedded fossilized pieces of brachiopods, clam-like shells, and fragments of crinoids, or "sea lilies," which are actually animals related to sea stars.

At Harpers Corner, compare the somber colors of the limestones and shales from an ancient sea that make up Whirlpool Canyon (to your left on the Green River), to those of Yampa Canyon, which are light-colored sandstone. The block you stand on was thrust high by faulting and the sandstone has now been eroded away. Geologists theorize that the Green and Yampa rivers were originally slow, winding streams on fairly level land before uplift occurred, and that their courses held while their waters sliced through the rising rocks to form deep, convoluted canyons.

Plants and Wildlife

Most of the spring color found along the drive is the yellow of arrowleaf balsamroot, but rabbitbrush (rabbits do like this), sagebrush, grasses, and alder trees are also easy to spot. Along the Harpers Corner Trail, notice the twisted shapes of pinyon pines and junipers, even some Douglas firs, and the splashes of colorful lichen on boulders. Native ricegrass and intruder cheatgrass are also visible. Though water is scarce on this narrow land peninsula above the rivers, spring and early summer reward the hiker with a proliferation of wildflowers—bluebells, gilia, paintbrush, and more. The wet edges of the rivers are habitat for cottonwood and box elder trees.

Bighorn sheep are found on the cliffs; Canada geese follow the linear oasis of the rivers. Other animal species include mule deer, coyote, yellow-bellied marmots, chipmunks, ravens, harrier hawks, and tree lizards.

Activities

Harpers Corner Scenic Drive

At monument headquarters, obtain the information guide that correlates to the numbered posts along this 31-mile drive to Harpers Corner. Several of the overlook areas have short trails.

The tour begins with wide expanses of smashing geology in both directions, with red buttes and mesas, and with rock layers once horizontal that have since buckled and tilted. The textures are incredible, with swirls of patterns, geometric shapes of triangles, lines, circles, half-circles, slants, parabolas, domes, pyramids, scallops, squiggles, and stripes of colors. It is a geological artistic collage near an intersection of the Colorado Plateau with the complex uplift of the Rocky Mountains.

The middle part of the drive is through cattle pasture with scattered tiny ponds among sagebrush, rabbitbrush, and balsamroot. Sage grouse live here but are difficult to see, though you may hear them clucking if you listen carefully. Mule deer frequently cross the road and ravens circle overhead. Aspen trees grow at the high point.

The last 11 miles of the drive are in canyon country, with an abrupt drop-off of 2,600 feet to the canyon floor cut by the Yampa River.

Harpers Corner Trail

At road's end is a parking lot for the 2-mile-round-trip trail that was named after a local rancher who used this narrow promontory as a corral for livestock. Beginning in a "pygmy forest" of pinyon pine-juniper, where the trees are actually hundreds of years old, the trail soon opens up to spectacular views of Echo Park—a cliff-rimmed alcove of meadow and trees near the merging of the Green and Yampa rivers. This easy, gently rolling trail wanders from side to side, with sheer drops on the edges; yet there is plenty of room for safe walking.

The trail destination is at the end of the rocky finger, where it drops off steeply above the meeting place of the two rivers, though don't confuse them because of their names. The Yampa is the green one, the Green is brown with sediment, though I remember it was green back in 1981. It is not unusual to see sunbathers and rafts on a sandbar near the confluence of the rivers, where echoes reverberate off nearby Steamboat Rock.

Hikers on the point have a magnificent view that encompasses the Canyon of Lodore, Steamboat Rock, and Whirlpool Canyon, where John Wesley Powell (in 1869) wrote that water "... is set eddying and spinning in whirlpools by projecting rocks and short curves, and the waters waltz their way through the canyon, making their own rippling, rushing, roaring music." An excellent view of the upturned layers of the Mitten Park Fault are visible in cross section, after it was sliced through by the Green River.

River Running

With its exciting white-water passages, some adventurous souls will want to run these rivers and experience that facet of their wildness, but you need a competent guide and a permit to float these turbulent and treacherous waters. Explorers and pioneers have left faint traces of their presence in the canyons and rock art of the Fremont Indians still survives on the rock walls.

Ecotouring and Safety Concerns

In the 1940s and 1950s, some people wanted to flood Echo Park by building a dam on the river, but concern for wildness won out. Wildness is a resource worth saving for the future. No camping is allowed along the scenic drive. Removal of plants, rocks, fossils, and other natural features is prohibited; the monument is a wildlife sanctuary.

Mariscal Canyon, Big Bend National Park

TEXAS

Big Bend National Park
TX 79834
(915) 477-2251

Attractions: Float trips, nature study, geology, photography
Hours/Season: Overnight; year-round
Fees: Entry fee per vehicle to park; extra daily fee for developed campgrounds
Visitor Center: One of several in the park is located at Rio Grande Village, with information (including some on fishing) and free river float permits available.
Picnicking: Rio Grande Village and Daniels Ranch picnic areas and along river during float
Camping: At 1,850 feet, the park's Rio Grande Village Campground (nearest to Mariscal Canyon) does not have hookups, but a concession trailer park near the Rio Grande Village Store does. Both are first-come, first-served, and very popular. Backcountry campsites are located at both Talley and Solis (permit required), at the beginning and end of Mariscal Canyon.
Access: North entrance at Persimmon Gap is 42 miles south of Marathon on US 385. West entrance is 82 miles south of Alpine on TX 118.

If you've never floated a river, Mariscal Canyon in Big Bend National Park is a wonderful place for your first expedition, assuming your timing is right. This gorge is where the Rio Grande makes the downward arc that dips into Mexico and gives the park its name. The river is a meandering oasis that flows through the Chihuahuan Desert.

Winter is often a good time for a float trip, with lots of sunshine and warmth, and an almost tranquil river. The experience of such a river run lets one really take in the surroundings, with only the fabric of the raft between you and the gravity-induced movement of the water. It is a time when all of your senses are intertwined with nature's; self is on the back burner. The rhythm of the water is soothing while glimpses of wildlife and geology engage the eyes.

The best seasons to visit the park are winter, spring, and fall. At those times, star-gazing is particularly good in the clarity of the nights. Summers are hot with the rainy season occurring from mid-June through October.

Geology

Though the complexity of Big Bend's geology induced some geologists to refer to it as the "eggbeater formation," the rocks are well exposed and much of the geological history has been deciphered.

15

Lower Cretaceous seas covered the Big Bend area, and the slow death of sea creatures left shells and skeletons that piled up to form massive layers of limestone. As the sea retreated, plant and animal life changed. (Fossilized bones tell of a time when dinosaurs, a huge crocodile-like creature, the Big Bend pterosaur, and other reptiles of all sizes squished, swam, and soared amongst the swamps and lush forest.) About the same time, a 40-mile trough, known as the Sunken Block, formed between Mesa de Anguila and the Sierra del Carmen.

During the Cenozoic Era, the land rose higher, a milder climate nourished lush grasslands and forest, and mammal species proliferated that are now extinct. This was a time of mountain building, erosion, deposition, and igneous activity. The Chisos Mountains were born in the center of the Sunken Block and erosion followed.

Was it the Rio Grande that did all the carving of Mariscal Canyon? Probably not. The Rio Conchos, which joins the Rio Grande today at Presidio just north of the park, is believed to have been the master carver of the park's river gorges in ancient times, and today supplies much of the water that flows down the Rio Grande.

Plants and Wildlife

The floodplain along the river encourages the growth of many plants, though the native plants suffer from competition with several exotics (tree tobacco, salt cedar, the bamboolike giant reed, and exotic species of cottonwood trees at Rio Grande Village). Trees in the legume family are abundant along the river plus some native lance-leaf cottonwoods; catclaw acacia and honey mesquite follow the washes and arroyos into the foothills. Desert willow, with its lovely orchidlike flowers, is often a companion of these trees in the arroyos. Narrow-leaf globemallow brightens the river floodplain, while yellow rock nettle drapes the nearby limestone cliffs. Prickly poppy and bicolor mustard are seen from the river to the foothills.

Farther from the river are many desert plants, including lechunguilla, yuccas, feather dalea, skeleton-leaf goldeneye, damianita, yellow trumpet flower, century plant, and creosote, which scents the air after a rain.

Survivors from long ago, garfish and some turtles, are living fossils still found in the river. Catfish are common. Beaver live in bank burrows along the river and leave their teeth marks on cottonwood and willow trees.

Big Bend is a bird watchers' paradise, with more than 430 species found here. And the best place to start spotting birds is along the green ribbon of the river. Look for gray hawks, red-tailed hawks, warblers, American coots, white-winged doves, mockingbirds, summer tanagers, painted buntings, vermillion flycatchers, cardinals, yellow-bellied sapsuckers, ladder-backed and golden-fronted sapsuckers, and the peregrine falcon. Sandpipers and killdeer are seen on the river's gravel and sandbars, and a variety of ducks fly by intermittently. Cliff swallows build adobe nests of river mud, and great blue herons stalk at water's edge.

Animals in the vicinity include: cougar, coyote, mule deer, javelina, kangaroo rat, desert amphibian, jackrabbit, cottontail, spadefoot toad, snakes, arthropods, and many lizard and grasshopper species, which the roadrunner is happy to devour. Cicadas may buzz in the daytime; crickets and katydid chirp and trill at night.

Hot Springs Float Trip

Activities   A short 2.5-mile float trip can be taken from the Hot Springs area to Rio Grande Village.

Mariscal Canyon Float Trip

The start of this float trip is reached via the backcountry River Road (high-clearance vehicles are best), which starts a few miles west of Rio Grande Village and passes the Mariscal Mine, where 894 flasks of mercury were produced between 1917 and 1919.

The put-in point is at Talley backcountry camp. This magical float can be done in a canoe, kayak, or inflatable raft; commercial outfitters are an option or you can go on your own with a permit. Sliding into the water, river runners quickly become confined within the steep limestone canyon walls that rise over 1,000 feet. The Rockpile is soon reached and requires some maneuvering (scouting might be necessary), but it is usually not difficult. Only one place requires some technical ability—the Tight Squeeze, normally a 10-foot gap between huge blocks of rock—but a commercial operator will help you scoot easily through the fast waters by hugging the Mexican border, or

Rafters enjoy the float through Mariscal Canyon of Big Bend.

if the river is wilder, it can be portaged. A sharp left turn must be made immediately after negotiating this gap to avoid another rock. Primarily, the float is an almost effortless glide between impressive, ever-changing rock formations, riparian vegetation, and wildlife.

It takes less than four hours to traverse the seven miles of the Rio Grande to the take-out point at Solis. A good lunch stop along the way is at a place where a large arroyo enters the canyon from the Mexican side. With the raft beached near a grassy meadow, petroglyphs can be observed on the nearby rocks. Floating again, the narrow canyon displays its tilting rocks and reflections of oranges and blues upon the green water. Debris from floods and the remains of a hermit's structure are visible high up in the rocks. Two miles before Solis, one exits the canyon. Visitors in the park can fish for catfish in the river, and no license is required.

Ecotouring and Safety Concerns

Always check with a ranger concerning river conditions. Do not camp in arroyos, washes, or other low spots, as they can become raging rivers. Ground fires and dogs are prohibited in the backcountry. No off-road driving is allowed. Swimming is not encouraged or prohibited, but strong undercurrents or drop-offs make it unadvisable.

2

SAND DUNES

Climb to the top of a high sand dune and your brain will ask questions. Why are sand dunes in this particular place? What type of dune formations are found here? What kind of sand is it and where did it originate? Can vegetation compete with blowing sand? What animals live here?

The answer to the first question is always the same. Sand dunes need lots of sand, wind, and space. Besides a considerable sand supply, the wind must be strong enough to move the sand around and pile it up as sand hills and dune formations that reflect the direction of the blow. And the terrain must be receptive—a place where sand and wind are the principal actors on an open stage. Though the mind's eye might envision scorching, inhospitable desert dunes, sand hills and ridges also occur in nondesert regions both inland and along coastal areas in temperate climates where the exploring can take place at comfortable temperatures.

For each of the suggested places to visit, the other questions have varied answers. In your explorations, remember that the dune landscape is very dynamic. It is not neat nor organized, but has transition areas, and something is always happening. One is lucky to witness this struggle, however, to see the forces of nature in operation. In desert dunes, the small amount of moisture eliminates any plant succession, which does occur amidst the Oregon dunes.

Sand dunes are like science fiction compared to your childhood sand box or your first sand castle, yet the fascination with sand is still there. (In fact, sandhills inspired the science-fiction writing of Frank Herbert in his *Dune* series). The dunes startle the eye and dare one to climb them. If you do, you will have fun, whether you go only a few steps from viewpoints or trek out for a day of strenuous climbing. And the scenery is grand.

Sand dunes are a haunting, daring change of scenery. At first, they seem to be just a bunch of sand, a possibly boring landscape, but close encounters show that this is not true. The visitor has to rethink ideas of trails, of walking, and of vistas. Dunes are a perfect place to practice orienteering skills while learning about this different landscape. But you must pinpoint yourself within the terrain and remember landmarks or you will be as lost as a blowing grain of sand.

Oregon Dunes National Recreation Area OREGON

Oregon Dunes National
Recreation Area
Siuslaw National Forest
855 Highway Avenue
Reedsport, OR 97467
(541) 271-3611

Attractions: Hiking, orienteering, backpacking, nature study, fishing, horseback riding, boating, canoeing, photography, off-road-vehicle (ORV) driving in certain areas, bicycling, campfire programs in some campgrounds
Hours/Season: Overnight; year-round
Fees: Only for camping
Reedsport Visitor Center: Information, exhibits, books, and maps available; open seven days a week during the summer, 8:00 A.M. to 4:30 P.M.; Monday through Friday throughout the rest of the year
Picnicking: Oregon Dunes overlook, Tahkenitch campground, Eel Creek campground, Sand Track picnic area, and Spinreel campground
Beach Access: South Jetty, Driftwood Campground, Winchester Bay, and Horsfall Road
Camping: From north to south, campgrounds are at Tyee (no ORVs); Lodgepole, Lagoon, Waxmyrtle, and Driftwood II are along Siltcoos Beach Access Road (all allow ORVs at sites); Carter (no ORVs); Tahkenitch (no ORVs); Eel Creek (no ORVs); Spinreel (ORVs allowed at sites); Horsfall (ORVs allowed), Bluebill (ORVs allowed), Wild Mare Horse Camp (corrals at each campsite), and Horsfall Beach (paved area for ORVs) are all accessed along Horsfall Dune and Beach Access Road. Call 1-800-280-2267 (TDD 1-800-879-4496) for reservations at some campgrounds. No hookups and a 10-day limit at forest service campgrounds. The campground at Jessie M. Honeyman State Park has hookups and showers. Backcountry camping is also allowed with a permit and certain restrictions.
Boat Ramps: Tyee Campground, Carter Lake, and Tahkenitch Lake
Access: Off US 101, between North Bend and Florence, see map

Surf-splashed cliffs, hidden coves with waterfalls, and magical sunsets over the ocean are only part of the intrigue of the Oregon coast. Between Coos Bay and the Siuslaw River on Oregon's central coast, lies a 40-mile strip of low coastal plains that has long invited the deposition of sand from the ocean's reservoir. In fact, sand dunes have penetrated as far as 2.5 miles inland in this region and it is now designated the Oregon Dunes National Recreation Area (ODNRA). Established in 1972, this 31,500-acre park includes freshwater lakes, forests, streams, wildlife, and plants that all complement the varied dune formations on the 14,000 acres of sand. One major river, the Umpqua, bisects the dune area at Reedsport.

These wonderful dune formations move and change dramatically with the summer winds and violent winter storms, when winds sometimes gust at more than 100 miles per hour and send avalanches of sand plunging down ridges. Yet, such winter dynamics are interspersed with sun-drenched days condusive to exploring when reflected solar heat bounces off the sand. Summers bring little rain but moderate temperatures to the dunes.

Geology

About one million years ago, a period of extreme submergence occurred along this coast, evidenced by the wave-cut terraces that are 1,500 feet above today's sea level. A period of uplift followed that lowered the shoreline approximately 300 feet below the present sea level. This lowering caused rivers and streams to cut trenches in the continental shelf.

Resubmergence to 160 feet above the present sea level followed and Pleistocene sand dune activity began in roughly the same location as the ODNRA of today but was even more extensive.

Cycles of glaciation caused sea level to rise and fall many times. The last major lowering of sea level, to 450 feet, was 17,000 to 20,000 years ago, at the peak of the Wisconsin glaciation. The melting of these glaciers produced the general features of the present coastline. As the sea advanced, sand dune activity began moving inland and reached maximum development about 6,000 years ago. Evidence indicates that the same seasonal wind patterns existed then as those that produce dune formations today.

Many coastal streams are characterized by drowned mouths and valleys. Sand movement blocked

Patterns and textures of the Oregon Dunes.

21

the mouths of some small streams and left lakes with their surfaces above sea level. Examples are Siltcoos, Tahkenitch, Clear, and Eel Lakes.

Sand Supply

The cracking and weathering of erupted rock by water, ice, wind, even clouds, send sediments down rivers and waterfalls to the Pacific, where currents and waves move them around. Both erosion of coastal cliffs and sediments of marine organisms add to the ocean's sand supply.

Sand pushed ashore by waves dries out and the tiny grains are blown inland by the strong winds of this area, smashing them into obstacles and each other until they are near-perfect spheres. Sand grains measuring between 0.1 mm and 1 mm in diameter seem to be the perfect weight for being blown into dune formations.

Most of the sand in the Oregon Dunes is translucent quartz, but there is some milky white feldspar, small amounts of colorful iron minerals, dark red garnet grains, and glittering specks of zircon, though most of these minerals are heavier and not easily airborne.

Dune Formations

In summer, fairly constant northwest winds pile sand into a succession of low, long parallel ridges that are perpendicular to the blow. These are called transverse dunes. Only about 6 feet in height, their crests may be 75 to 150 feet apart, but it varies greatly. The steep side, where the sand is falling, is called the slip face.

Winter winds come out of the southwest in furious, wild storms that erase and turn the transverse ridges and work them into bulging, fat snakes that waddle imperceptibly toward the inland forest, some as long as a mile in length and 165 feet in height. These are oblique ridges; they are oblique to both summer and winter winds; each year they grow larger and longer. Only here in the Oregon Dunes do these particular variations in wind produce this exact landform.

In moving sand inland, the wind scours hollows, or deflation plains, to expose the water table. These clear shallow circles of wetland are translucent mirrors that reflect the sky.

Each year, the sand advances 3 to as much as 18 feet, in an overall northeast direction, and meets the coastal forest at the precipitation ridge, where the wind is deflected and drops its load of sand. Steep dunes along the edges of the many lakes will eventually fill them with sand.

When the wind tears a hole in the vegetation cover where it meets a large sand mass, a parabola dune can form. Shaped like the curve of half of a watermelon, these dunes are the highest ones, some more than 500 feet, where the wind is blocked in all directions except one.

Plant Succession

It turns out that this recreation area provides an excellent outdoor laboratory for understanding plant succession in the all-year temperate climate where snow is rare and water is available.

Native beach grasses are pioneer plants that grow on shifting, blowing sand and tolerate the ocean salt spray while sending rhizomes—underground creeping stems—deep into the sand to anchor themselves. Exotic European beach grass, or marram grass, grows profusely, stabilizing dune areas and causing the unnatural formation of the foredune along the edge of the ocean, which threatens to cut off the sand supply to the dunes. Other pioneer plants of the open sand are yellow abronia, silver beach weed, sea rocket, beach morning glory, large-headed sedge, beach pea, beach knotweed, and sweet wild strawberries. All of these pioneer plants have special adaptations—deep roots, creeping stems, thick stems, large seeds—to aid them.

Once these plants have somewhat stabilized the shifting sands with their root systems and enriched the sand with nutrients after they die, other less tolerant plants can grow. Microenvironments change as the soil holds more water and erosion subsequently becomes less of a problem. One moss can prepare the way for kinnikinnick, and then lodgepole pine seedlings sprout. Shrubs soon arrive, including salal and evergreen huckleberry, but the Western rhododendron is the dominant shrub, with its vivid pink flowers in sharp contrast to the adjacent sand dunes in June. In time, Douglas fir trees start to grow.

Different plants grow where the sand is wetter, such as rushes, monkeyflowers, and twisted orchids, even the sundew of bogs. On deflation plains, coast willow, and wax myrtle are important intermediates in the plant succession to a climax forest where Sitka spruce is one of the first trees to flourish.

Wildlife

In this transition zone between coastal waters and coastal mountain forest, the sand records the early morning scurry of insects and small animals, erratic tanglings of animal encounters, nocturnal paths of deer, raccoon tracks at the wet edges of deflation plains, imprints of birds, and the curving trace of a garter snake moving across a dune. Flying squirrels and deer mice can be found on the forest islands.

Fish-eating ospreys and bald eagles fly overhead and river otters swim in creeks. Swallows swoop across the sand scouting for insects. Tundra swans are residents from November through March and are often found just south of the Siuslaw River.

Of the 426 wildlife species in the 26 distinct habitats of the ODNRA, 247 are birds, including many migratory birds. More songbird species, with a greater density, are found here than in the coastal mountain forests. The 50 species of terrestrial mammals include the rare white-footed vole and the Pacific jumping mouse, which is fun to watch if you are lucky enough to find one, which I was. Coho salmon, largemouth bass, yellow perch, rainbow trout, bullhead catfish, crappie, cutthroat, steelhead, and bluegill are found in the lakes and streams. And strangely enough, a wild gray mare roamed the dunes for years before her death in 1984.

Orienteering

Activities

Hikers soon learn that some sand surfaces are packed and hard while others are soft and sinkable due to the wind rearranging the formations. When it is windy, the valleys between dunes are calm and warm. Photographers will be enchanted by the tracks, textures, and patterns on the sand; the crossbedding swirls created when the winds change; the shapes sculpted by the scouring of wet sand during winter storms; and the smearing of sunset colors across the dune formations and circles of waters.

Birdwatchers and anglers should head for the creeks, lakes, and rivers that punctuate the golden sand hills. Tenmile Creek, Threemile Lake, Siltcoos River, Eel Creek, Cleawox Lake, Tahkenitch Creek, and Carter Lake are all good choices.

Bluebill Lake

Take the Horsfall Dune and Beach Access Road just north of North Bend and the McCullough Bridge to Bluebill Campground. A 1.2-mile trail circles a pond and then jogs into the forest, skirting sand dunes, before returning to the campground. Listen for green frogs—they sing in the rain. Some years the pond has no water, only memories.

Umpqua Dunes Scenic Area

Accessed from the Eel Creek campground, this is my favorite place in the Oregon Dunes. It is pristine, with few visitors, and offers exceptional dune-building observations among some of the highest dunes, up to 400 feet in elevation—and no ORVs are allowed.

The Umpqua Dunes Trail to the beach begins at the campground via a 0.25-mile forest hike. Climb the nearest tall dune and head west for 2 miles across an unmarked sand area. Pass the distant "tree island" to the north and look for route markers (poles with blue bands) that head north at the edge of the vegetation deflation plain. Take the path that turns west to the beach. This vegetated area is rich with bird life and small mammals.

Umpqua Lighthouse

Follow the signs to Umpqua Lighthouse State Park south of Winchester Bay. Built up higher on safer ground than the earlier 1857 structure, the present lighthouse was constructed in 1894 and shines its beacon 19 nautical miles out to sea. A good whale exhibit with information on their behavior, migration, birthing, and different species overlooks the water. Adjacent Lake Marie has a 1.3-mile trail circling it and is a popular summer water playground. A trail spur leads on to the sand dunes and ocean beach.

Tahkenitch Dunes

Two hiking trails begin at the Tahkenitch Campground. The 2-mile Tahkenitch Dunes Trail leads north through forest and then on to open dunes west to the mouth of Tahkenitch Creek.

The Tahkenitch Lake Trail branches off to the south and wanders first through second-growth conifer forest to a bench at the Elbow Lake overlook and then crosses a parabola dune slip face before opening up to views of the ocean and a deflation plain. At about 1.25 miles, another bench at 400-foot elevation offers a vista of Butterfly Lake and the mouth of Tahkenitch Creek. After crossing a bridge at 2.5 miles, it is only 0.25 miles to the end of the trail on the crest of an oblique dune overlooking Threemile Lake, where fishermen will find cutthroat trout and yellow perch. Backpackers will find good campsites in this area as well. Good route finders can hike a 6.5-mile loop by returning via the beach and the dunes trail. This area is closed to ORVs.

Oregon Dunes Overlook

Besides being a good stop for auto touring, the 1-mile Overlook Beach Trail begins here, crosses a quarter mile of open sand, and then goes through a vegetated deflation plain wetland (with good bird-watching opportunities) to reach the beach. Bridges over standing water make this a year-round hike. A longer option branches off to the south and eventually follows Tahkenitch Creek to the beach, passing a freshwater marsh and the estuary of the creek—good hunting grounds for raptors, including ospreys and bald eagles. If one continues north on the beach for about a mile to the Overlook Beach Trail, a 3.5-mile loop can be trekked. Watch for the wreckage of a Pacific trawl ship near the beach. No ORVs are allowed in this area.

Siltcoos Dunes and Estuary

Accessed via the Siltcoos Dunes and Beach Road, this area consists primarily of stabilized sand dunes with the added attractions of the Siltcoos River estuary and salt marsh, plus a freshwater lagoon. Three short trails begin at the Stagecoach Trailhead, a site that commemorates the route of pioneer travel across the Siltcoos River. ORV routes are numerous north of the river.

Siltcoos Lake Trail

East of US 101, across from the Siltcoos Dunes and Beach Road, a 5-mile trail traverses second-growth forest on the way to Siltcoos Lake.

Mountain bikes can use this path and six primitive campsites are located near the lake.

Jessie M. Honeyman State Park

One of Oregon's most popular state parks, Honeyman, is a magnet for recreation seekers. Near the dunes is Cleawox Lake, which is excellent for canoeing and rafting and an illustrative example of sand blockage of a coastal stream. To reach open sand, climb the steep sand dune that plunges downward to the lake. Many people just explore this adjacent open sand area where no ORVs come close, but I enjoy heading for the long oblique dune and following its waddling crest—with beautiful views of the ocean—as it heads for the beach.

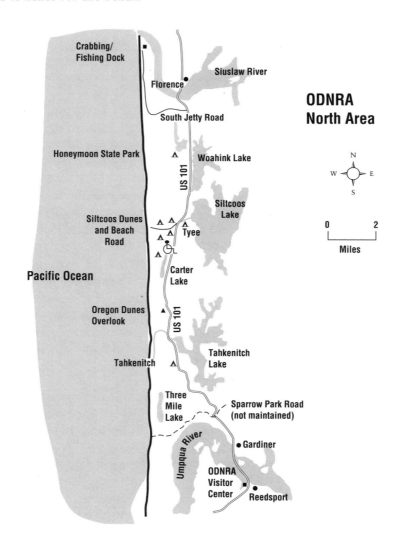

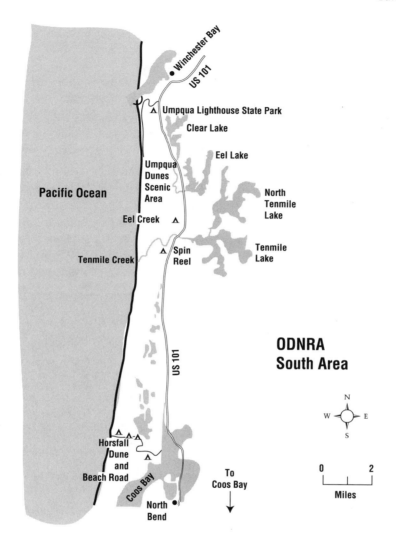

Pacific Ocean

Winchester Bay
US 101
Umpqua Lighthouse State Park
Clear Lake
Eel Lake
Umpqua Dunes Scenic Area
North Tenmile Lake
Eel Creek
Tenmile Creek
Spin Reel
Tenmile Lake

US 101

ODNRA South Area

N
W — E
S

Horsfall Dune and Beach Road
Coos Bay
North Bend

To Coos Bay

0   2
Miles

Carter Lake

Carter Lake Campground is situated at the beginning of the Carter Dunes Trail. Take the 0.25-mile hike through conifer forest to open dunes that roll westward for a mile to the edge of the deflation plain that backs the beach and its foredune.

The new Taylor Dunes Trail, near the entrance to the campground, offers a firm surface designed for visually-impaired as well as physically-impaired people. This trail leads to a boardwalk overlook of Taylor Lake. A more strenuous uphill grade continues to a bench overlooking the dunes and the ocean.

Ecotouring and Safety Concerns

Do respect the pristine quality and vastness of the dune-fields. People can get lost, so continually be alert for landmarks and let people know where you are going. Hikers must choose ORV-restricted dune areas or put up with numerous noisy, dangerous confrontations.

A decision in 1994 left 5,930 acres open to ORVs, with another 4,455 acres where ORVs are restricted to designated routes. Stop at the visitor center for a copy of the "Off-Road Vehicle Guide to Sand Areas of the Siuslaw National Forest." All motor vehicles are required to have both current registration and off-road use permits. Vehicles, except for motorcycles, are required to have a red flag mounted at least nine feet above ground. Respect vehicle closure areas that protect pedestrians, wildlife, and water quality. One particular wildlife concern is that of the snowy plover, a threatened species that nests on open sand.

Coral Pink Sand Dunes State Park
UTAH

Coral Pink Sand Dunes State Park
P.O. Box 95
Kanab, UT 84741-0095
(801) 874-2408

Attractions: Hiking, photography, nature study, OHV driving, geology study
Hours/Season: Overnight; year-round
Fees: Charge for either day use or camping
Visitor Center: Entrance station has numerous brochures, a bottled collection of various sands from around the world, and exhibits of a few animal specimens, such as live salamanders and scorpions—safely enclosed. A ranger is accumulating a fine file of labeled, dried area plants.
Picnicking: Picnic area with tables and water at nature trailhead
Camping: Park campground has restrooms with showers (Easter to late October).

Would you like to roam among rose-colored hills of sand edged by the Vermillion Cliffs where you can see huge hummocks of yellow-flowered mule ears bloom in late spring? If so, head for Coral Pink Sand Dunes State Park, established in 1963, in the White Cliffs Bench of Utah. Camp there and enjoy nighttime star gazing.

Geology

The sand of the park is derived from Navajo sandstone created during the Middle Jurassic period. Various cycles of sand to sandstone have occurred over time. Ninety-eight percent of Navajo sandstone consists of grains of quartz crystals that were once part of loose sand dunes. With time, a cement of lime, iron oxides, and clay substances bonded these grains together into a hard material. Weathering and erosion of these sandstones produced sediments carried here by winds to form sand dunes estimated at 10,000 to 15,000 years old.

Dune Formation

The same iron oxides and other minerals that color Utah's red rock country are responsible for these photogenic sand hills, the only major dunefield on the Colorado Plateau today. At 6,000-foot elevation, some 2,000 acres of park dunes are the result of winds funneling through a constricting notch between the Moquith and Moccasin mountains (south of the park) that increases the wind velocity, a phenomenon known as the "Venturi effect." Once the wind reaches the open valley, the velocity decreases and sand is deposited in this open space. Another wind blows east between Moccasin and Harris mountains and adds to the boiling effect as currents merge and drop sand. Formations found at Coral Pink include barchans, parabolas, and a star dune (caused by winds coming from several directions).

Hikers descending sand dune at Coral Pink Sand Dunes State Park.

Plants and Wildlife

Two vegetation zones are found within the park. At the lower elevation of 6,000 feet is the pinyon-juniper zone, with yucca, cacti, mule ears, sunflowers, and wildflowers. Those interested in nature study should ask a ranger for places to hike in the dunes where a threatened species of milkweed sprouts on sandy hillsides near a stand of ponderosa pines.

The second life zone is that of the ponderosa pine, at elevations of 6,900 feet and above. Small pools of water attract animals in these upper dunes.

Bird tracks are visible on the sand, along with the uniform footprints of the camel cricket and scurrying beetles. Animals of the area include spadefoot toads, tiger salamanders, ravens, eagles, hummingbirds, rattlesnakes, mule deer, coyotes, bobcats, kit foxes, kangaroo rats, jackrabbits, and other small animals.

Activities

Nature Trail

This easy 0.5-mile hike begins at the boardwalk located at the day-use area, and has numbered interpretive signs with information about this dune area.

Two Dunes Trail

Cross the sand from the day-use area to two enormous dunes that one can climb, a barchan and a star dune that are both approximately 200 feet high. Most people choose one or the other of these energetic ascents. The round-trip covers about 1.5 miles.

South Boundary Trail

Obtain a hiking brochure from the visitor center for this strenuous 5.5-mile-round-trip hike that begins at the day-use parking lot, curves south around the edge of the dunes, and then returns straight across the dunefield.

OHV Areas

An access road for OHVs begins near the campground. Other areas along Sand Dunes Road also offer access points for both off-highway vehicles and hikers.

Ecotouring and Safety Concerns

This state park is noted for enforcing Utah OHV regulations, so it is recommended that you are aware of both these rules and the areas open to vehicles. Since the sand is so fine-grained here, vehicles are mostly dune buggies, but 4-wheel-drive vehicles are acceptable if equipped with super-wide flotation tires. All vehicles using the dunes are required to have a whip with flag measuring 8 feet from the ground. Vehicles must stay at least 10 feet away from any vegetation and 100 feet away from pedestrians. No vehicles are allowed in the fenced natural area. All vehicles must remain on the pavement while in the campground. Quiet hours are from 10 P.M. to 9 A.M., with no vehicles, generators, or loud disturbances allowed during this time.

White Sands
National Monument
NEW MEXICO

White Sands National Monument
Superintendent
P.O. Box 458
Alamogordo, NM 88310
(505) 479-6124

Attractions: Hiking, orienteering, nature study, backpacking, photography
Hours/Season: From Memorial Day to Labor Day, hours are 7:00 A.M. to 9:00 P.M., with an hour allowed to leave the park. During the rest of the year, hours are from 7:00 A.M. to 5:00 P.M., with an hour allowed to leave the park; closed on Christmas Day.
Fees: Entry charge per vehicle
Visitor Center: Information, interpretive programs, museum, exhibits, audio-visual programs, gift shop, soft drinks
Picnicking: Picnic area along loop drive
Camping: Only a primitive backcountry walk-in site requiring registration at headquarters. A good campground, Oliver Lee Memorial State Park, is located 10 miles south of Alamogordo, off US 54.
Access: 15 miles southwest of Alamogordo, off US 70

One quickly suspects that the sand is different at White Sands National Monument. This stark white landscape is the world's largest gypsum dunefield. It is an ecological island of some 300 square miles that is surrounded by open prairies, ebony lava flows called Malpais, and jagged buttes of the Tularosa Basin. The dunes form a dazzling wave of moving hills across the sun-drenched northern edge of the vast Chihuahuan Desert. The park was established on January 18, 1933.

Geology

Approximately 10 million years ago, a huge block of the Earth's crust began to settle in this area as fault lines, running roughly north to south, gave way to create the Tularosa Basin. Left exposed were the layered sedimentary cliffs of the Sacramento Mountains to the east and the San Andres Mountains to the west. Called a "graben" because of the way it was formed, the basin has no outlet for its water.

For eons, rain and melting snow washed eroded sediments from the surrounding mountains into the basin, and a large body of water, Lake Otero, was formed. It was saturated with a specific salt, gypsum (hydrous calcium sulfate), that water had dissolved from certain layers of the cliffs.

What was once a cold and wet terrain changed gradually as the climate became warm and dry. As a result, about 30,000 years ago, the lake slowly evaporated, leaving a remnant body of water now called Lake Lucero—the lowest part of the basin and gravity's strongest hold—and a surrounding valley floor of exposed gypsum. About 20,000 years ago, the stage was set for the subsequent gusting winds to play their role in the formation of the dunes.

Dune Formation

When Lake Otero evaporated, gypsum crystallized into a form called selenite, a three-layered structure similar to that of mica, which today can be found around crusty Lake Lucero, a dry lake bed most of the year. After weathering flakes the crystals of selenite, the wind picks up the fine chips and tumbles and blows them into fine grains of sand (a word that only defines size).

At White Sands, the southwest winds are the driving force that causes the gypsum sand to skip and hop, causing other grains to move as they land, as the entire dune surface flows or creeps to the northeast. Sandstorms in early spring, with gusts of more than 45 miles per hour, play a major role in moving sand; the rest of the year the breezes blow at a mild 5 miles per hour. Except for some late-winter northerly storm winds, when short-lived counter dunes are formed atop larger dunes, the dunes are formed primarily by unidirectional winds from the southwest.

The dunefield is 97 percent gypsum. Simple mounds near Lake Lucero move on to form transverse dunes, which can break apart to give rise to barchan formations (crescent shaped with pointed tips or horns), and vegetation can then invert these formations to produce parabolic shapes. The transverse formations are the largest ones here and can be 400 feet thick, with heights of 40 feet, and crests that run 800 feet long.

Plants and Wildlife

Although plants in this region must endure minimum shade and shelter, heat, dryness, shifting sand, and few soil nutrients, at least 62 species have adapted to these conditions on or between the sand hills of the dunefield. Water arrives during violent events, with more than half of the annual 7 to 8 inches falling during the thunderstorm months of July, August and September. The water penetrates the sand rapidly, but due to capillary action, it sinks to a certain level and no lower. Blue-green algae may flourish after a rain and give a slight tint to the dunes.

The cleverest adaptations are seen in the elongated stems of skunkbush, sumacs and soaptree yuccas, the sand stabilizing roots of rubber rabbitbrush, the stunted Rio Grande cottonwood trees, and the low-growing rosemary mint.

It is easy to spot the yuccas, which have clusters of large, cream-colored blossoms in early summer, and observe their growth (as much as 30 feet high) in response to the advancing sand. A wonderful demonstration of interdependence is seen in the pollination of the yucca by the pronuba moth. As part of a symbiotic exchange, the moth larvae feed on the seeds of the yucca plant. Also resident are delicate Indian ricegrass—the best protein source for animals in the dunes—and jointfir, which is better known as ephedra or Mormon tea.

Look for short-lived pedestals of gypsum hardened by rain that are held together by the roots of skunkbush, cottonwood, or yucca plants. After these plants elongated, the sand moved on and left these pedestals behind.

More than 90 percent of the animal species inhabiting the monument area are birds and insects, and these are also the most obvious. Most intriguing is the darkling beetle, with its distinctive tracks that can be found all over the dunes. Rarely seen in the daytime are the bannertail kangaroo rats, snakes that hibernate in winter, and some toads and rodents that estivate underground during summer hot spells. Though rarely seen, the western hognose snake has a snout for digging out dormant desert toads. More easily spotted are the swift insect-eating lizards that scoot about the dunes, seeking shade during the day. Burrowing is a common practice used to escape the heat of day and the cold of the desert night.

The most frequently seen mammal is the kit fox, but coyotes, badgers, porcupines, rabbits, and skunk hunt in the fringe areas around the dunes. The three poisonous species of reptiles and amphibians—the rare desert massasaugua, and the diamondback and prairie rattlesnake—are scarce and live primarily outside the dune area.

The birds are keenly aware of the snakes, lizards, rabbits, and insects because they are excellent food sources. Predator birds include the great horned owl, Swainson's hawk, roadrunner, loggerhead shrike, nighthawk, western kingbird, and flycatcher. Patient birders can also spot the golden eagle, sparrow, oriole, mockingbird, and meadowlark.

An interesting camouflage adaptation is manifest in the white dunes habitat. To escape predation, natural selection favors animals that are difficult to see. Two species of lizard and some mice are almost pure white. Many other animals are lighter in color than expected, a nearly transparent cricket, for example. The darkling beetle, however, is apparently a contradiction.

Heart of Sands Loop Drive

Activities

Begin this 16-mile-round-trip tour at the visitor center (4,000-foot elevation), where you can obtain an interpretive guide keyed to numbered posts along the road.

Notice the San Andres Mountains to the west, the Sierra Blanca to the north, and the Sacramento Mountains to the east as you drive past dunes stabilized by vegetation. At Post #5, the main dunefield is reached. The road here is of hard-packed gypsum. Pull over only in established areas to explore on foot; do not stop on the road. Look for successful plant species both on the dunes and between them, where the water is closer to the surface and some of the gypsum has dissolved.

Big Dune Trail

Stop along the loop drive to hike the 1-mile Big Dune Trail, a self-guiding nature hike complete with interpretive brochure. Two moderately steep dune climbs occur along the trail. These are good places to stop and ponder the formation of these dunes. Listen for birds and the powerful wind. As you walk, look for the tracks of lizards, pocket mice, roadrunners, and the cryptic prints of the darkling beetle. You will see firsthand how soaptree yucca and cottonwood trees have adapted to the moving sand. As the largest plant of the dunefield, the cottonwood tree attracts birds (some nest in its branches) like the great horned owl, and porcupines that nibble away at the tree itself. In certain places you can find fragments of fossilized roots and stems, remains of gypsum sand pedestals (some encased in gypsum), and other fragments with the inclusion of these mineral crystals. And did you smell the sweet scent of hoary rosemary mint along your hike?

Ecotouring and Safety Concerns

Removal of archeological or natural objects, sand, selenite crystals, plants, or animals is prohibited. Driving or parking on the dunes or outside established parking areas is prohibited. Do not tunnel into sand, since it may collapse. Never sand surf near roadways. And do not get lost on foot excursions. Do bring good sunglasses along for exploring. Ground fires are prohibited.

Great Sand Dunes
National Monument
COLORADO

Great Sand Dunes
National Monument
11500 Highway 150
Mosca, CO 81146
(719) 378-2312

Attractions: Hiking, backpacking, horseback riding, sand skiing, photography, nature study, 4-wheel-drive tour, campfire programs, ranger-guided tours
Hours/Season: Overnight; year-round
Fees: Entry fee and additional charge for developed campground use
Visitor Center: Information, exhibits, maps, books, terrace talks. The visitor center is being expanded in several phases, and will soon offer more interactive, updated exhibits and facilities. Hours are 8:00 A.M. to 5:00 P.M. daily (except for federal holidays in winter), with extended hours from Memorial Day to Labor Day.
Picnicking: Main picnic area is adjacent to dunes, near the visitor center. Two other sites are located along the Medano Pass Primitive Road (no water or restrooms available).
Camping: Pinyon Flats Campground is open all year, first-come, first-served, restrooms but no showers or hook-ups (water is available only from April to October). Group site C and two individual campsites at the Pinyon Flats Campground are wheelchair accessible. With a permit (tags on parked vehicles required), varied backcountry camping (free permit required) is allowed at designated sites and in the dune wilderness (no open fires permitted). In 1994, a wheelchair-accessible backcountry campsite was constructed east of Medano Pass Road in Sawyer Canyon. The trail, picnic table, and vault toilet are all wheelchair accessible. Collecting firewood is prohibited, but wood can be purchased.
Access: 38 highway miles northeast of Alamosa, either north on CO 17 and then east on Six Mile Lane, or east on US 160 and then north on CO 150

No two dune destinations are the same; each has its own surprises. The view on arrival at Great Sand Dunes National Monument in south central Colorado is awesome, and not just because the 700-foot-high dune formations are North America's highest. Nestled in the curving ridge of the snow-peaked Sangre de Cristo Mountains, with the glittering shallow waters of Medano Creek between you and the beginning of the dunes, the scene is a photographer's dream landscape. The creek is seasonal, usually skirting the dunes from the time snowmelt begins in April and lasting for about four months, though it varies yearly depending on the summer rains. In a rare year, the creek forms the foreground for autumn foliage colors.

Geology

For centuries the Rio Grande flowed through the San Luis Valley, carrying eroded bits and sediments that were fed to the river primarily via tributary streams coming down from the volcanic San Juan Mountains, where the headwaters of the Rio Grande are located. Some sediments were also left by glacial deposition during the Ice Age. As often happens, the Rio Grande changed course, leaving behind great amounts of exposed sediments and sand. For thousands of years, the wind influenced the movement of this sand and produced 39 square miles of dunes in this area.

Dune Formation

Throughout most of the year, southwest winds move across the San Luis Valley, pushing and bouncing sediments and sand grains to the northeast. The 14,000-foot Sangre de Cristo Mountains, however, quickly put a stop to any further sand movement, though fine dust particles did make it over some of the mountain passes. The result is a spectacular pileup of dune formations, which is intensified when brief storm winds roar down the peaks from the northeast. These gales cancel the slow work done by weaker winds. As a result, the windward and lee faces are suddenly reversed and the dunes fold back on themselves. Unable to migrate due to space restraints, these dunes grow higher and higher. Fair amounts of moisture also inhibit dune movement, though surface sands move freely.

Wind from one direction produces crescent-shaped barchans and linear transverse dune formations, which require a larger sand supply than barchans. Reversing dunes result from two wind directions and slip faces can form on either side of the existing formation. Multiple wind directions result in star dunes that grow vertically and have three or more slip faces. A complex network of star dunes is located in the northwest lobe of the dunefield—formed at the base of Mount Herard, which separates the Music and Medano passes where winds fluctuate.

The dunes are composed of various minerals, with 51.7 percent from volcanic rock fragments. Quartz accounts for 19.1 percent, followed by 8.9 percent feldspar, 2.5 percent sandstone, and the remaining 5.2 percent of other minerals. Sand grains in the park are quite small, between 0.2 and 0.3 mm in diameter.

Plants and Wildlife

Few plants grow on the dunes in this high, parched valley. Blowout grass, Indian ricegrass, scurfpea, yucca, and bright yellow prairie sunflowers are a few that have adapted to the sand. Around the dunes are grasslands and pinyon and juniper trees, and cottonwoods frequently line creeks. The Pinyon Flats Trail to the dunes is a good place to look for plants and wildflowers. Along the

Montville Nature Trail are Rocky Mountain maple, quaking aspen, white fir, mountain spray, thinleaf alder, and several edible fruits—chokeberry, gooseberry, currant, wild rose, and skunkbush (which the pioneers used to make a lemonade-like drink).

The dunes themselves are not very hospitable to animals, but two well-adapted species of insects are endemic, the Great Sand Dunes tiger beetle and the giant sand treader camel cricket—both roamers over sand. On the fringes of the dunes, small rodents (including the kangaroo rat), bobcats, coyotes, and pronghorn antelope find suitable habitat, though many animals are nocturnal; watch for tracks. Mule deer are not skittish at all and often come to the flats near the campground. Birds—warblers, kinglets, siskins—find hospitable habitat in the vegetation near Mosca Creek. Ravens and blackbilled magpies fly the skies.

Activities

Orienteering

An obvious recreation choice is the challenge of climbing these massive, aerobic-demanding dune formations, especially since they occur at 7,900-foot elevation. Even if one can not reach the high points, a sampling will capture some of the dune magic. And if the season is right, who can resist some cool wading, splashing, and sand castle building in the creek area?

The dunes offer the solitude and exhilaration of backcountry exploring, with star gazing on crystal-clear nights, and dune play that includes jumping,

Splashing through Medano Creek at Great Sand Dunes National Monument.

body surfing, private sunbathing, and even some skiing—yes, on the sand hills.

People with disabilities will be happy to learn that the "Friends of the Dunes" have provided an all-terrain wheelchair for negotiating sandy trails and the dunes (with assistance). This can be checked out free of charge at the visitor center.

Picture Point Trail

This short walk begins at the visitor center and leads to the picnic area.

Pinyon Flats Trail

This trail connects Loop 1 of the campground with the dunes, with another path branching off to the dunes parking area adjacent to the picnic area.

Montville Nature Trail

For hikers only, this easy 0.5-mile hike is accessed a short distance northeast of the visitor center. It offers an opportunity to get out of the sun and into the forest, an appealing walk of varied vegetation, views of the dunefield, and a crossing of Mosca Creek. Some interesting history of pioneer settlement in this area is pointed out along the trail.

Mosca Pass Trail

Accessed from the interior of the Montville Nature Trail, the 3.5-mile Mosca Pass Trail follows Mosca Creek through the Rio Grande National Forest, and into the newly designated (1994) Sangre de Cristo Wilderness Area as it climbs to a pass, at 9,740 feet elevation, over the Sangre de Cristo Mountains. Pioneers coming west used this pass, which was once a toll road and gated. Near the beginning of the trail, a log cabin store and post office once stood.

Wellington Ditch Trail

The 1-mile Wellington Ditch Trail—once an irrigation canal for pioneers—takes off north from the Montville Nature Trail as a connecting route to Pinyon Flats Campground, an easy walk at the edge of forest vegetation.

Little Medano (Spanish for "dune") Creek

Starting from the north end of Loop 2 of the campground, one can hike 1 mile to the Point of No Return Trailhead (PNR). Return to the campground via the primitive road or continue another 3.9 miles on the Little

Medano Creek Trail. Both hikers and horseback riders can use the trails north of the Point of No Return Trailhead. There is parking there.

Sand Creek Trail

Near completion, this 6.4-mile trail continues from Little Medano Creek to Sand Creek. Marked by brown posts, it offers great dune and mountain views, and traverses dunes, ponderosa forests, aspen groves, creeks, and timbered bottomlands. Habitat for elk, bear, cougar, and deer is passed along this 10.5-mile route from PNR, with four new backcountry campsites.

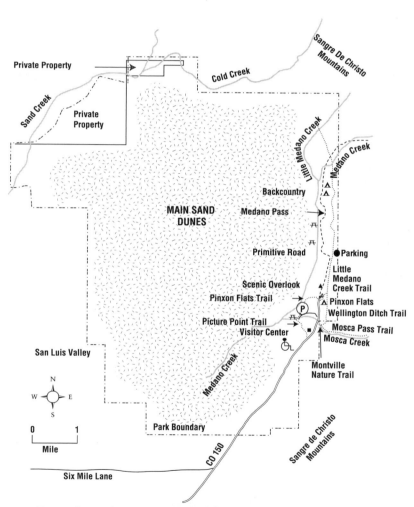

Great Sand Dunes National Monument

Medano Pass Primitive Road

This 12-mile, four-wheel-drive road begins near the campground. It follows the eastern edge of the dunes, crosses Medano Creek, and climbs to Medano Pass (10,030 feet) and into the Rio Grande National Forest. The drive offers spectacular views of the dunes. Reduced tire pressure makes for easier negotiation of the soft sand. (Air is available near the campground.) From May to September, a park concessionaire operates tours on this road. In the mountains, this primitive road splits the Sangre de Cristo Wilderness Area.

Ecotouring and Safety Concerns

Do wear shoes, or take them along, on dune hikes because sand temperatures can reach 140 degrees Fahrenheit under the hot sun, though nights in the dry air are cold. When it is hot, hike in the early morning or evening. Watch for ticks. Avoid the dune area during thunderstorms because lightning frequently strikes the dunes. Off-road driving and mountain biking is prohibited in the park. Horses and llamas are not allowed in designated backcountry camping sites.

Baja White Dunes
Baja California

Backcountry Discovery
Near Guerrero Negro
Baja California Sur

Attractions: Beachcombing, photography, wildlife viewing, boating
Access: From town of Guerrero Negro (471 miles south of Tijuana), west off Mexico 1, take C. Allendre west from the center of town and continue northwest on a gravel road for a total of 8 miles to the Old Wharf at Estero de San Jose.

I discovered these pristine dunes in an isolated area strictly by a stroke of serendipity when I chartered a whale-watching excursion boat in the town of Guerrero Negro. The Old Wharf is at the end of a narrow finger of land extending into Estero de San Jose, and was a scene of considerable interest. I found Mexicans fishing without poles, twirling the lines out to cast them some distance. Children danced to silent music. Picturesque old boats were beached along the shore and osprey carried twigs to nests perched on abandoned cement towers.

The objective of the day, however, was whale watching from a charter boat. For some unknown reason, the gray whales were late in migrating south to birth and breed in Baja's warm lagoons. Since Captain Mario had guaranteed whale sightings—and we saw none—he motored us over to a stretch of coast accessible only by boat to let us explore. And it turned out to be a pristine stretch of exquisitely patterned, white sand dunes.

Geology

This coastline (some 15 miles or so) is part of a T-shaped peninsula connected to the mainland by a narrow, swampy piece of land—not an access route. The dunes are composed of calcium-containing remains of marine organisms that have washed ashore. The Pacific Ocean offshore curves to form the bowl-shaped Bahia de Sebastian Vizcaino. Waves bring the sand into the bottom of this bowl and form dunes on the land.

Plants and Wildlife

The drive to the Old Wharf offers good bird-watching as long-legged egrets and tricolor herons move silently through the grasses of wetlands. Take binoculars and plan to return at sunset for some good photo opportunities. Do try to hit the peak of the whale-watching season to view the gray whales.

Visiting the Dunes

Activities

Adventurous and experienced travelers with their own boat or raft might access these dunes from the Old Wharf. Do check with local people about directions and cautions (I have not done this). Check with charter operators to see whether they will take you there. Surf exists at the mouth of Estero de San Jose, which is to the north, so caution should be exercised by taking a more westerly heading to the dunes. Large seashells were discovered on a walk among these soft slopes.

Scammon's Lagoon

If you travel to this area anytime from January through March, do check out gray whale watching at nearby Laguna Ojo de Liebre (Eye of the Hare Lagoon or, more notoriously, Scammon's Lagoon), though this is best done on a well-organized boat tour. This area is the first designated gray whale sanctuary in the world, courtesy of the Mexican government, a 7.2-million-acre reserve that encompasses much of the peninsula's Biscayne Desert and extends into the open sea.

Ecotouring and Safety Concerns

If you boat to these dunes yourself, use caution and check out the situation. Do not visit these white coastal dunes unless you go with reverence and leave them uncluttered.

Pristine white sand dunes along the Pacific Ocean and Estero de San Jose.

3

TEMPERATE RAIN FORESTS

West

With so few temperate rain forests in the world, those found in the Pacific Northwest take on a very special role as a valuable ecosystem. The best way for humans to have any real knowledge or appreciation of such rain forests is to visit them, to put on hiking boots and walk softly amongst their quiet happenings, preferably in all seasons.

The magnificent trees suck in that worrisome carbon dioxide, use solar energy to power growth, and throw away oxygen. Lungs breathe easily and safely in the unpolluted air. Trees creak in the gentle wind.

Mushrooms grow under sheltering trees from spores that squirrels and mice have inadvertently planted. Below ground, a mutually beneficial exchange occurs between the entanglement of tree roots and these fungi. High in the forest canopy, lichens pull nitrogen from the atmosphere and drop it as fertilizer. Leaves form cups for holding water. The lush vegetation sparkles with morning dew as sword ferns, sorrel, and rhododendrons edge the trails. Snags open a sun path to new seedlings and offer homes for wildlife.

Stimuli flood the hiker's senses—the majesty of conifers, the sound of water rushing down maidenhair fern-lined canyons, the contrasting touch of bark and mosses, the fragrance of a vanilla plant, and the taste of wild thimbleberries.

Humans build cathedrals; nature constructs temperate old-growth rain forests that seem like temples when one walks through them. There is no better place to feel at peace and to connect with the spirit of all life. If a poem can not match the magnificence of a tree, how can we describe the totality of a temperate rain forest?

The Pacific Northwest temperate rain forest is not just trees, but a web of life that supports more than 200 wildlife species and more than 1,500 types of invertebrates. One old-growth tree is home to a hundred different plant species, and these forests bring more breeding birds to the Northwest than to any other part of North America. The northern spotted owl is only an indicator of the forest's health, like the canary that served miners. Remember as you explore, however, that it is easy for wildlife to hide in this forest. Yet, take time for quiet observation and perhaps you'll be lucky, as I was once in these forests, and see a mountain lion strolling down the path. It will no doubt be gone as quickly as retina and brain register its presence, as long as you are quiet and don't panic.

Travelers fly round the world to see an endangered tropical rain forest, but they can easily experience the wonders of the Pacific Northwest old-growth rain forest, with campgrounds nearby. This forest is a easy place to walk, and to stop and ponder thoughts shoved aside in today's fast-paced life.

Because the redwood forest is also a temperate rain forest of the Pacific Northwest, it will be included. Though restricted to a smaller area, it has many of the same plants and animals, as well as a history associated with similar geological changes. It seems appropriate to begin with the general geology and fossil record.

Geology and the Fossil Record

We know now—from the fossil record—that redwood, fir, cedar, spruce, and hemlock trees and their ancestors have been around for a very long time. They were part of a major plant community—a diverse number of both needle-leaved and broad-leaved species—called the Arcto-Tertiary Geoflora that was prevalent up to 40 million years ago spanning from today's San Francisco latitude across the northern United States and into Canada and Alaska.

Then, at the beginning of the Oligocene Epoch, the climate began to change, to become cooler with less rain in the summer. Some inland forests were replaced by grasslands. The uplift of the Cascades, coast ranges, and Sierra Nevadas began about 20 million years ago, and these ranges considerably blocked inland rainfall from reaching the Great Plains.

A major natural sculpturing, with profound influence upon the climate and geography of North America was caused by glaciers that began to appear 2 million years ago. The vast Arcto-Tertiary Geoflora split into distinct communities (with some species replaced or lost), and the broad-leaved trees found preferable habitat in the East while the conifers (including the redwoods) were localized to the north and west areas of North America. The redwood forest is now found only from near San Francisco north to just over the Oregon border. The temperate rain forest extends along the Pacific coastal strip into Alaska.

River Corridors of the Olympic Peninsula WASHINGTON

Olympic National Park
Superintendent
600 East Park Avenue
Port Angeles, WA 98362
(360) 452-4501

Quinault Ranger District
Olympic National Forest
353 South Shore Road
Quinault, WA 98575
(360) 288-2525

Attractions: Hiking, backpacking, nature study, wildlife viewing, boating, paddling, river and lake fishing, photography, interpretive programs, campfire talks

Hours/Season: Overnight; year-round

Fees: Entry charge per vehicle to Hoh area, free entry to Quinault (in Olympic National Forest); charge for camping

Visitor Centers: Quinault Ranger Station on south side of Lake Quinault, open daily; Hoh Rain forest Visitor Center, open daily

Picnicking: Hoh Rain forest, Lake Quinault

Camping: Five forest camps are located along Quinault Lake and two more are on the Quinault River; national park campground near Hoh Rain forest Visitor Center and two forest camps along the Hoh entry road; backcountry sites are along both the Quinault and Hoh rivers, with permits required.

Access: Lake Quinault is just east of US 101, 38 miles north of Hoquiam; Hoh River is 14 miles south of Forks on US 101 and then 19 miles east on the park road.

The rain forest along the lower elevations of the Hoh, Quinault, and Queets rivers on the Olympic Peninsula is world-renowned, and rightly so. We are talking about vast acreages of forest that are pretty much protected for the future, allowing many visitors to feel their power and majesty.

Begin your exploration with a visit to the Lake Quinault Ranger Station or the Hoh Rain forest Visitor Center. The rustic lodge at Lake Quinault is an impressive timber construction where President Franklin D. Roosevelt stayed in 1937 on a fact-finding trip prior to establishing the national park. The lodge offers an opportunity to savor some fresh grilled salmon and to paddle a canoe across the glacier-carved lake.

It was at Lake Quinault that the 1889-90 Press Expedition led by James Christie ended, after a five-and-a-half-month north–south trek across the park. The trip today, now that we know more about the wilderness area of this park, can be made in five days.

Plants and Wildlife

The predominant trees include Douglas fir, western hemlock, western red cedar, and Sitka spruce—all of which grow here to gigantic proportions—with sword ferns very showy in the understory of the forest. Sitka spruce is the predominant coastal tree, rather than the redwood as one heads north from California. Bigleaf maple and alder prefer the wet edges of streams. One acre of this forest can grow some 6,000 pounds of moss, lichens, and epiphytes. Vanilla leaf, western trillium, salal, Oregon grape, and Pacific bleeding heart all provide flowers. Huckleberries, salmonberries, thimbleberries, and blackberries are tasty edibles that grow wherever they can get some sun.

Those health indicators of old-growth forest—the northern spotted owl and the marbled murrelet—are found here. Winter wrens scurry about on the forest floor. And kinglets, varied thrushes, chickadees, finches, vireos, and other small birds are heard more often than seen. Large mammals include black-tailed deer, Roosevelt elk, black bear, cougar, bobcat, and mountain goats, though the latter are not native. Deer mice are everywhere. The Pacific salamander is a creature that can rattle, scream, or yell. Watch for a green flash that could be a tree frog.

Activities

Quinault Rain Forest

Several trails provide access to excellent examples of temperate rain forest. The 0.5-mile Rain forest Nature Trail, in the designated wilderness, is accessed from a parking area on South Shore Road, a short distance south-

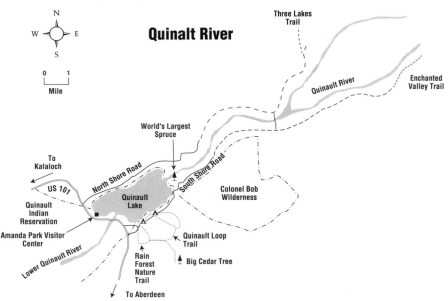

east of the entry road to Willaby Campground, or from the lower end of the same campground, which makes the trail closer to a mile. If one takes the longer trail, it passes under the road and initially is above a gorge with a waterfall on Willaby Creek. For a longer excursion to immerse oneself more completely into this habitat, take the Quinault Loop Trail, which can be hiked in several ways for a 4- to 8-mile hike; it begins across South Shore Road from Quinault Lodge and is also entered from the south shore campgrounds (maps are available at the nearby ranger station). Several longer trails are located upriver, including the 13-mile Enchanted Valley Trail that follows the river upstream to a chalet set in a spectacular gorge rimmed with waterfalls. This trail continues to the world's largest western hemlock and on to Anderson Pass. Another trailhead in the Quinault area leads to the world's largest yellow cedar.

Hoh Rain Forest

The Hall of Mosses Trail (0.75-mile round-trip) reveals that "jungly" atmosphere associated with mosses and ferns hanging from giant trees and lush vegetation caused by more than 140 inches of rain annually, as does the nearby Spruce Nature Trail (1.25-mile-round-trip)—wheelchair traveled with assistance. An easy 0.5-mile paved mini-trail loop can be done by wheelchair-confined people. For a more peaceful connection with the ecology of this forest, try a bit or all of the 17-mile Hoh River Trail that climbs to Glacier Meadows

Dew on rain forest maidenhair fern.

and summer wildflowers, and Blue Glacier—the shortest route to Mount Olympus.

Ecotouring and Safety Concerns

Know wilderness regulations if you plan to enter a wilderness area. Stop, stay calm, and do not run if you spot a cougar. Plan carefully for long hikes into the inner Olympics, drink only potable water or boil it, consider the possibility of a good rain, and leave only footprints.

▼ *Trip Tips*

Lake Quinault is part of the Quinault Indian Nation and a special permit is required from them for lake fishing.

Manning Provincial Park
British Columbia

Zone Manager
Manning Park, B.C.
VOX 1RO, Canada
(604) 840-8836

Attractions: Hiking, photography, horseback riding (only on designated trails or with guided tours), paddling (canoe rentals), swimming, fishing, mountain biking (only on certain routes), skiing, nature study, wildlife viewing, interpretive programs, campfire programs, lodging, store
Hours/Season: Overnight; year-round
Fees: Charge for campsites
Visitor Center: Open daily summer and winter
Picnicking: Summalo Grove
Camping: Four campgrounds in park available first-come, first-served (Lightning Lake has showers and is very popular; arrive early); group and winter campground at Lone Duck; designated wilderness campsites
Access: Hwy 3 goes through the park, with Hope 26 kilometers (16 miles) west of the west entrance and Princeton 48 kilometers (29 miles) east of the east entrance.

Manning Park spans a large chunk of the interior landscape of British Columbia that includes wet rain forest in the west to the drier climate on the eastern side of the Cascade Mountains. A couple of easy trails—one for wheelchairs—provide illustrative samples of the rain forest and should not be missed if you are in the area.

History buffs can trek on the Dewdney, Whatcom, or Hope Pass trails, explorer routes through the Cascades that were connecting links between the coast and the interior until the early 1900s.

Plants and Wildlife

Great old-growth red cedar and Douglas fir trees are featured at Sumallo Grove, along with western hemlock, Sitka spruce, cottonwood, alder, vine maple, sword fern, spring wood fern, mosses, foamflowers, mushrooms, devil's club, rotting trees, and ginger, with its distinctive smell. Included in the animals are shrews, crows, and other typical inhabitants of a temperate rain forest.

Sumallo Grove Trail

Activities

Located just off Hwy 3, 10 kilometers (6 miles) from the West Gate of the park, this 700 meter, wheelchair-accessible loop (0.5 mile) offers an insight into the components of the temperate rain forest. The short drive from the highway weaves through large trees and is reminiscent of roads among the redwoods in California.

Sumallo Grove is a self-guiding interpretive trail through old-growth forest, about a 20-minute walk. A picnic area is situated along the Skagit River.

Rhododendron Flats Nature Trail

Typical in many rain forest areas because they are also dependent on lots of rain, rhododendrons are featured on this 20-minute forest walk. Though especially beautiful if you are able to see them bloom in late spring, the trail is still interesting at other times and an exemplary rain forest tract along the Skagit River. I found rein orchids blooming in late July. Rhododendrons are found worldwide with some 1,000 different species. Access this trail seven miles east of the West Gate off Hwy 3.

Ecotouring and Safety Concerns

Flowers, trees, plants, and even rocks are part of the park's natural resources that are protected under the Park Act. Check with angling regulations at Park Headquarters for fishing in the Similkameen, Skagit, and Sumallo rivers. No hunting is allowed in Manning Park. Horseback riding and mountain biking are only allowed on a few trails; do check which ones. Power boats are prohibited in the park.

Oregon State Parks

Oregon State Parks & Recreation
Department
525 Trade Street SE
Salem, OR 97310
(503) 378-6305

One of the reasons for the establishment of Oregon State Parks was to preserve its native trees. That policy was set back in 1929 as follows:

> To create and develop for the people of the state of Oregon a state park system, to acquire and protect timbered strips on the borders of state highways, rivers, and streams, to secure in public ownership typical stands of the trees native to Oregon, to maintain the public right to the use of the sea beaches of the state, to seek the protection of our native shrubs and flowers and to preserve the natural beauty of the state.

The traveler will be overjoyed to find that several parks along the coast manage to satisfy all of these requirements, with several representative swatches of old-growth rain forest.

Humbug Mountain State Park

Attractions: Hiking, nature study, wildlife viewing, beachcombing, surf fishing, photography
Hours/Season: Overnight; year-round
Fees: No day-use fee at this park; fee for camping
Picnicking: Day-use area is 1 mile south of campground, off US 101, on the backside of the mountain.
Camping: Park campground has both tent and full hookup sites available first-come, first-served, and a hiker/biker camp.
Access: Off US 101, 6 miles south of Port Orford

The last grove of uncut old-growth rain forest on the southern Oregon coast is found on the slopes of Humbug Mountain, which slides right into the Pacific Ocean. The picnic area encompasses a lush meadow—where Port Orford children hunt for Easter eggs—surrounded by tall trees on the back side of the mountain. The campground is only a few steps from a long stretch of ocean beach that invites beachcombing. The trail to the summit of the mountain is a wonderful excursion for all seasons.

Plants and Wildlife

Big-leaf maples (a large, water-loving, broad-leaved tree common in the rain forest) are seen at the beginning of the Humbug Mountain Trail. Two rare, prized trees are found along the trail—Port Orford cedar and myrtlewood (which flowers in spring)—along with old Douglas firs, western hemlock, and huge rhododendrons.

Early spring brings pink wild currant blossoms, flowering red elderberry, and the first lovely trilliums edging the trail, followed by other wildflowers that include fairy lanterns, false Solomon's seal, vanilla plant, yellow violets, smilacinas, and bleeding hearts. White flowers of sorrel carpet the forest floor. Splotches of red or orange on decaying wood are from slime molds; yellow is from fairy cups or witches butter. Lichens and liverworts add subdued contrast as well as contributing minerals. Berries—blackberries, thimbleberries, huckleberries, and salmonberries—find enough sun along the edge of the path to flourish. Tanoak trees are dominant along the upper trail on the mountain.

Listen for the odd two-note song consisting of eerie, quavering whistles belonging to the varied thrush, which Edwin Way Teale called the "true voice of the rain forest." Chickadees chatter, and Douglas squirrels (chickarees) sometimes shrilly protest your presence. The forest floor looks like the debris in an unkept house, but it decays and becomes nutrients in a rich soil with decomposers such as fungus, millipedes, bacteria, and insect larva that work slowly at these cooler temperatures where logs pile on top of each other. This is not like the tropical jungle where decomposition is speeded up and nutrients are used up quickly, leaving a depleted soil. The biomass in the temperate forest exceeds that of the tropical forest, but the number of species is less. The forests of the lonely southern coast of Oregon have vast numbers of black-tailed deer. From the summit, binoculars help spot gray whales migrating along the coast.

Humbug Mountain Trail

Activities   A parking space along US 101 is located at the trailhead. Or access this trail in the middle of the campground (part of the Oregon Coast Trail) by crossing a walkway that spans Brush Creek and passing through a tunnel under US 101. Then start climbing 1,748-foot Humbug Mountain past lovely trees with occasional tree-framed glimpses of the coast in the vicinity of Port Orford. This is a fairly strenuous, though not difficult, 3-mile climb with a grand view south from a grassy knoll at its summit (take a lunch, even a book if you'll be alone). The best of the old growth is near the beginning, where green moss drape over tree limbs.

Recreation Trail

Not many visitors know about the 2.6-mile Recreation Trail (also part of the Oregon Coast Trail) that uses some of the road bed of the old coast highway in this area (a hazardous stretch for truckers). Walk to the east end of the campground, past the toll booth, to the signed trail. After crossing a small creek, the path goes uphill and west at the edge of forest.

Wonderful views are soon the norm as the trail follows a flat shelf above the ocean until it descends the short distance to its end, which is just across from the good clamming area at Rocky Point.

Oswald West State Park

Attractions: Hiking, nature study, wildlife viewing, surfing, fishing, geology, photography
Hours/Season: Overnight (except in winter); day use year-round
Fees: Charge for camping
Picnicking: One picnic area on east side of US 101; a walk-in picnic area overlooking Short Sand Beach is reached via a trail from US 101.
Camping: Walk-in sites (with tables and restroom) are available (wheelbarrows provided for 0.25-mile paved walk).
Access: Off US 101, 10 miles south of Cannon Beach

Rub Aladdin's lamp and you couldn't ask for a better 4-mile stretch of coast. Within the 2,474 acres of Oswald West State Park, this spur of the Coast Range has incomparable geology, ancient forest, majestic views, Cape Falcon, Neahkahnie Mountain, Arch Cape, and Smuggler's Cove. Short Sand and Necarney creeks merge at the sea at Smuggler's Cove, where surfing is an option. Take the forest trail to Cape Falcon, where you'll want to linger for the scenery. Don't cancel your hike on account of a misty rain, because the green cathedral of trees will shelter you and let you feel the pulse of what nourishes this rain forest.

The park name honors Governor Oswald West (1911–1915), whose leadership preserved Oregon's beaches for public use. With 13 miles of the Oregon Coast Trail wandering through the park, consider the walk-in campsites as a base since they are centrally located in the park and near the creeks and beach. They are popular, however.

Plants and Wildlife

Lush vegetation comprised of huckleberry, salmonberry, and salal bushes surround the campsites. This rain forest has the typical tree species and the usual large numbers of sword ferns and representatives of other fern species. A mammoth shell of an ancient tree is visible along the Cape Falcon Trail. Be on the alert for nurse logs—fallen trees that are decomposing and often provide nourishment for young trees to spout and grow from them. As the log rots away, the trees seem to hug a now non-existent entity, roots above ground reaching down into the rich humus.

Stellar jays, kingfishers, and hairy woodpeckers are numerous near the camp-sites. Water ouzels, or dipper birds, are seen at the creek areas, while forest birds include Wilson warblers, chestnut-backed chickadees, and winter wrens. A herd of Roosevelt elk roams the area near Mount Neahkahnie. When walking in the rain forest, keep an eye out for banana slugs on the trail. One doesn't want to step on these large, slippery snails without shells. Seals, sea lions, and whales are often spotted from the cape trail viewpoint.

A view of trail's end at Cape Falcon from Smuggler's Cove at Oswald West State Park.

Activities

Cape Falcon Trail

The 1.8-mile trail to 750-foot-high Cape Falcon starts just beyond the Short Sand Beach Picnic Area. As you near the tip of the cape, take the left spur where the trail divides. This goes out onto a vegetated knoll, where you can wander among paths through very thick bushes to overlook points on this very scenic coast. The sound of the surf is background music. Smuggler's Cove is below, with Point Illga to the south. The right spur on the trail is the continuation of the Oregon Coast Trail. It goes another 5.6 miles through dense woods over Arch Cape, crosses the highway, and then descends through ancient forest via an old mail route to the town of Arch Cape.

Neahkahnie Mountain Trail

Neahkahnie Mountain is the north coast's only peak to rise directly above the sea. To climb to its 1,661-foot summit from the campsite and creek area, follow the signs 1.3 miles through woods and then through the Neahkahnie Punchbowl to the highway. Legends of shipwrecks and buried treasure abound in this vicinity, and there is some evidence that Norsemen visited here in A.D. 1010. Cross the highway and continue uphill on a moderate grade for 2.5 miles to the summit where one has a wide-open spectacular view of Nehalem Bay and the Pacific Ocean. On a clear day, you can see for 50 miles. The Oregon Coast Trail continues south another 1.8 miles through lush forest with views of ridges of the Coast Range to intersect again with US 101.

Ecotouring and Safety Concerns

Preserve the pristine quality of the two streams and their environs near the campground in Oswald West State Park; do not dig for treasure in this park without a permit. The trails up Humbug and Neahkahnie mountains have many switchbacks; do not take shortcuts and contribute to causing erosion. It is a fine thing to keep, this rain forest wilderness. It is full of questions yet unasked, entities undiscovered.

Trip Tips

Other coastal Oregon state parks with good rain forest trails nourished by rainy winters and fog-dripping summer days are Ecola State Park (day use) and Cape Lookout (day use and camping).

Redwood National Park
CALIFORNIA

Redwood National Park Headquarters
1111 2nd Street
Crescent City, CA 95531
(707) 464-6101

Attractions: Hiking, nature study, wildlife viewing, photography, bicycling, fishing, swimming (in Smith River), interpretive campground programs
Hours/Season: Overnight; year-round
Fees: Day-use fee to access Fern Canyon; fee for shuttle to Lady Bird Johnson Grove and Tall Trees Grove; fee for state park campgrounds
Picnicking: (north to south) Hiouchi Area, Crescent Beach Picnic Area, Crescent Beach Overlook, Lagoon Creek Picnic Area, Klamath Overlook Picnic Area, Fern Canyon Picnic Area, Elk Prairie Picnic Area, Lost Man Creek Picnic Area, Redwood Creek Trailhead Picnic Area, Redwood Information Center Picnic Area
Camping: (north to south) Jedediah Smith Redwoods State Park, Mill Creek Campground (Del Norte Coast Redwoods State Park), Elk Prairie Campground

and Gold Bluff Beach Campground (Prairie Creek Redwoods State Park); all of these campgrounds have showers and restrooms, but no hookups. Designated backcountry camps and an environment camp are available with a permit.
Summer Camping Reservations: Call Mistix at (800) 444-7275
Access: Off US 101, from California-Oregon border south

With its 100 or more inches of annual rainfall and summer fog, the northern California coastline is a superb habitat for redwood forest, a special type of temperate rain forest dominated by the tallest trees in the world. These magnificent trees routinely grow to 300 feet or more, and are often 500 years old; some may live as long as 2,000 years. A few redwoods are also found along the southern Oregon coast.

Aim for this park (a World Heritage Site) in late spring when the pink-purple flowers of rhododendrons are blooming underneath these red-barked trees and the sweet scent of azalea flowers adds to the ambiance. Certainly, these trees are easily seen while driving the highways through Redwood National Park, but those who walk some of the miles upon miles of trails in the park will come away with a more profound experience, one that includes the tapestry of nature woven around these giants, which includes the wildlife. I remember my euphoric feeling one winter day when the first light of day sparkled on frosty meadows next to magnificent redwood trees while Roosevelt elk grazed for breakfast amongst the splendor.

Plants and Wildlife

It is interesting that the redwood trees are magnificent in many memorial groves in Jedediah Smith Redwoods State Park, which is some miles inland and primarily sunny. It would seem that the wet, often flooding conditions near Smith River and its confluence with Mill Creek make up for the absence of foggy summer weather. When conditions are not optimal for the redwoods, they mix with other typical trees of the rain forest—western hemlock, Douglas fir, western red cedar, and Port Orford cedar in the north. The understory is dominated by rhododendrons, azaleas, ferns (especially sword ferns) and a carpet of redwood sorrel, with its white to pink flowers. Blueblossom ceanothus (wild lilac) is found at the forest edge, a species that does not grow in the northern temperate rain forest. Big-leaf maple and red alder are found near creeks.

The numerous Roosevelt elk are certainly the most obvious wildlife stars for viewing in the park, as they linger in meadows adjacent to US 101 by Elk Prairie Campground. In winter, when the campground was empty, I've found them nestled among the campsites. The elk are also seen in the Gold

Bluffs area, where magnificent bulls may be observed if one is lucky. The park elk population totals about 2,000 animals. The Indian word for elk is *wapiti,* which means white rump. Black-tailed deer, bobcats, squirrels, chipmunks, raccoons, and the occasional black bear live in the forest. Salmon, steelhead, and trout spawn in the creeks. Streamside is the place for birdwatching, with more than 260 species identified in the park. The osprey and belted kingfisher are possible sightings, and the pileated woodpecker with its unusual sound and appearance will startle you into joy. Both the spotted owl and the marbled murrelet (the park is considered an oasis for them) are dependent on old-growth forest. The Smith River is an excellent place to spot river otters, which are such fun to watch as they play in river riffles.

Circle of tall trees in Redwoods National Park.

Activities

Fishing

Anglers will find good fishing in the Smith River for rainbow and cutthroat trout from late August until the rains begin. From October to February, salmon and steelhead provide challenging excitement. A fishing license is required.

Stout Grove Trail

This wheelchair-accessible trail is an easy 0.5-mile-round-trip excursion to a superb grove of redwood trees. The largest, the Stout Tree, is 340 feet high and 20 feet in diameter. From north of Crescent City, turn east off

US 101 and travel approximately 6 miles on US 199 to Howland Hill Road; turn right and continue 2 miles to the trailhead parking. From July to September, a footbridge is put in place over the Smith River and access is available by trail from Jedediah Smith Redwoods Campground. (Free maps are available from Jedediah Smith Redwoods State Park, (707) 464-9533.)

Revelation Trail

Between the Elk Prairie Campground and the park office is an unusual trail for both the blind and the sighted. The walkway is edged by wood and rope hand-rails that run the length of the 0.2-mile loop. "Touchable" features are described on signs and in a braille handbook available at park headquarters.

Fern Canyon Loop Trail

The 0.6-mile trail through Fern Canyon is a major attraction of Prairie Creek Redwoods, a one-of-a-kind magical walk. The eroding water of Home Creek caused a natural cut through bluffs and a lush profusion of five-fingered ferns cover the 50-foot-high walls. The trail is reached by driving 8 miles on narrow, unpaved Davison Road, where trailers and vehicles over 24 feet in length or 8 feet in width are prohibited (vehicles pulled by motorhomes do come in handy). The trail can also be accessed by a wonderful trail loop for those willing and eager for a longer excursion that penetrates deeper into the mysteries of the rain forest. From the Prairie Creek Campground area, hike the James Irvine Trail (4.5 miles) to Fern Canyon; go south on the Beach Road past Gold Bluffs for a little over a mile; and then take Miners Ridge Trail (4.2 miles) back to the campground. This is a fairly long trail, but an easy one, and the rewards are many, including the starbursts of light piercing through the magnificent trees. Besides the majestic trees, you will see lush, boggy carpets of tiny mushrooms, mosses, and flowers. Free maps are available from Prairie Creek Redwoods State Park, (707) 488-2171.

Redwood Creek Trail

Three miles north of the Redwood Information Center (at the south end of Redwood National Park), a spur soon goes off the Bald Hills Road to the trailhead. This 17-mile-round-trip trail accesses the Tall Trees Grove, where the tallest redwood tree (367 feet high and approximately 600 years old) is found. Whether you plan to reach the grove on this trail or not, do sample this fine path for at least a mile or two as it follows the creek and gets you close to possible spottings of ducks, herons, hawks, ruffled grouse, and bald eagles. The Tall Trees Grove is more easily reached via a steep 2.5-mile-round-trip trail off Bald Hills Road, where trailers and motor homes are prohibited. (Parking for RVs is available at the Redwood Information

Center, just to the south on US 101.) Other vehicles may use the road only with a limited number of permits, best obtained before 10 A.M. in summer. A shuttle bus runs between the information center and the trailhead to alleviate traffic (donation fee) from May through September.

Lady Bird Johnson Grove

A lovely stand of redwood trees is seen by walking the 1-mile nature trail loop reached via the steep Bald Hills Road. (See Redwood Creek Trail for notes on vehicle restrictions. The shuttle bus stops here before continuing on to the Tall Trees Grove.)

Bicycle Trail

A 19-mile combination of roads and trails has been designated a bicycle trail. From the Elk Prairie Campground, follow the campground road and link up with the jogging trail, which takes you through the forest to Davison Road. Ride this road to the Beach Road at Gold Bluffs and on to Fern Canyon, and then continue north on the Coastal Trail to Ossagon Trail. This last trail climbs steeply up to the Newton B. Drury Scenic Parkway. Head south on this road back to the campground. Be alert for hikers along the trails and show them respect. Do not ruin their experience of the redwood forest.

Ecotouring and Safety Concerns

Please note that all plants and animals are protected. Do not approach the wild and unpredictable elk on foot. You are permitted, however, to pick and enjoy the wild berries along trails. Pets are prohibited on trails. Watch for logging trucks on the roads. Do not take trailers or large campers on roads other than the main highway without checking with authorities about road conditions.

Trip Tips

Note that some trails involve stream crossings with footridges that are in place only in summer.

4

THE SONORAN DESERT

West

The Sonoran Desert is an enigmatic place first defined by its meager rainfall. Yet a Papago Indian once commented that "the desert smells like rain" since powerful scents fill the air as water releases the aromatic oils from creosote bushes and other desert plants.

Exaggerated myths merge deserts with stories of Gila monsters, sand dunes, hot sun, scorching winds and dust storms. Though some of all these myths are found in the desert, the Sonoran Desert in particular holds enchanting beauty and wondrous things. Of North America's four major rain-starved deserts, the Sonoran is the richest in diversity of life-forms and habitats, with 2,500 plant species. And strange organisms have responded to the challenge of scarce water. Eggs of small crustaceans (fairy shrimp, for example) can remain dormant for years; seeds of annuals sprout only in years with ample rain; buried spadefoot toads "hear" when the rain is sufficient to allow them to pop out and reproduce.

The Sonoran Desert covers 120,000 square miles and includes the southeastern corner of California, the southwest one-third of Arizona, the state of Sonora in Mexico, and much of Baja. The habitats include the low, hot desert (with less than three inches of precipitation annually) along the lower Colorado River, yet it has surprisingly fine wildlife viewing in the lush wetlands edging the waterway. The Sonoran region also includes block-faulted mountains, cinder cones, and even forests in the basin and range areas. The largest and driest sand sea in North America, El Gran Desierto, is found just south of the border in Baja and Sonora, Mexico. A large dunefield (two hundred square miles), the Algodones, trends north/south in the southeast corner of California, where Ajo lilies periodically adorn them. And the Gulf of California contains desert islands, complete with migrating birds and marine life.

Rain, in years when it does arrives, is either the usually gentle "female rains" of winter or the dramatic thunderstorms or "male rains" of summer (names that the Navajo Indians call them). Nature throws curves, however, and I encountered a thunderstorm in January, when sunbeams splintered the gray storm clouds all afternoon. From my campground at Picacho Peak State Park I had a marvelous seat for a magnificent light show. Evening sunset volleys flashed through the gray to wash Newman Peak clean and bright and paint a mammoth Saguaro with soft pinks and purples. It was not an evening of vivid color but one where the light had a special illuminating quality that revealed the openness and enchanting character of the Sonoran Desert.

And then the thunderstorm broke loose. Lightning and rain reverberated through the darkness until finally morning rose fresh and clear—more typical weather for this landscape—with a cactus wren singing from its perch on a saguaro.

Spring and fall are the driest seasons, good times to visit when the temperatures are not as hot. Winter also has its good days. Summer can bring extreme heat, exceeding 120 degrees Fahrenheit, with surface temperatures approaching 200 degrees, at the lowest elevations near the lower Colorado River.

Nature writers are often drawn to the mystique of the desert. Ann Zwinger wrote that easy landscapes like lawns and forests stifle her; she prefers "the absences and the big empties ... the crystalline dryness and an unadulterated sky strewn from horizon to horizon with stars." Edward Abbey balanced his periods of human contacts by retreating to the solitude of the desert, where other things could be forgotten.

Rare margay cats are one of the inhabitants of the Sonoran Desert.

Anza-Borrego Desert State Park

CALIFORNIA

Anza-Borrego Desert State Park
P.O. Box 299
Borrego Springs, CA 92004
(760) 767-5311

Attractions: Hiking, nature study, photography, wildlife viewing, backpacking, interpretive programs and hikes, campfire programs
Hours/Season: Overnight; year-round (though summer is very hot with off-season camping rate)
Fees: Day-use fee (additional for dog) in some areas; no fee for Visitor Center; addition fee for developed campgrounds and for primitive Bow Willow campground
Borrego Springs Visitor Center: Open daily 9 A.M. to 5 P.M. from October through May; open the same hours but only on Saturdays, Sundays, and Holidays from June through September; slide show on wildflowers, video on bighorn sheep, information, desert exhibits
Picnicking: A picnic area is accessed by going through the campground area on the way to the Borrego Palm Canyon Trailhead, at other developed campgrounds and at the primitive campgrounds of Bow Willow, Sheep Canyon, and Fish Creek.
Camping: Borrego Palm Canyon has group, tent, and hookup sites (flush toilets and showers); Tamarisk Grove has shaded sites plus flush toilets and showers; Vernon V. Whitaker Horse Camp has 10 campsites (flush toilets and showers) and 40 corrals; nine primitive campgrounds are scattered through the park; open camping is allowed throughout the 600,000-acre park (at least one car length from road where no plant damage can occur, and not near water holes or developed areas); for reservations call (800) 444-7275; to cancel, call (760) 452-5956.
Access: The Visitor Center, Borrego Palm Canyon, and campground are off County Road S22 (1.7 miles west of Borrego Springs) on Palm Canyon Drive.

California has done a fine thing in preserving this 600,000-acre swatch of Sonoran Desert as a state park—the largest one in the West. For one thing, it provides a sizable chunk of needed habitat for bighorn sheep. For another, it offers varied recreation from short exploratory trails near developed camping to vast expanses of desert where solitude, thoughtful contemplation, and individual discovery is possible. Perhaps you will find petroglyphs and pictographs, or sleep under the stars. Elevations vary from 200 feet at Fish Creek just west of the Salton Sea to 3,400 feet at Culp Valley.

The terrain includes colorful badlands, trickling water, mountains, alluvial fans, a sandstone canyon, and washes that can flood with rain and nourish wildflowers.

The best times to visit—and avoid scorching heat—are from November through April. Early March is the best time of year for wildflower displays.

Geology

Several geological features are seen in this park. County Road S22 follows California's most active fault line. And Split Mountain is just that—a mountain split by a fault allowing visitors to see the twisted red walls and layered cobbles that resulted from the rupture.

Anza-Borrego has an exceptional fossil record, with more than 225 different types of organisms identified, from marine plants to large mammals. The Carrizo Badlands Overlook lets people view an area once roamed by sabertooths, zebras, camels, and mastodons.

Plants and Wildlife

Elephant trees are found near Split Mountain Road, and it may surprise hikers to find palm trees at the Borrego Palm Canyon, but water furnishes that magic. Desert ironwood and smoke trees are also found there. Ocotilla, a relative of the boojum tree, grows leaves for photosynthesis after a rain and then drops them when it is too dry. The reddish flowers of the ocotilla are a bright addition to the desert terrain in spring. A variety of cacti and wildflowers are abundant here—desert lily, monkeyflower, chicory, phacelia, verbena, brittlebush, and sunflower.

Borrego cimarron, the desert bighorn sheep of the Peninsular Range, is the park's symbol. Though well adapted to harsh desert conditions, the bighorn is having some problems—which researchers are addressing—because of habitat fragmentation, threats of livestock disease, and diminishing water sources. Five distinct populations that total between 300 and 400 bighorn reside in the park . Probably the easiest sighting possibility is afforded by hiking the trail into Borrego Palm Canyon and scanning the heights. Mountain lions are

Backed by masses of yellow blooms, red flowers of this ocotilla stand out against a blue sky at Anza-Borrego Desert State Park.

around, predators of bighorn. Coyotes are predators of smaller animals. Desert iguana is one of largest lizards in the park and zebra-tailed is the lizard most frequently seen. The waterhole at Yaqui Well makes it one of the best birding spots in San Diego County. Twenty or so long-eared owls nest in the trees at Tamarisk Campground annually.

Activities

Visitor Center Trail

From Site #71 in the campground, a 0.6-mile hike wanders through creosote scrub flora, taking two forks to the Visitor Center.

Borrego Palm Canyon Trail

This very popular 3-mile-round-trip trail (brochure at Visitor Center) starts near the west end of the campground area and leads to an oasis with native fan palm trees, a waterfall plunging between large boulders, and mountains in the background.

Elephant Trees Discovery Trail

This flat, sandy 1-mile loop trail leads visitors to three elephant trees, rare in this part of the Sonoran Desert (others are found by some orienteering west off the trail). The trailhead is reached by driving 5.9 miles south of CA 78 on Split Mountain Road to the signed turnoff for the trailhead, which is another mile.

Yaqui Well Trail

To see ancient ironwood trees, bird life, wildlife, and a varied display of cactus and desert wash plants (with interpretive signs), hike the 0.8-mile trail to this desert waterhole. From Borrego Springs, drive south on Yaqui Pass Road (S3), park in Tamarisk Grove Campground, and walk across the road to the trailhead.

Cactus Loop Trail

Across from Tamarisk Grove Campground, this self-guiding 1-mile loop is moderately strenuous with expansive views of the San Felipe Wash and surrounding mountains.

Narrows Earth Trail

This easy 0.4-mile walk in a small canyon wash is a place to see faultlines, alluvial fans, and to consider human relationships to such geology. Some of the oldest rocks in the Anza-Borrego Desert are exposed here. It is located on the south side of CA 78, 4.7 miles east of Tamarisk Grove.

Equestrian Trails

The horse camp is the hub of many riding trails. Check with the park ranger at the Visitor Center for other trails and backcountry trips. The possibilities are vast.

Ecotouring and Safety Concerns

Sturdy footwear is recommended. A comb is useful for removing burrs that attach to clothes. No dogs are allowed on trails. The detailed park map available at the Visitor Center is most helpful in this large park.

Trip Tips

Mail a self-addressed, stamped postcard-in-a-letter to WILDFLOWERS, Anza-Borrego Desert State Park, P.O. Box 299, Borrego Springs, CA 92004, and you will be notified about two weeks prior to the expected peak bloom.

Picacho Peak
State Park
ARIZONA

Picacho Peak State Park
P.O. Box 275
Picacho, AZ 85241
(520) 466-3183

Attractions: Hiking, nature study, wildlife viewing, geology, photography, campfire programs
Hours/Season: Overnight; year-round
Fees: Entry fee per vehicle or campground fee
Picnicking: Ramadas and picnic sites on Barrett Scenic Loop, De Anza Picnic Loop, across from the new campground, and adjacent to Sunset parking area
Camping: Campground has 95 campsites, some with full hookups and nearby flush toilets and showers, though chemical toilets were temporarily all that was available for the tent sites in 1995; a group campground can be reserved.
Access: Off US 10 at Exit 236, 40 miles northwest of Tucson

Picacho Peak is easy to spot from US 10. It pops up sharply from the desert floor at 2,000 feet, a landmark that early Spanish explorers used to their advantage. Climbing it did and still does provide an excellent lookout point, whether it is for an Indian scouting the territory or a modern traveler eyeballing the terrain.

The interstate highway roughly follows what was once a well-traveled wagon road. It was constructed by a Mormon Battalion in 1848, under the command of Captain Philip Cooke, and used by the Jackass Mail (1857), Butterfield Overland Mail (1858–1861), and those going to the California gold fields. Picacho Pass was the site of one of the three battles of the Civil War in the Southwest. The 3,400-acre state park features a reenactment of these battles during a March weekend, complete with artillery, cavalry, and medical demonstrations.

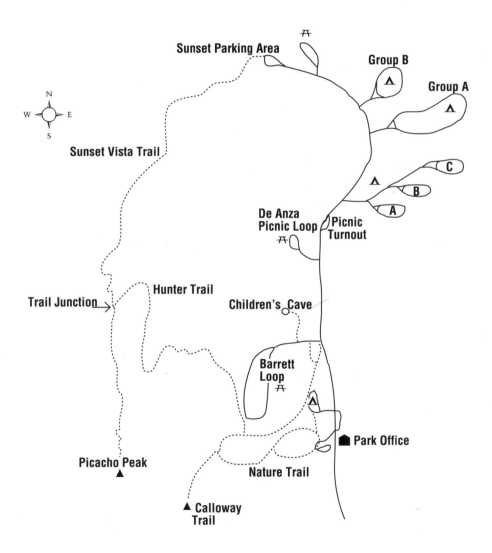

Picacho Peak State Park

Geology

Picacho Peak is an eroded, resistant lava flow interlaid with a thin strata of sedimentary rocks. The mountain, about 22 million years old, was tilted toward the northeast, then faulted and eroded. These rocks are now exposed as part of the High Picacho Mountains block, with loosened rocks buried beneath valleys or basins.

Plants and Wildlife

The nature trail offers a good chance to become acquainted with the small paloverde tree, which has green bark that harvests sunlight with its photosynthesis components. When dry, it drops its leaves and saves its chemical energy for wetter times. Sometimes there is no rain for two years in certain areas of this desert. Saguaros are numerous in the park, along with other typical Sonoran Desert vegetation—cholla, prickly pear, and creosote bush. Wildflowers bloom on the slopes of the peak.

A ranger talk concentrates on the myths and truths about the smaller, more elusive animal life. For instance, the Gila monster, one of only two toxic lizards in the world (the other is the Mexican beaded lizard, also of the Sonoran Desert), is so elusive and secretive that your chances of coming across one are minimal. The myth that it won't let go of you, if provoked and cornered, is not true. It's just that it needs to take a slow bite and grind it jaws to inject its toxin effectively. The danger of the gentle tarantula spider is a Hollywood myth, as it is actually an important eco-link—food for even an enterprising wasp—that tries to avoid humans; its toxin has little effect upon them. The scorpions are dangerous, though nocturnal.

And the rattlesnakes are not aggressive. They are a favorite meal for the roadrunner. Though this bird looks like the comedian of the desert, it is a ferocious survivor, a seeming contradiction since it can run at speeds of more than fifteen miles an hour to elude a predator and it subdues a rattlesnake by beating it against the ground or a rock until the snake's venom is all used up, then pops it into its mouth, the spent rattler dangling outside. The park lists 19 species of birds frequently seen, 27 occasionally seen, and 19 species rarely seen.

Self-Guiding Nature Trail

Activities

A road loops near the park entrance to access this trail, or one can take the connecting path from the campground. Interpretive signs identify the desert vegetation and inform those who might have questions.

Hunter National Recreation Trail

This strenuous 2-mile trail climbs from 2,000 feet to the 3,374-foot summit. Twelve sets of cables (gloves are useful) are in place to assist hikers on the more difficult portions of the trail. Those wanting a taste of the climb and better vistas will enjoy the first part of the trail; the final climb to the saddle and then on to the summit is more difficult. Park officials suggest that hikers allow four to five hours for the round-trip. A hike to the upper saddle and back is easier and only takes about an hour and a half. Check with a ranger for present conditions at the top. The hike is accessed from the Barrett Scenic Loop, with a connecting trail from the campground, which obviously makes it slightly longer.

Calloway Trail

Also accessed from the Barrett Scenic Loop or the campground, the 0.7-mile Calloway Trail climbs leisurely to a lower saddle of Picacho Peak with the reward or an immense view east. I found it a perfect place for a lunchtime snack.

Sunset Vista Trail

A recent hiking addition is a 3.1-mile trail that begins at the Sunset parking area and wanders through scenic desert terrain, away from the noise of the railroad and US 10, for more than 2 miles on the back side of Picacho Peak. It then climbs and joins the Hunter Recreation Trail for the last strenuous mile to the summit.

Ecotouring and Safety Concerns

If you put your hands or feet into rocky areas without observing what is there, you might startle a scorpion or rattlesnake. It is a good idea to shake out your shoes before putting them on. The cautious hiker is an alert and watchful one and will be rewarded with more discoveries.

Saguaro West National Park

ARIZONA

Saguaro West National Park
36933 South Old Spanish Trail
Tucson, AZ 85730
(520) 733-5100

Attractions: Hiking, nature study, birdwatching, wildlife viewing, scenic drives, photography, guided hikes, ranger talks
Hours/Season: Open 24 hours a day, but no overnight camping; year-round
Fees: Free
Red Hills Visitor Center: Open daily, except Christmas, from 8 A.M. to 5 P.M.; exhibits, information, books, and 12-minute slide program on desert habitats
Picnicking: Four picnic areas are located along park roads; one is reached by trail.
Camping: Gilbert Rey Campground (electrical hookups) in adjacent Tucson Mountain Park, off McCain Loop Road
Access: South of the park, from Ajo Way (AZ 86) by going northwest on Kinney Road a short distance west of Tucson; from US 10 by taking Exit 242 at Avra Road to a left turn on Sandario to the park (well signed from freeway); or taking Exit 257 west (Speedway) and then continuing over Gates Pass to Kinney Road

Also known as the Tucson Mountain Unit, Saguaro West National Park is a showplace for the Sonoran Desert, a place to wander amongst a forest of tree-sized cacti that have great individual variety, akin to aliens in a strange land. The stands of accordion-pleated saguaro cacti are impressive, even awesome. Yet, this forest has an openness that reveals the Tucson Mountains in the background and the exquisite colors of cacti blooming near the ground. The park is in the Arizona Upland part of the desert with considerable mountainous terrain.

As one hikes the longer trails in the park through this basin and range province, it is not difficult to envision the task of pioneer travelers who had to find the best routes, where mountain ridges seemed to pop up as often as freckles on a fair-skinned youngster.

Much of southwestern Arizona is Papago Indian country (with a 71,000-acre reservation on the western edge of the park). Their culture practiced ways of using the little rain to their advantage in planting crops, working around nature's erratic schedule and going to where the water was, in the mouth of washes. (Ethnobiologist Gary Paul Nabhan has sympathetically observed how the Papago Indian still wants to fulfill his "responsibility as a Tohono O'odham to tend the Earth and help the desert yield its food" (see

References). The Papagos have long harvested the saguaro fruit for making syrup, jam, and ceremonial wine, which they drank while dancing to invoke rain for their crops. These Indians used 450 species of the Sonoran Desert's vegetation for food, revealing a considerable knowledge of the plant life that perhaps might be of some value to other humans. For instance, the flower buds of cholla are rich in calcium.

Do stop at the new Red Hills Visitor Center and watch the slide show. The building itself is a joy of light, color, and striped shadows upon the landscape, framing saguaros and surrounded by desert plants. Since much of the wildlife of the desert is elusive, the nearby Arizona-Sonora Desert Museum—neighbor of the park—is covered under the activities.

A wonderful way to immerse yourself in the desert environment 24 hours a day is to stay in the Gilbert Ray Campground, on the southern edge of the park. This provides a bonus of nature's desert sunsets.

Geology

Several million years ago, a phase of tectonic activity opened the Gulf of California. Huge blocks of rock slowly sank as a result of faulting in the continental crust. Slowly, a series of broad, flat valleys (basins) and abrupt mountain ranges took form as a result of much sinking, uplifting, and erosion. The Sonoran Desert is superimposed on top of this geological region. The Tucson Mountains within the monument were formed during eruptive periods but they are not active today because there is no longer any thermal activity. The drive over Gates Pass traverses the remnants of an ancient volcano.

Plants and Wildlife

Each fascinating individual saguaro cactus has anywhere from two to 50 arms—one abnormal type, the cristate saguaro, has a fanlike top—which begin as buds only after 75 to 100 years when they are twelve to twenty feet high. The saguaro may grow to 50 feet and weigh several tons, hoarding water, when available, in its interior. The many spines of these plants are vital for protection, but more so for shading the plant against the hot sun. In May, many magnificent creamy, yellow-centered blossoms decorate each arm, followed by tasty fruit that, over the course of a century, will produce 22 million seeds, which turns out to be enough to produce one more mature plant, on average.

For the 24 hours that the flowers bloom—first opening at night—the nectar feeds bats, moths, ants, wasps, bees, birds, and butterflies. The sweet fruit, like a ripe fig, provides a glorious feast for many animals of the Sonoran Desert—squirrels, packrats, pocket mice, coyotes, fox, skunk, javelina, birds, and the kangaroo rat—including humans.

The saguaro plant is an excellent example of the interconnections in nature. The white-winged dove, nurtured by the nectar and fruit of this cactus, is the major distributor of its seeds. Other birds use the saguaro as their home. Gila woodpeckers and gilded flickers are so fussy when building a cavity nest in the saguaro that they discard some of the nests that other birds are wise enough to use. Those who compete for these cavities are sparrow hawks, Lucy's warblers, cactus wrens, elf owls, western kingbirds, phainopeplas, and purple martins. Honeybees are also attracted to the holes. Red-tailed and Harris hawks assemble bulky nests in the saguaro's arm joints. The saguaro condo—with its insulated walls and cool interior (warm in winter)—has a assortment of residents who live in close quarters.

Even in death, the saguaro has value because its interior column of wooden ribs have proved useful in building structures and fences. Notice them on your wanderings.

If you are alert, you might notice that some animals are lighter colored in the desert than they would be in a dark forest. I found a distinct illustration of this adaptation at my campground site when I saw a very light-colored ground squirrel and its same-colored young, almost albino in appearance.

Majestic saguaro cactus at dusk in Saguaro West National Park.

Cactus Garden Trail

Activities   Beginning at the Red Hills Visitor Center, a collection of desert plants are easily viewed along this nature trail.

Desert Discovery Nature Trail

Located a short distance northwest of the Red Hills Visitor Center, walk this 0.5-mile nature trail and become in awe of the varied saguaro population. See how many variations you can detect.

A Suggested Loop Hike

Explorers will become more intimate with this desert by hiking one or more of the trails to the highest point in the Tucson Mountains (4,687-foot Wasson Peak, which is inside the park). Try this 8-mile loop trail that takes in parts of three trails around the peak.

Leave your vehicle in the parking area across Kinney Road from the Arizona-Sonora Desert Museum (not in the museum lot) and start the King Canyon Trail, This path initially follows an old jeep trail north (closed to vehicles), staying above and to the right (east) of the canyon floor, and arrives at the Mam-A-Gah Picnic Area in 0.9 mile. From the trail register here, continue on the King Canyon Trail, as it forks to the right. The trail then ascends for 1.4 miles along the flanks of several minor ridges to a saddle where it turns northwest, left, and switchbacks uphill near some sharp drop-offs to intersect the Hugh Norris Trail in 0.9 mile. A 0.3-mile spur goes right (northeast), and 200 feet higher, to the summit of Wasson Peak for a 360-degree view of the mountain ranges scattered among the basins of this part of the Sonoran Desert Arizona Upland. After descending the summit spur, continue west on the Huge Norris Trail for 1.9 miles, where it intersects the Sendero Esperanza Trail. One can guess from a distance where this trail cuts across the ridge in a shallow saddle. Turn left and descend on an old mining road in a southeast curve for 0.5 mile to reach the Mam-A-Gah Picnic Area (my sweet pear tasted mighty good at this point) before returning on the King Canyon Trail to your vehicle. Open mine shafts in this area are a hazard, but those near the trail are well marked.

Hugh Norris Trail

From 0.3 mile east of Sus Picnic Area, along Bajada Drive, this 9.8-mile-round-trip hike goes to the summit of Wasson Peak.

Bajada Loop Drive

Northwest (1.5 miles) of the Visitor Center, the paved road terminates at Bajada Loop Drive, a 6-mile graded dirt road, with guidebook available, which passes Apache Peak, two picnic areas, and the short Valley View Overlook Trail. Those with motorhomes or trailers should first check at the information center for road conditions.

Arizona-Sonora Desert Museum

Travel 2 miles south of the park on Kinney Road and be prepared to allot a big chunk of time when you visit this incredible museum. Photographers may want to spend days, watching the animals and observing behavior that would elude them in the wild. Here, a jaguar (now found only in Mexico) and mountain lion are neighbors. William Carr, the cofounder of the museum, was the ghostwriter for a newspaper column under the byline "George L. Mountainlion." It was Carr who defined the aim of the museum as he realized that education of the public was the necessary first step toward thoughtful conservation.

The small cat canyon with its simulated rocks and crevices includes the small spotted margay, an agile and secretive creature in the wild, but quite viewable here. The ocelot cat can also be spotted—a protective coat feature in its habitat—but has a natural coat that is so attractive it once was a prime object for hunters, though this is now illegal under the Endangered Species Act. The jaguarundi is a dark-colored cat that looks more like a weasel and is usually found further south.

Near the entrance is one place where visitors can safely view those "scary" creatures of the desert—scorpions, lizards, rattlesnakes, Gila monsters, tarantulas, and so on. Actually, they're quite interesting. The chuckwalla lizard in particular seems quite a show-off as it peers about alertly.

The underwater viewing of river otters and beavers will hold your attention for some time, as will the walk-in aviary, where a wondrous variety of birds go about the daily business of living, even assembling nests, within four representative habitat areas that occur in the Sonoran Desert.

The magnificent desert bighorn sheep appear to be posed for photos in their cliff and canyon enclosure that re-creates a rocky area called "White Tanks" west of Phoenix. A social community of prairie dogs are full of playful interaction. Other animals include the tortoise, Mexican wolf, deer, javelina, badger, kit fox, and coyote.

In addition to the geology and mining exhibits, the Earth Sciences Center contains man-made "wet" and "dry" limestone caves, complete with stalactites and stalagmites. Besides the human use of caves in this region for at least 10,000 years, the packrat is a frequent occupant. This animal spends much time nest-building—using most anything available—and it turns out to be one of "our first curators." Artifacts that are 10,000 to 14,000 years old have been found in limestone caves in huge nests cemented with urine, which preserves them.

Vegetation displays are not neglected. Included are boojum trees, saguaros, grassland plots, a Papago Indian exhibit, and a Demonstration Desert Garden, which demonstrates the use of native plants for home landscaping.

One could wander for years in the Sonoran Desert without seeing and learning what takes only a few hours to absorb at this museum. Don't miss it. The museum also has many educational programs and engages in scientific research to benefit conservation efforts.

Ecotouring and Safety Concerns

The park is a sanctuary where you are welcome to explore, with respect. To avoid close encounters at night, carry a flashlight. Observe speed limits on park drives. Pets are not allowed on trails. Horseback riding is permitted on all trails. No matter how hot the days get, the nights can still be cold, so be prepared with the correct sleeping gear.

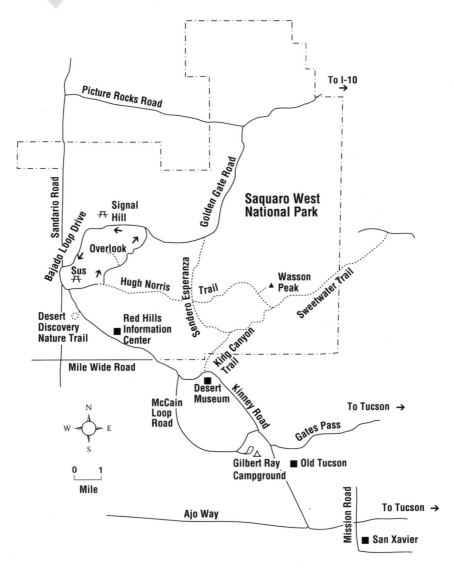

Organ Pipe Cactus National Monument
ARIZONA

Organ Pipe Cactus
National Monument
Superintendent
Route 1, Box 100
Ajo, AZ 85321
(520) 387-6849

Attractions: Hiking, backpacking, nature study, photography, wildlife viewing, geology, historical sites, visitor center, campfire programs
Hours/Season: Overnight; year-round
Fees: Fee per entry vehicle and for camping
Picnicking: Four picnic areas along Ajo Mountain Drive, and two at Bonita Well and Senita Basin off the Puerto Blanco Drive
Camping: 208 sites in the monument campground, available first-come, first-served; backcountry camping with permit
Access: 5 miles south of Why on AZ 85 to monument boundary, 22 more miles to Visitor Center

More than 330,000 acres of rocky canyons, stark mountains (three major ranges), outwash plains, creosote flats, and dry washes or arroyos in this monument might make one think it is a barren waste, but it is not so. It is a living land where the vegetation intrigues and even enchants. Spring is the best time to visit, however, before the intense heat of summer.

The area's human history is a rich one that dates back to 12,000 years ago based on the stone implements, pottery fragments, and ancient campsites that have been discovered. Spanish explorers, missionaries, and colonizers moved through this section of the Sonoran Desert, beginning in the middle 1500s, and California gold-seekers passed this way from 1849 to 1860. The journey was a hot, thirsty, and dangerous one (even bandits) that earned the route the name Camino del Diablo—the Devil's Highway.

The park's namesake, organ pipe cactus—which is common in the Baja desert—has ignored international boundaries and found just the right habitat for its growth across the border in Arizona. In a place where the sun is intense, organ pipe intensifies light exposure by growing on south slopes, though that fact also keeps it out of any winter frost. Like the saguaro, wonderful, huge flowers open during the cool of early summer night on the many up-stretched arms. Their fruit is valued by the local Indians for its tasty uses.

The monument is an International Biosphere Reserve, which is fortunate since areas of the Sonoran Desert that are not preserved often become overgrazed, cow pie–studded places of tattered vegetation. The eastern boundary of this desert wilderness abuts the Papago Indian Reservation.

Geology

Some 50 million years ago, molten lava was forced upward and encrusted parts of this area. Faulting, upthrusting of blocks, and fracturing of this volcanic rock followed to produce this basin and range country. Wind and rain further sculptured the rock formations and summer thunderstorms caused the eroded rock and gravel to fan out around canyon mouths. These fans eventually conjoined to become sloping outwash plains called bajadas. The assemblage of desert plants here is estimated to be about 4,000 years old.

Plants and Wildlife

Visitors can observe the convergence of three distinct Sonoran Desert divisions throughout the varying elevations of the monument, a complex that includes six major plant communities. The lower Colorado division includes creosotebush, bursage, saltbush, brittlebush, and foothill paloverde. The area fanning out from the campground is mostly Arizona Upland, where organ pipe, saguaro, prickly pear, and cholla grow on bajadas. Higher in the Arizona Upland, in the canyons of the Ajo Mountains, are jojoba, agave, rosewood, ironwood, and juniper. A small pocket of exotic Mexican species—elephant tree, senita cactus, limberbush, and organ pipe—is situated near the Senita Basin Picnic Area. A total of 26 cacti species have adapted to the hot, arid environment of the monument.

Annual wildflowers adapted to the desert by mechanisms where seed germination is controlled. The soil is full of seeds that remain dormant until the right amount of rain washes away the seed inhibitors. Sometimes bacteria are involved in the removal of these inhibitors. The best place for viewing flowers here is along the Ajo Drive. Once or twice in a decade, extraordinary fields of resplendent growth includes gold poppies, pink owl clover, desert dandelions, and goldfields, though some color is found annually. Cacti blooming adds to the visual magic.

Unlike plants, animals can choose to avoid the intense sun by roaming at night—which the elf owls, kangaroo rats, and most snakes do—or opt to be active during the early and late daytime hours— which the bighorn sheep, most birds, and lizards do while finding a shady rest spot during the heat. Coyotes, javelinas, and the desert tortoise are not so particular about when they're out, if it's not too awfully hot. Hummingbirds are around when the cacti and wildflowers are in bloom. Bird life includes 35 permanent resident species and more than 260 migratory species. The curve-billed thrasher and canyon wren are somehow able to nest in the chainfruit cholla, which provides protection for them.

Activities

Visitor Center Nature Trail

A 0.1-mile wheelchair-accessible path with guide pamphlet introduces the desert and its plants.

Desert View Nature Trail

This 1.2-mile loop climbs up to a ridge with vistas of Sonoyta Valley and the pink granite Cubabi Mountains in Mexico. Trailside signs describe various features along the way. Saguaros add interest to the beautiful sunsets that can be photographed from the vantage point of the ridge.

Victoria Mine Trail

Starting from the south side of the campground perimeter loop, this fairly easy 4.5-mile-round-trip trail wanders up and down rolling hills—take time for some nature study—to the site of the monument's richest and oldest gold and silver mine, where a remnant stone structure and various artifacts are found.

Estes Canyon–Bull Pasture Trail

Accessed from Ajo Mountain Drive, this strenuous 4.1-mile-round-trip trail climbs from weird-shaped saguaros and other interesting vegetation to a high plateau where ranchers used to bring their cattle. Excellent vistas.

Campground Perimeter Trail

A 1-mile loop around the campground is just right for leisurely strolls, even with pets.

Paloverde Trail

Pets are permitted on this 2.6-mile-round-trip hike through the desert to the Visitor Center.

Ajo Mountain Drive

This 21-mile auto tour on a mostly one-way, graded dirt road climbs to the edge of the sixth vegetation community, including an impressive number of organ pipes. About midway along the drive, a natural arch is visible. In the Ajo Mountains, notice the darker basalt and the ribbons of light yellow, compressed volcanic ash or "tuff." No motorhomes over 25-feet long or trailers are advised. Even smaller RVs can experience difficulties on these winding, up-and-down roads. Guidebooks are available at the visitor center. Don't miss this interesting tour.

Puerto Blanco Drive

A long and winding dirt road loops 53 miles around the Puerto Blanco and Sonoyta mountains, and the La Abra Plain, edging the Mexican border on the final leg before a spur leads off to Senita Basin. Along the way lies Golden Bell Mine and Quintobaquito Spring. Plan to take at least a half day to cover this road, which is mostly one-way. The same vehicle cautions, as in Ajo Mountain Drive above, apply to this drive.

Alamo Canyon

A short drive accesses this canyon where the remains of a brick structure and a corral are situated. Wander about and follow the rocky Alamo Wash, which carries water down from the adjoining Ajo Range during rains.

Cross-Country Hiking

Check with a park ranger on trip possibilities best suited to your ability.

Ecotouring and Safety Concerns

Be careful to avoid any physical contact with the cacti, especially the cholla. If impaled by this, do not try to remove it with your fingers, use some implement (pliers are handy to have along). Human visitors are not as well adapted to the heat as other organisms and there is little available water; so do carry some, wear a hat, and bring sunscreen. If you travel either or both of the dirt drives in the park, carry emergency tools. Avoid flooded areas (yes, this can happen in the desert) and never drive off the park roads. Do not even think about digging up even the tiniest cactus to take home.

Baja Sonoran Desert
BAJA CALIFORNIA

Backcountry Discovery
Baja California

The vast continuation of the Sonoran Desert into Baja California has enticements found exclusively in this region. Only the northwest corner and the tip of Baja are excluded from the Sonoran Desert designation. Though some areas of this desert are fairly flat, much evidence of past volcanic activity exists and picturesque cliffs, fringe bays, mountain ridges, and volcanic cones punctuate the desert. Consider that the Baja desert is adjacent to both the Pacific Ocean—with surf and sunsets—and the Gulf of California, with warm, quiet bays and sunrises. From a primitive campsite edging the gulf at Bahia de Los Angeles or from a waterfront spot on Bahia de la Concepcion, campers can walk into the desert amidst breathtaking surroundings. The exploring opportunities are vast.

Plants and Wildlife

The Baja vegetation is intriguing. Imagine a cactus shaped like an enormous upside-down carrot. This plant was named the boojum tree by geographer Godfrey Sykes, who was inspired by Lewis Carroll's use of the name. This strange plant is endemic to Baja and Sonora, Mexico. The "king" of cactus is the cardon, larger even than the saguaro. The ocotilla, Baja fairy duster, mesquite, ironwood, paloblanco ("white stick," related to the paloverde farther north), and the elephant tree are other plants to keep an eye out for. Many of these species can be spotted while walking in the rock garden near Catavina, where huge picturesque boulders punctuate the desert terrain. Several endemic plants are also found on the desert islands in the Gulf of California.

An ecosystem comprised of water, vegetation, shore birds, and sea life is found on the desert islands in the Gulf of California, with large numbers of nesting and migrating birds, including terns, gannets, tropicbirds, Heermann's sea gulls, and both the brown- and blue-footed booby (a name given by sailors because they were so easy to catch). California sea lions breed and birth in the safety of these gulf islands. Gray whales breed and birth in lagoons inland from the Pacific Ocean. The Indians of Baja have long called these cetaceans the "desert whale" because their spouts rise above the surrounding Sonoran Desert.

The Baja desert, particularly near water, provides intriguing birding. Brown pelicans, in their colorful breeding plumage, can be seen diving for fish. Caracara hawks soar overhead and ospreys nest on abandoned cement towers.

Activities

Consider taking a mountain bike along on your auto tour to explore the dirt roads that branch off from the main highway. Kayakers can paddle near the shore in the Gulf of California, or in the inland lagoons, and make occasional stops to explore the desert. Check out the sand dunes north of San Felipe in the El Gran Desierto. A few miles north of Catavina, take a break amdist a collection of large reddish boulders that form a rock garden—the Catavina Boulder Field—a great place for examining the boojum and elephant trees, in the company of a colorful shrine of the Virgin Mary painted on one of the rocks. There are even some petroglyphs on the boulders. Allow time to hike out into the desert. A lush palm oasis is located at Mulege, along the Santa Rosalia River. After a rain, take a wildflower walk to discover what colorful blossoms have popped up on the desert landscape.

Ecotouring and Safety Concerns

You are a visitor in a foreign country in Baja and should treat the residents and their customs with respect; the fragile desert deserves that consideration also. Always carry enough water for the situation, even while auto touring.

5

PACIFIC COAST TIDEPOOLS

It is difficult to imagine a more fascinating and dramatic place to check out the biodiversity of living organisms than the intertidal pools of rocky shores, which are so prevalent along the Pacific coast. Two major environments merge and invite organisms to select from the varied real estate.

Visit at a high tide, however, and you'll have little indication of what you can walk amongst during a low tide, when a time slot opens and beckons visitors to make discoveries before it slips away and they must wait for the next picture show.

The low tide is really the retreat of a slow wave produced by the moon and the sun as they engage in a tug of war over the ocean's fluid motion. During one revolution of the moon, two high tides and two low tides occur. The most dramatic of these tides occurs when the sun and moon are in line with each other—the "spring" tides (which do not refer to the season).

The life-forms that survive here have adapted to considerable stresses, enough to discourage most organisms, yet complexities often spur biological molecules to adapt. Intertidal life must meet the challenge of the often-violent surf; variations in sunlight, salinity, and temperature; shifting sand and sediments; and periods of living under water alternating with times in air. Each living marine organism has adapted to a niche and developed strategies for survival.

The prime requisite for the survival of rocky shore intertidal creatures is the ability to hold on in the face of surf action. Sea stars possess hundreds of tube feet for suction attachments to rocks. Mussels secrete elastic byssal threads to secure their shells. Limpets prefer suction; barnacles manufacture cement for this hanging-on purpose. Different species, different approaches to the problem. Anyone who harvests mussels for food knows the effectiveness of their anchoring devices; it takes some hefty prying to loosen them.

When you walk toward the sea during a minus tide, notice how you pass through zones of different organisms that depend on how much time is air time.

The first zone constitues the spray area where organisms get showers only during the highest of water levels, and life is more a matter of air than water survival. Storm surges provide good growing conditions while dry summers stress living here. Black lichen, periwinkles, limpets, and acorn barnacles are found in this highest zone—the penthouse apartment.

Next is a region where life-forms spend time underwater daily at high tide. Black turban snails, mussels, ochre sea stars, and tiny porcelain crabs that scurry about—sometimes chasing each other—are among those organisms that stay put much of the time.

Closer seaward, black leather, lined and mossy chitons; green and aggregating anemones; and sea staghorn seaweed abound.

Finally, the lowest zone is exposed only during minus tides—those below the average low water mark—with purple urchins, sea cucumbers, many-rayed sea stars, and bull kelp proliferating. These representative species are only the most obvious, the most easily found.

Part of the allure of tidepools lies in the beauty of the arrangement of the organisms in watery cracks of rock surfaces and in miniature swimming pools. Colors contrast—purples, oranges, off-whites, browns, lime greens, shiny silvers, pinks, blacks, and blood reds. Designs and textures offer a clue as to individual plants and animals as well as the collage that makes up each tidepool.

Take time to listen, too. Put your ear next to a patch of mussels or barnacles on a rock surface and hear the hissing sound of water and the working of valves as these sessile creatures close up tight to retain water during the inactive period. Air time is fasting time. Food comes via seawater, and facing into the waves—like the bow of a ship—expedites eating for filter-feeding animals such as mussels, clams, tubeworms, and barnacles.

As you become more interested in these creatures, you might learn about their unique and extraordinary strategies: how the sea star squeezes its stomach into a tasty bivalve to digest its meat; how the flowers of this ecosystem—the sea anemones—capture small prey with stinging nematocysts that are released on touch and fired as projectiles with an acceleration 10,000 times that experienced by astronauts at liftoff; and how barnacles have a unique sex life by having both male and female gonads present in the same individual. Plants and invertebrates of the intertidal region have responded to the dynamics of the sea's edge with some unusual life cycles, some even a little bizarre.

Microscopic happenings of tiny organisms and larvae of intertidal animals are not obvious to the naked eye, but are nonetheless incredibly varied and intriguing to those who wish to delve deeper into the ecology of the tidepools.

All of these destinations have varied tidepool organisms, some easy to discover, others found by the more inquiring and persistent explorer. Tidepools are an arena of diverse life exposed for viewing, for learning, for wonderment. And the rocky coastal scenery is a bonus, providing some of the West's most spectacular seascapes.

In conjunction with exploring natural tidepools, consider expanding your knowledge by visiting one of the world-class aquariums, where so many species can be viewed during one visit; Monterey, California; Tacoma, Washington; and Newport, Oregon all have excellent facilties.

Coastal Strip,
Olympic National Park
WASHINGTON

Olympic National Park
600 East Park Avenue
Port Angeles, WA 98362
(360) 452-4501
Mora Ranger Station:
(360) 374-5460

Attractions: Tidepools, beach walking, wildlife viewing, beachcombing, backpacking, clam digging, surf fishing, smelting, photography, exhibit information, campfire talks
Hours/Season: Overnight; year-round
Fees: Charge for developed campgrounds
Picnicking: Rialto Beach
Camping: Kalaloch has 177 campsites and restrooms (fee); Mora has 94 campsites and restrooms (fee); South Beach offers primitive oceanfront camping and restrooms (free); Backpackers (with free permits) may camp on the beach except between Ellen Creek and Rialto Beach and on all beaches south of the Hoh River.
Access: All tidepool, picnicking, and camping locations are accessed from US 101 on the northwest coast of Washington (see the map for specific locations).

Imagine a pristine wilderness coastline where wave watching is spectacular on the rocky sea stacks and headlands. Realize your visions on the 57 miles that are part of Olympic National Park. Dynamic changing scenery and vibrant adaptations of wildlife add to the charm, especially if the sun is shining. The fury of the surf comes in raw from 5,000 miles of open ocean and often hides the wonder of the tidepool areas that are exposed at low tide. Experienced hikers can opt for strenuous backpacking along this coast to views rarely seen.

Remember that the massive quantities of rainfall make this a very wet place much of the year, with some snatches of sunshine and vibrant sunsets in summer, with the best possibility of fair weather in August. These times are very special.

Geology

The Pacific Coast that we see today has only existed for about 25 million years, not really very long geologically speaking. The continent of North America continues to move northwestward a few centimeters per year, widening the Atlantic Ocean while narrowing the Pacific Ocean as the lighter continental substance rides over the sea floor of the Pacific Ocean, causing it to submerge and often precipitating volcanic eruptions as hot magma is thrust upward through weak spots below the continent.

Plants and Wildlife

The warm waters of the Kuroshio (the Japan ocean current) meeting the upwelling of cold waters off northern California results in a coastline habitat with similar intertidal animals from Sitka, Alaska, to Point Conception (north and west of Santa Barbara, California). Discover tidepool plants and animals on a walk to Hole-in-the-Wall with a park naturalist. Some unlikely edibles are resident here and you will learn about them—pickled kelp, anyone? The tidepool habitat is so successful that 4,000 animals belonging to 20 species may inhabit a single square foot of seashore. One intriguing animal of these pools is the two-spot octopus, which grows to about 12 inches long and changes color with its mood.

Watch for sea otters offshore and birds such as gulls, black oystercatchers, and bald eagles. And don't be surprised if you discover a raccoon snatching shellfish at low tide or footprints of deer, river otters, or even bear.

Beach 4

Activities

A good, short paved trail leads to this sandy beach where a short stretch of walking takes one to rocks where discoveries include sand dollars, fittings from shipwrecks, green anemones, and hermit crabs. In spring, be alert for glass floats swept ashore by currents. Razor clam digging, smelting, and surf fishing are good options here. The Big Cedar Tree is just a short distance north, reached by a short gravel road on the east side of the highway.

Ruby Beach

A short downhill trail is easily negotiated that terminates at a choice beach location. This place is named for its pinkish sand that contains tiny garnet crystals. Consider clamming, surf fishing, and smelting at appropriate times.

Wandering through the intertidal area at Ruby Beach in Olympic National Park.

Second and Third Beach

It can be confusing, but these two much-photographed scenic stretches of beach and rock formations within the park are located south of La Push (a fishing village on the Quileute Indian Reservation) and are accessed by trails. Both have tidepool areas. Second Beach is a 0.6-mile hike through coastal forest; Third Beach is reached via a 1.2-mile trail.

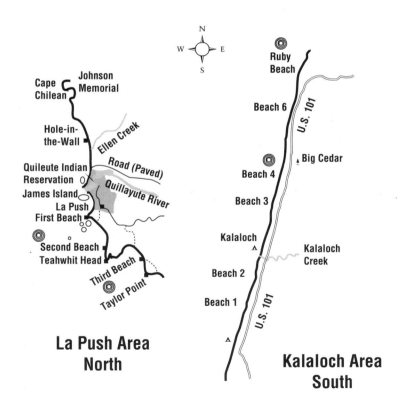

La Push Area North

Kalaloch Area South

Olympic National Park Coastal Strip

Rialto Beach

This beach consists primarily of round, polished stones stacked on top of each other. Picturesque James Island lies just offshore, sometimes reachable at low tide, but part of Indian land. Walk 1.5 miles north from Rialto Beach to reach the tidepools on a rock reef at Hole-In-The-Wall, a sea tunnel. Cross Ellen Creek along the route, usually easy to wade at low tide. You can join a ranger-led hike to this area in summer.

Ecotouring and Safety Concerns

Though it is permissible to turn over rocks while looking for intertidal organisms, it is important that these rocks be returned to their original position to prevent causing deaths. One is allowed to collect a handful of unoccupied shells. Long-distance trails on the beach often involve going over headlands that can not be rounded by shore and these are marked by orange and black targets. Due to minimal maintenance, caution is required on the often steep and muddy climbs. Do obtain a detailed park map of the coastal strip before undertaking these hikes and carry a tide schedule.

Devil's Punch Bowl State Park
OREGON

Oregon State Parks and Recreation Department
1115 Commercial Street NE
Salem, OR 97310-1001
(503) 378-6305

Attractions: Marine gardens, unusual geology, whale and storm watching, beachcombing, hiking, surfing, bicycling, photography
Hours/Season: Day use; year-round
Fees: Free
Picnicking: A picnic area overlooking the ocean is adjacent to Devil's Punch Bowl.
Camping: No camping in this park, but Beverly Beach State Park (1 mile south) offers 138 tent, 76 electrical, and 53 full hookup campsites, plus restrooms with showers.
Access: Off US 101, 8 miles north of Newport, on the Otter Crest Loop—a scenic alternative to US 101 and part of the Oregon Coast Bike Trail; the parking area for the marine gardens is 2 blocks north of the day-use and viewpoint area for the punch bowl.

The marine garden at Devil's Punch Bowl State Park is one of the most popular tidepool areas on the Oregon coast. The park is situated on the lower edge of Cape Foulweather—named by Captain James Cook on a stormy March day in 1778—where a expansive rock shelf is exposed when the tide is out.

Various species of seaweed populate the tidepools.

An exuberance of colorful living organisms have attached themselves to the rocky surface and crevices where one can walk cautiously past slippery sea weeds on a path of barnacles. Boulders rise above the hard surface. Channels and pools of sea water occur where there are depressions. The surrounding geology is fascinating and adds to the lure of these gardens. The undulating rocky shoreline next to the picnic area consists of soft sedimentary rock, with varied formations that make for good wave watching as the surf bounces off the cliffs.

Geology

Though the interactions of tectonic plates were a slow process that created the present Pacific coastline of North America over a period of millions of years, the more recent great ice ages greatly influenced the present appearance of the Pacific coast. Vast quantities of water were periodically locked up in sheets of ice on the North American continent. Continental shelves were laid bare. Sea levels dropped during ice ages (between 100 to 130 meters during the last one). The melting of the ice between ages left terraces and scars above today's sea level where water lapped high upon the landscape.

Cape Foulweather rises steeply at the north end of this broad rock bench. To the south, a golden cliff of sandstone fronts sea caves. The forces of erosion tore holes in the 15-million-year-old sandstone roof of these caves to the point where they collapsed. Further shaped by surf, the cave now looks like a giant punch bowl, a caldron for the brews of a giant wizard. But that wizard turns out to be Neptune, and he floods the bowl with swirling seawater at high tide and empties it on the ebb tide.

Plants and Wildlife

Those interested in seaweeds will find the marine garden an invaluable aid in identifying the various species in different tidal zones.

Look for round holes carved in underwater rocks. This is where sea urchins live. If you approach the pools of water silently, you can see tiny sculpin fish swimming around. The ubiquitous sea anemones and sea stars are obvious, but closer inspection will acquaint the visitor with many other diverse organisms. Once in a while a giant Pacific octopus is visible in these tidepools—a fascinating creature best visited in an aquarium. Shore birds and gray whales provide additional entertainment when seen in the area.

Tidepool Walk

Activities

A trail leads downhill from the parking area to a sandy beach, a beach mostly inundated with waves except at low tide, and provides access to the marine garden. Head seaward through the various zones of the intertidal area. The floor of the punch bowl can be entered from the south end of this beach, and you can see the tunnels where the water enters. Offshore are rock formations, one imaginatively called Otter Rock.

Gray Whale Watching

Volunteers are available to answer questions and help visitors spot whales offshore at this wheelchair-accessible site during the last week of the year and during spring break. This is when the gray whales are migrating south and later returning north. These charismatic cetaceans attract thousands of visitors worldwide, including 62 foreign countries, who have signed logs in the past, in a quiet cultural exchange.

Oregon Coast Trail

A wooden stairway on the south side of the day-use area descends to the beach and to a 5-mile section of the Oregon Coast Trail connecting this park and Yaquina Head (no access to this headland). The beach is easily traversed except for a promontory just north of Yaquina Head, but this can be rounded easily at low tide. The access to the beach from Beverly Beach State Park is only 1.2 miles so it is feasible to stay overnight at the campground and visit Devil's Punch Bowl via a beach hike.

The rock shelves of the intertidal area of Devil's Punch Bowl State Park.

Ocean Surfing

Surfers may want to bring their boards as the beach to the south of the punch bowl provides fine ocean surfing.

Cape Foulweather Wayside

Drive another 1.25 miles north on Otter Crest Loop to see Cape Foulweather with its impressive view of the marine gardens, punch bowl area, and the surrounding seascape.

Ecotouring and Safety Concerns

This is a protected marine garden and any collection of organisms is prohibited, even by scientists or educators. Wear rubber boots and walk with caution.

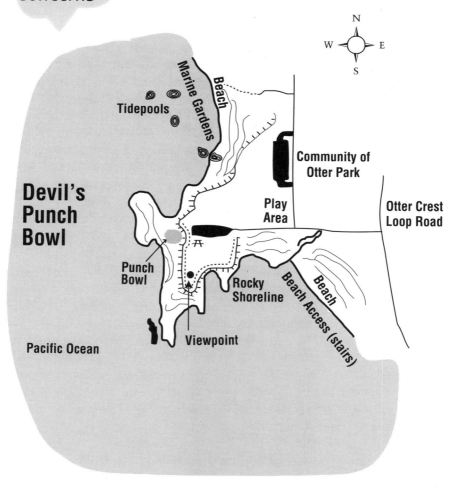

Yaquina Head Outstanding Natural Area
OREGON

YHONA
P.O. Box 936
Newport, OR 97365
(541) 265-2863

Attractions: Marine garden, Yaquina Head Lighthouse, barrier-free tidepool path, wildlife viewing, exhibit information, visitor center (under construction)
Hours/Season: Day use; year-round
Fees: Free (this may change)
Picnicking: No facilities
Camping: Campsites for tents and with full hookups (restrooms and showers) are available at Beverly Beach State Park, 3 miles north of this headland.
Access: Off US 101, 3 miles north of Newport

Sometimes nature presents biologists and naturalists with catastrophic events—such as the volcanic eruption on Krakatau—that wipe out all life-forms. The stage is then set for visitors to observe organisms reestablishing themselves, an exciting and informative process. Nothing quite so dramatic happened on Yaquina Head, but a former rock quarry has been reclaimed by breaking up a three- to four-acre area of basalt rock and subsequently digging it down to let the sea in—a Bureau of Land Management (BLM) project. Part of the 100-acre Yaquina Head Outstanding Natural Area (YHONA), one now can watch what happens as tidepools become slowly populated along the world's first barrier-free walkway through a reconstructed intertidal zone. This is good news for all travelers, particularly those with physical disabilities who must view nature from a wheelchair, and for adults pushing strollers.

Also found at Yaquina Head are the Yaquina Head Lighthouse (recently renovated), a Fishermen's Memorial, an adjoining intertidal area by a cobble beach, and the dramatic offshore rocks of a national wildlife refuge. This coastal headland is indeed outstanding.

The lighthouse was built in 1873 and is still active. The original plan was to put the lighthouse on Cape Foulweather, but it proved too difficult to transport materials there. Yaquina Head was not an easy destination either and supplies were transported up to the point via a staircase hacked out of solid rock with a windlass and derrick. In 1977, a Nancy Drew television production focused on ghost stories associated with the lighthouse.

Geology

Waves and rain are the major short-term forces that act rapidly and dynamically to continuously shape Pacific seascapes. Though sand and cobble beaches change from day to day, rocky beaches and headlands are more slowly eroded by this action. The fury of storms brings explosive surf action upon coastal rock formations, with the softer rocks becoming more easily eroded. The harder rocks of basalt, which include the offshore sea stacks, resist this energetic wearing away longer, but not forever.

A major El Niño occurrence during the spring of 1983 washed around 50 feet of coastal bluffs in one night in one area of the Oregon coast. When winter storms, high tides, and a strong El Niño converge, abnormally high waves batter the coastline.

The central Oregon coast in this particular area remained submerged long after the rest of the Coast Range had risen above sea level. This particular headland results from a lava flow that originated at least 14 million years ago in eastern Washington and Oregon before spreading to the ocean.

Plants and Wildlife

Already—as of 1995—tiny fish, crabs, shrimp, barnacles, and diatoms inhabit the newly-created tidepools, with seabirds, larger fish, and harbor seals as visitors. A full range of intertidal creatures are accessed near the lighthouse. Many harbor seals haul out on nearby Seal Rock, and interpretive exhibits are displayed along the observation area of the headland. BLM volunteers answer questions during the summer.

The headland overlooks Yaquina Head Rocks National Wildlife Refuge, part of the offshore Oregon protective system where hundreds of thousands of seabirds find refuge and human access is prohibited. These offshore nesting rocks are very close—not distant, binocular-requiring sea stacks—so it is easy to see young, nondescript seagulls parading about in the spring. The large seabird rookery just offshore is named Colony Rock, and nesting species include pigeon guillemots, sea gulls, common murres, and cormorants. One can also spot black oystercatchers, auklets, storm petrels, and spectacular tufted puffins showing off their breeding plumage. This headland is also an official whale-watch site. Some "resident" gray whales stay during the summer to feed.

Barrier-Free Tidepool Walk

Activities

This well-planned, 1,500 feet of curving walkway gently slopes into the water, covered at high tide, but all walkable during a good low tide when tidepools are exposed. Overlooks, rock benches, and even elevated pools—for those who can't bend down—add to the enjoyment. Imagine being able to see how nature slowly populates these newly established tidepools. It is enough to lure you to visit often to follow the processes. Wayside displays and an interpretive center are planned for the near future.

Black Cobble Beach

Near the lighthouse, a wooden stairway leads to this beach composed of large black cobbles. This marine garden is explored often by school children on educational trips and gets considerable traffic.

Ecotouring and Safety Concerns

All public entry is strictly prohibited on Oregon's offshore rocks, islands, and reefs, in order to protect nesting seabirds.

Westport-Union Landing State Beach and MacKerricher State Park
CALIFORNIA

Westport-Union Landing
State Beach
MacKerricher State Park
P.O. Box 440
Mendocino, CA 95460
(707) 937-5804

Attractions: Tidepools, beaches, surf fishing, bird-watching, whale watching, abalone diving, spear fishing, and hiking. MacKerricher has horseback riding, bicycling, ranger-led hikes and bike rides, wheelchair-accessible boardwalk trail, mussel-gathering, and campfire programs.

Hours/Season: Overnight; MacKerricher is open year-round; Westport-Union Landing is closed in winter.

Fees: Fee for camping at both parks, though more at MacKerricher, but no day-use fee at either park.

Picnicking: Picnic area at MacKerricher, and tables are numerous at Westport-Union Landing.

Camping: MacKerricher has 143 developed campsites (restrooms with showers) and 11 walk-in sites. Westport-Union Landing has 130 primitive sites and vault toilets. Call Mistix at (800) 444-7275 for reservations from April through September.

Access: Westport-Union State Beach is 2 miles north of Westport, off CA 1, with several entry roads, some marked by a Vista Point sign. MacKerricher State Park is a short distance south, 3 miles north of Fort Bragg, off CA 1, near Cleone.

Just a few miles apart on the northern California coast, these two California parks both have spectacular rocky coastal scenery and several intertidal areas with tidepools to explore, but each park offers quite different facilities. Westport-Union Landing is a quiet 41-acre park with a narrow 2-mile stretch of ocean frontage along coastal cliffs that the locals will share with the occasional traveler who discovers it. One of its seven campgrounds—just north of Howard Creek—has primitive sites available that are right on the edge of a bluff overlooking fantastic ocean views; other sites are not far back. MacKerricher, on the other hand, is a well-developed park with an extensive campground area in the midst of forest vegetation located a short distance from the ocean. This 1,600-acre park has 8 miles of beach and various recreation areas, including delightful freshwater Lake Cleone, a lagoon affair with enticing wetland areas.

Ten Mile Dunes, just south of Ten Mile River, occupies a large segment of northern MacKerricher, a collecting point for sand swept ashore from the ocean's reservoir.

Geology

The San Andreas Fault lies a short distance offshore in this area of northern California—the notorious boundary between tectonic plates where stresses have shaped the coastline and produced coastal mountains.

Resistant rocks that become headlands receive the focused energy of surf action, wearing them down gradually to form beaches and coves. The cove where the boardwalk begins was most likely created by erosion near Laguna Point. Now the waves sweep into this deep cove. Holes in coastal volcanic rocks fill with mineral matter brought by circulating water, and sometimes agates, more often zeolites, are frequently washed onto beaches.

Plants and Wildlife

The vegetation between Lake Cleone and the ocean is a colorful ground cover of ice plant that blooms yellow in spring and dries pink. In spring, reddish purple owl clover, golden orange California poppies, violet-colored lupines, and numerous sunlit yellow flowers color the shoulders and meadows near CA 1. The intertidal plants at both parks include various species of algae, commonly called seaweeds, which are quite varied and vital photosynthesizers in the shallow water of the tidepools.

Numerous coastal birds, harbor seals (capable of diving to depths of 600 feet and for periods up to 23 minutes), and whales (in season) are seen from the beaches of both parks. Typical Pacific coast tidepool animals resode in the intertidal areas.

Freshwater Lake Cleone at MacKerricher is stocked with trout and popular for fishing. Ducks are plentiful; some migrate from Mono Lake. MacKerricher has a gray whale skeleton on exhibit near the entry station of the park. (Whale-watching boat trips are offered from Fort Bragg in April.) The lush vegetation of the campsites lures birds that enhance your relaxation with their songs.

Intertidal Areas

Activities

Several steep trails to the beach have been cut by visitors from sites on the cliff at Westport-Union Landing, but an easy access to the beach is just north of Howard Creek, with stairs and informative signs about the tidepools. The shallow creek must be waded to reach the shoreline. An even easier entry point—and gentler trail—is reached south of Howard Creek without wading through the creek. A long stretch of beach invites walking and observation, with sea stacks and rocky shelves near the sand providing intertidal habitat. Tidepool areas are accessed at MacKerricher via the boardwalk trail to Laguna Point.

Wheelchair-Accessible Boardwalk at MacKerricher

From a parking area overlooking a spectacular wave-watching cove, this walkway borders a bluff and leads to Laguna Point to a seal-watching station. Gray whales travel south in the winter and return north in the spring; rangers are on hand to assist whale-watchers.

Lake Cleone Trail at MacKerricher

A 1-mile, hikers-only trail circles this pretty lake where the scenery includes cypress trees and marshes, and offers good bird-watching at the right time of day. It is accessed from the adjacent picnic area and from both Cleone and Surfwood campground areas. Part of the trail is wheelchair accessible.

The "Haul Road" at MacKerricher

This abandoned logging road (vehicles are prohibited) extends from the southern end of the park at Pudding Creek day-use area to the northern edge of the park, approximately 8 miles available for hiking.

Ecotouring and Safety Concerns

Do check the tide times and go out at low tide—preferably one of the lowest or minus tides—about an hour earlier so you can explore for a couple of hours before the tide comes in. Always be aware of incoming tides so you will not get stranded on an offshore rock when the water returns. Be cautious on coastal cliffs; some are not stable. No hunting is allowed in the state park system.

6

SUBALPINE MEADOWS

West

It is interesting that the ancient Greeks' idea of heaven—the Elysian Fields—was a meadow of flowers at the edge of woods, where people walked about and enjoyed the sunshine, the long evenings, and the stars.

Earth was for so long a place of rather drab colors; there were no flowers. And then, 100 million years ago, as Loren Eiseley wrote, "All over the world, like hot corn in a popper, these incredible elaborations of the flowering plants kept exploding." The wonder of these angiosperms is in the myriad of different seed cases and the variety of their fruits, though colors were often the enticement that lured interconnections with animals and insured pollination.

Bees smear pollen on their bellies and make honey. Some insects use the yellow centers of flowers as landing pads. Even mosquitos can pollinate flowers. Birds find a source for their high energy needs from both the plants and their respective interactive insects. These angiosperms, with their concentrated and diversely packaged foods, are even up to the task of firing the brains of warm-blooded animals and humans, whether they are brightly colored flowering plants or not. Mammals are nourished on the grasslands, including humans. Elk graze, and black bears eat fruits, grasses, and dandelions. Coyotes keep the population of small mammals in check so that the wild garden is not stripped clean. These angiosperms anchor the soil, then enrich it when they die down over winter.

And yet, much of this utility is painted with the brilliance of a master painter who dips into a palette of rainbow colors. We humans work hard to make our flower gardens a thing of beauty and solace, but nature plants and nourishes these wild gardens with no assistance from us—though other life-forms do help—and we can simply visit and enjoy them. Probably the most striking gardens are the mountain meadows where snowmelt from mountain peaks spurs a brilliant display of wildflowers of high elevations in the short summer, when sweet scents are often in the air.

Many mountain ranges in the West have vivid wildflower displays and trails—long and short—for exploring. Suggested are a few destinations that are quite special. Since best flowering times vary slightly, even from year to year, travelers may want to check with authorities when planning trips. Bring a small pocket magnifying glass to entertain the children; flowers often have exquisite tiny designs inconspicuous to the naked eye.

Hurricane Ridge and Deer Park, Olympic National Park
WASHINGTON

Olympic National Park
Superintendent
600 East Park Avenue
Port Angeles, WA 98362
(360) 452-0330

Attractions: Hiking, backpacking, wildlife viewing, nature study, naturalist walks, photography, geology, visitor center, campfire programs
Hours/Season: Overnight; summer for meadow experiences (skiing in winter)
Fees: Park entrance fee per vehicle and at Heart O' the Hills Campground
Picnicking: Tables and food service available at Hurricane Hill Visitor Center, tables also at Deer Park
Camping: The park campground (no hookups), Heart O' the Hills (1,807-foot elevation), is 5 miles south of Port Angeles on Hurricane Ridge Road, first-come, first-served, with restrooms; also 10 sites at primitive campground at Deer Park (5,400-foot elevation).
Access: From US 101 in Port Angeles, Hurricane Ridge is 19 miles south on Hurricane Ridge Road. To reach Deer Park, go 6 miles east of Port Angeles on US 101 and then south 17 miles on Blue Mountain Road (mostly unpaved, a narrow, winding road for experienced mountain drivers-no trailers or motorhomes).

One of the earliest western subalpine flower displays begins in late June at Hurricane Ridge (5,225-foot elevation) in Washington state's Olympic National Park. The Olympic Mountains, the vital core of the park, are unusual in that they are so near the coast with moist, temperate weather moving in across the Pacific Ocean. With Mount Olympus drawing some 200 inches of precipitation annually (mostly as snow), conditions are right for wildflower gardens in the meadows of Hurricane Ridge and Deer Park to flourish. Colors continue into October as huckleberry bushes turn red and mountain ash becomes golden.

Both Hurricane Ridge and Deer Park have superb mountain scenery adjacent to subalpine meadows. Though the tallest of these peaks, Mount Olympus, is only 7,965 feet high, the multitude of peaks and ridges is quite impressive. Myth hints that the park became the new home of the god, Jupiter, when he became disenchanted with his mountain in Greece.

Geology

The craggy-looking Olympic Mountains are among the youngest mountains in the world, only 12 to 30 million years old. Forced upward by the collision of two giant plates, compressed ocean-floor sediments were the building ingredients of these mountains. Lava, rather than spewing from volcanic cones, was vented up through underwater fissures. A colossal dome some 60 miles in diameter was scraped off the sea floor and thrust against the shore to become a mountain range that was powerfully fractured, folded, and overturned to become today's jumbled peaks. Later, a series of glaciers added the final sculpturing touches to this high landscape of horn peaks, knife ridges, and rocks smoothed by moving ice. About 50–60 year-round glaciers are still present, seven of which are on Mount Olympus. Tarns remain where basins were scooped out by ice.

Plants and Wildlife

Due to the geographical isolation of the Olympic Peninsula on three sides by water, several unique plants have evolved. Endemic flowers (relics of pre-glacier days) are Flett's violet, Piper's bellflower, and the Olympic Mountain daisy. The first flowers to bloom in summer, avalanche lilies, store energy in below-ground bulbs and taproots and then pop up through the snow. Other subalpine flower species include yellow fawn lily, owl clover, yellow cinquefoil, glacial lily, red paintbrush, bistort, mats of phlox, fireweed, purple lupine, pearly everlasting, yarrow, columbine, and monkeyflower. Last to bloom are the blue gentians.

The Olympic marmot is a unique animal species of the Olympic high meadows that does not defend its territory, but rather forms a

Black-tailed deer are easy to spot at Hurricane Ridge in Olympic National Park.

95

social group with much friendly and playful interaction that is fun to observe on meadow walks. Stop and listen to their sharp, piercing whistles. Black-tailed deer seem tame near Big Meadow and this is one of the most opportune places to see a young fawn in June. Grouse and the Olympic chipmunk are frequently observed partaking of the wild garden on Hurricane Hill and at Deer Park. Other possible wildlife spottings include mountain goats near Klahhane Ridge, elk herds, black bear, cougar, bobcats, Douglas squirrels, snowshoe hares, and deer mice. Birds familiar with these higher elevations are rosy finches, horned larks, olive-sided flycatchers, nuthatches, sparrow hawks, swallows, swifts, and gray jays.

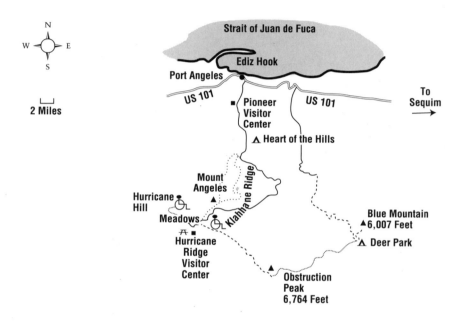

Hurricane Ridge/Deer Park

Big Meadow Loops

Activities

Across from the Hurricane Ridge Visitor Center are several easy trails that weave through a typical subalpine environment thick with wildfowers in early summer.

Klahhane Ridge Trail

This 2.7-mile trail to 6,454-foot Mt. Angeles also originates across from the Visitor Center and wheelchairs can be negotiated (with assistance) for the first part of it, which is steep yet paved. The dirt trail then continues on the side of a slope that has excellent views—a delight.

Hurricane Hill Trail

At the end of Hurricane Ridge Road, a neat 1.6-mile trail ascends Hurricane Hill, (5,757 feet), with meadows and views that stretch across the Strait of Juan de Fuca and into Canada. It is paved and wheelchair accessible for the first 0.5 mile, but has steep dropoffs.

Deer Park Meadows

Flower discoveries are plentiful when exploring near the campground and around Blue Mountain, reached by a short spur near the road's end.

Obstruction Point Trail

Accessed from Deer Park, this is a 7.6-mile trail to Obstruction Point, but this easy flower-edged hike—with great mountain views—can be done for a short distance with great enjoyment.

Backpacking

More than 600 miles of trails are available for backcountry experiences. Check with a ranger and obtain the required permit for overnight travel.

Ecotouring and Safety Concerns

The black-tailed deer seem so tame at Big Meadow that visitors feed them the strangest things, even potato salad, which is definitely not good for their health. Signs remind people *not* to feed the animals; please care enough about the wildlife to just observe them. Deer may not look dangerous, but they have sharp hoofs that can be lethal.

Manning Provincial Park
BRITISH COLUMBIA

Zone Manager
Manning Park, B.C.
VOX 1RO Canada
(604) 840-8836

Attractions: Hiking, photography, horseback riding (only on designated trails or with guided tours), paddling (canoe rentals; power boats prohibited in park), swimming, fishing, mountain biking (only on specified routes), skiing, nature study, wildlife viewing, interpretive programs, campfire programs, lodging, store
Hours/Season: Overnight; year-round
Fees: Charge only for campgrounds
Visitor Center: Open daily summer and winter
Picnicking: Subalpine meadows

Camping: Four campgrounds in park available first-come, first-served (Lightning Lake has showers and is very popular; arrive early); group and winter campground at Lone Duck; designated wilderness campsites
Access: Hwy 3 goes through the park, with Hope 26 kilometers (16 miles) west of the west entrance and Princeton 48 kilometers (29 miles) east of the east entrance.

Encompassing more than 27,000 acres of rugged mountains, forest, rushing whitewater, and lake recreation areas, Manning Provincial Park is as magnificent a destination as many a national park. Two major rivers are birthed within the park—the Skagit flowing west and the Similkameen winding east to flow into the Columbia. Miles and miles of trails are open in the cool summers and the winters bring excellent snow for cross-country skiers and snowshoeing.

The park is known as one of only two places in British Columbia with spectacular subalpine wildflower meadows. From late July to mid-August, a multi-hued carpet of flowers—up to 5 kilometers (3 miles) in width—stretches 24 kilometers (14 miles) long from Blackwall Peak to Three Brothers Mountain along the Heather Trail in the high country.

Complementing these colors are the high peaks of the Cascade Mountains, which encircle popular Lightning Lake. Launch a canoe into these waters shortly after dawn when a mist is rising and you may surprise a doe and her fawn along with a community of ground squirrels popping out of their holes to see what's happening.

Geology

The Paintbrush Trail begins on the Hozameen Range of the Cascade Mountains, where peaks were shaped by the last Ice Age and this ridge was under several hundred meters of ice. Nearby summits more than 2,100 meters (7,000 feet) high poked their tops above the ice sheet and have since retained their jagged appearance.

Plants and Wildlife

While on your walks keep in mind that subalpine plants and animals arrived after the last glaciers retreated. Sitka valerian, lupine, hellebore, lance-leaved stonecrop, wooly pussytoes, spreading phlox, fan-leaf cinquefoil, and red heather are some of the subalpine flowers. A rare find in these high meadows is the deciduous conifer, alpine larch, but whitebark pine and subalpine fir are common. Often overlooked, tiny Piper's woodrush, green-leaf fescue, and showy sedge have reddish leaves from the presence of the pigment anthocyanin, which serves as a sunscreen protection against the strong ultraviolet rays at this elevation.

Inhabiting the park are black-tailed and mule deer, snowshoe hare, pika, hairy marmot, squirrel, chipmunk, northern pocket gopher, meadow mole, moose, black bear, beaver, coyote, elk, and 206 bird species, with Clark's nutcracker prominent wherever it finds whitebark pine seeds.

Blackwall Road

Activities   Accessed just west of the Visitor Center, on the north side of the highway, this 15-kilometer drive (9 miles) takes you to the subalpine meadows. The first part of the drive goes to Cascade Lookout. It is a paved, winding, steep-edged road on which caution is required since there is just barely room enough to pass. A large exposed parking lot allows views of the Cascades to the south, with identification information available. The remaining 6 kilometers (4 miles) to road's end is signed as being a narrow road, but for the most part it is wider than to Cascade Lookout—though now gravel, it still requires considerable caution.

Paintbrush Interpretive Trail

This self-guiding 1.5-kilometer loop (0.9 mile) begins at the Naturalist Hut at Blackwall Peak where brochures are available, though it can also can be accessed from the lower parking lot. Common red paintbrush provides plenty of nutritious nectar for the energetic rufous hummingbird, but try to see how many other species you can identify. Peak wildflower bloom lasts from mid-July to August, though the western anemones bloom as soon as the snow melts and by late July their seed heads dot the meadows before their feathery parachutes are dispersed into the wind. Snow-peaked mountains in the distance add to the charm of the trail.

Heather Trail

At the lower parking area by Blackwall Peak, the Heather Trail traverses a vast subalpine meadow and reaches Buckhorn Camp in 5 kilometers (3 miles). The trail continues on for a total of 21 kilometers (12 miles) to Nicomen Ridge and Nicomen Lake, another backcountry campsite, with other return options available. Day hikers can sample a portion of this hike to savor the many wildflowers and then turn around whenever they wish.

Strawberry Flats Trail

For those not wanting to drive to the subalpine meadows, yet desiring a walk among summer wildflowers, trek the easy 1.8-kilometer (1.1 miles) path that heads for the Gibson Pass Ski Area—and continues on to see waterfalls—off Gibson Pass Road past Lightning Lake. After a initial stroll past columbines and lilies edging a path backed by forests, the trees recede and the strawberry flats area (aptly named) emerges replete with

99

lupine, yarrow, cow parsnip, and a good representation of the park's many flower species.

Rein Orchid Trail

This 500-meter (0.3 mile) trail, located off Gibson Pass Road just west of the amphitheater parking lot, has much to offer within a short distance. Smells are of the forest. Many blooming rein orchids are seen June through July, along with horsetail, bunchberry, fireweed, and other wildflowers, and the added attraction of a surprise pond and wetland area. Notice where a squirrel has eaten nuts and the huge bear claw marks on a tree.

Ecotouring and Safety Concerns

As always in the fragile subalpine meadows, please stay on the trail. No open fires are allowed along the Heather Trail. Be especially careful to keep the park's lakes and streams clean; they provide the drinking water. Food scraps, fish guts, dirty plates, and even "biodegradable" soaps pollute the water. You are not allowed to sample the good-eating berries of the park; these are to be left to the birds and wildlife. (For determining which ones are prime in permissible-eating areas, the park Visitor Center has an identification booklet available.)

Paradise and Sunrise, Mount Rainier National Park WASHINGTON

Mount Rainier National Park
Tahoma Woods
Star Route
Ashford, WA 98304
(360) 569-2211

Attractions: Hiking, nature study, wildlife viewing, photography, geology, mountain climbing, ranger-led walks, campfire programs

Hours/Season: Overnight; summer for wildflowers (only road open in winter is to Paradise from Nisqually Entrance (2,003 feet)

Fees: Entry fee per vehicle; additional charge for campgrounds

Visitor Centers: Paradise is open daily April to December, weekends January to March; Sunrise is open only until roads are closed by snow.

Picnicking: Cougar Rock, Paradise, White River, and Tipsoo Lake picnic areas

Camping: Cougar Rock (in the forest) has 200 sites (5 group sites); White River (along rushing river) has 117 sites.

Access: Nisqually Entrance (southwest corner of park) is 10 miles east of park headquarters at Ashford on WA 706.

Part of the charm of Mount Rainier's Paradise area is the mystery that unfolds if one is lucky enough to arrive early on a quiet weekday and ascend the Skyline Trail as the mountain flirts with swirling clouds. Though snow-clad Mount Rainier is enchanting, it has a tendency to hide amongst the clouds. The path edges the greatest of subalpine flowering meadows, according to John Muir. One soon realizes why Longmire (who discovered the area and mineral springs in 1883 and built a hotel) named this place Paradise (5,400 feet elevation).

It is usually late July before the trails that begin near Paradise Inn are clear of snow and the wildflowers begin their progression of diverse blossoms through the short season. Walk slowly to savor the changing clouds, mountain views, and spectacular areas of wildflowers. Sunlight is harvested by the plants as it warms the hiker.

Mount Rainier disturbs a great amount of maritime air and causes it to dump snow, with the greatest accumulations being at Paradise, usually enough to bury the 3-story inn up to its roof. A record snowfall in 1971-1972 measured 93.5 feet. To see how the amount of moisture influences floral displays, compare the meadows on the drier site of Rainier at Sunrise (6,400 feet elevation), which is in the rain shadow in the northeast area of the park. Stop at Tipsoo Lake along the way.

Geology

Mount Rainier (14,410 feet elevation) is a volcano that has erupted in the past, and could erupt again. Two craters on its summit have caves along their rims where steam melts tunnels in the summit ice cap. Warm steam caves have been used by climbers as refuge during blizzards. The mountain has the largest glacier system (35 square miles) in the contiguous states, with 27 named glaciers.

Plants and Wildlife

Lovely western pasque flower blooms early, followed by white American bistort, red and magenta Indian paintbrush, and lavender lupine—colors of the flag spontaneously assorted at Paradise. Yellow splashes are added by Mount Rainier lousewort, fanleaf cinquefoil, and glacier lily. Rose elephants head, Queen Anne's lace, Rainier pleated gentian, Cascade aster, and masses of red and white heath grow across the landscape. One area along Golden Gate Trail often nourishes large numbers of blooming beargrass (as do other high meadows or parks). Thick mosses border Edith Creek and lush grasses edge Reflection Lakes.

Watch for the many butterflies sucking nectar and marmots (large furry rodents who are not disturbed by hikers) snacking on apparently delicious lupine flowers. Black-tailed deer with their fawns are frequent visitors at Reflection Lakes and throughout the park. Some patient glassing above Paradise or Glacier Basin may discover mountain goats who manage sheer cliffs with suction-cup pads on their hooves. The ptarmigan fits into its habitat by changing the color of its feathers with the seasons, from white to blend with the deep snow to the mottled gray of the rocky summer terrain. Gray and Stellar jays are both common and bold. Look for frogs near the creeks. The raven, subject of so much Indian folklore, circles above, and rufous and calliope hummingbirds can be heard and seen among the flowers.

Beargrass blooms on a hillside below Mount Rainier.

Activities

Skyline Trail

This 5-mile loop is the highest meadow trail at Paradise and climbs to Paradise Point, with views of Mount Adams, Mount St. Helens, and the Nisqually Glacier. It returns via Sluiskan Falls. An alternate return on the Golden Gate Trail cuts one mile off the loop and takes hikers into the Edith Creek Basin. This trail connects to the route to Camp Muir, a mountaineering base.

Nisqually Vista Self-Guiding Trail

For a good view of the snout of the Nisqually Glacier, follow this 1.2-mile loop at Paradise.

Alta Vista Trail

A 1.5-mile loop at Paradise lets the hiker gaze at stunning flower fields and views from a prominent knoll overlooking volcanic peaks to the south.

Reflection Lakes

Trails descend from Paradise to Reflection Lakes, but travelers may elect to drive just east of Paradise since the lakes are adjacent to the road. A spectacular early morning trip rewards the stroller with mist rising from the water and the sun bursting above trees. One can also explore a glorious bog where the snow-topped mountain and lake are great scenic components.

Glacier Basin Trail

This 3.5-mile trail follows the Inter Fork of the White River from the White River Campground (park in the day-use area) and ascends to the meadows of Glacier Basin, where experienced climbers may be seen making their way up the Inter Glacier to Steamboat Prow. A spur near the beginning leads to a view of the Emmons Glacier.

Sourdough Ridge Trail

From the Sunrise Visitor Center, a 0.5-mile nature trail accesses subalpine meadows with a panoramic view of four peaks.

Tipsoo Lake

A refreshing stop between Paradise and Sunrise is Tipsoo Lake, just inside the eastern entrance via the Mather Memorial Parkway. Flowers circle this small tarn near Chinook Pass.

Ecotouring and Safety Concerns

Please stay on paved, dirt, or rock-lined trails. Flower meadows are extremely fragile environments. The park uses jute as a giant bandage to repair damaged areas. Wear boots if there are snowfields to cross. Be forewarned that the sun can be intense at these high altitudes. No pets are allowed on trails.

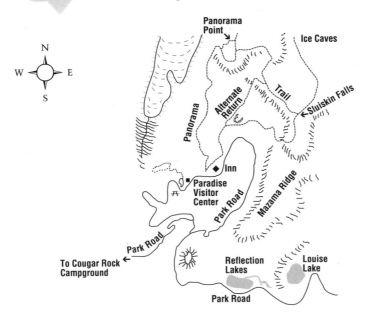

Paradise—Mount Rainier National Park

Green Lakes, Three Sisters Wilderness

OREGON

Deschutes National Forest
Bend Ranger Station
211 Northeast Revere
Bend, OR 97701
(541) 388-5664

Attractions: Hiking, backpacking, nature study, photography, waterfall, obsidian flows, mountain climbing
Hours/Season: Overnight; summer for wildflower meadows (snow is usually gone by August at 6,500 feet)
Fees: None
Camping: Ranger permit required for overnight, select appropriate wilderness site (no campfires within a mile of Green Lakes); several popular forest camps nearby along OR 46
Access: West of Bend on Cascade Lakes Highway (also called Century Drive and OR 46), approximately 25 miles to trailhead on the north side of the highway, just past Soda Creek Campground

Though accessible only by hiking, Green Lakes is a special destination to an area of subalpine meadows in the Three Sisters Wilderness—a fine choice for a first-time backpacking trip, though it is easily done as a family day hike. This area attracts too many people on weekends and holidays in summer, so try to plan your trip for other times. South Sister and Broken Top mountains seem so close, one wants to reach out and touch them. The lakes actually do look green, a color resulting from the finely ground silt from Lewis Glacier on South Sister. Consider backpacking and toting a small inflatable raft for use on the larger of the three lakes.

Slight elevation changes influence flower bloom times. Be aware that mountain weather is unpredictable. When the summer sun is out, weather is grand; but a cloudy, rainy day can be quite cool and snow can fall during any month. By late summer the mosquitos will be dying and some flowers still blooming.

Cascade Lakes Highway should be explored further if time permits. Highcountry lakes, boating opportunities, wildlife observations, and wilderness trails abound in this spectacular nearness to the Cascade peaks.

Geology

Broken Top (9,175 feet elevation) is a young composite volcano that is so eroded one can see what was once the interior alternating colors of red cinder and black lava. The area is strewn with circular blobs of lava and football-sized pieces of exploded magma that cooled in flight. Near South Sister (10,358 feet elevation), flows of glassy, black obsidian are visible. Several glaciers can be seen around South Sister.

Plants and Wildlife

The July and August bloom of subalpine flowers varies through the season and depends on moisture conditions. Look for white avalanche lily, marsh marigold, western pasque flower, red elephants head, shooting star, yellow monkeyflower, rose Lewis monkeyflower, columbine, larkspur, cat ears, wild sunflower, blue lupine, red Indian paintbrush, alpine buckwheat, and saxifrages. Notice which plants prefer the wetter spots.

The large expanse of this wilderness encourages shy animals such as cougar, wolverine, mink, and bald eagles to find habitats to their liking, in addition to the various smaller animal species. A little orienteering in the open country will find springs with dipper birds, or water ouzels.

Activities

Photography

Photographers will want to schedule the first and last light of day for taking morning reflection shots of South Sister on Green Lake or soft light photos illuminating the colors of Broken Top in the evening. These photo opportunities are often possible near a carefully chosen tent site.

Campers at Green Lakes are rewarded with reflections of South Sister at dawn.

Fall Creek Trail #17

Following Fall Creek, hike from a meadow at 5,500-feet elevation that soon crosses the creek, and then climb gently to a vibrant waterfall. The trail continues amidst views and interesting rock formations—look for obsidian along the way—for 4.5 miles to the subalpine-flowered meadows around Green Lakes, at 6,500 feet; elevation gain is only 1,000 feet.

Mountain Climbing

Neither Broken Top nor South Sister are technically difficult for experienced mountain climbers. South Sister can supposedly be hiked without technical equipment via a long trail from the Green Lakes Basin. It is best to check with a knowledgeable ranger at a U.S. Forest Service Station for more specifics and prevailing conditions at the time. Climb these peaks only in perfect weather.

Ecotouring and Safety Concerns

This destination is within a designated wilderness area. If you camp overnight, do follow all regulations for wilderness areas.

Castle Crest and Annie Creek, Crater Lake National Park

Crater Lake National Park
P.O. Box 7
Crater Lake, OR 97604
(541) 594-2211

OREGON

Attractions: Hiking, nature study, photography, wildlife viewing, geology, Visitor Center on Rim Drive, campfire programs at Mazama Campground (wheelchair accessible)

Hours/Season: Overnight when free of snow; year-round (skiing and snowshoeing in winter)

Fees: Entry fee per vehicle and additional fee for Mazama Campground, lesser fee for Lost Creek Campground

Picnicking: Nearest park picnic areas by the Godfrey Glen Trailhead and near Rim Center by Crater Lake

Campgrounds: 198 campsites at Mazama Campground (camper store, laundry, and pay showers) with wheelchair-accessible restrooms (no hookups)

near south entrance station; 15 tent sites at Lost Creek Campground with water and composting toilets, off East Rim Drive on the Pinnacles Road
Access: The Annie Spring entrance station (south) is reached from either Medford or Klamath Falls via OR 62, and is open year-round. The north entrance road is reached from the west via OR 230 and from the north via OR 138, with the Rim Drive open when the snow is cleared, usually in July, but it has varied from late April to mid-August.

During winter, snow blankets the area around Oregon's Crater Lake and contrasts with the stunning royal blue of the lake. With an average of more than 44 feet of snow falling annually, the snowmelt is certainly sufficient to cause the dormant seeds to sprout and flower in July and August, when Castle Crest and Annie Creek meadows are a lush carpet of many colors.

Crater Lake has much to offer including Rim Drive, Mount Scott to climb (the best and highest viewpoint in the park), the Pacific Crest Trail, and just the awesome sights at its many viewpoints. Many visitors, however, miss the two glorious wildflower trails. Summer weather is often quite grand, with the afternoons full of puffy white clouds framing the magical blue sky and mountain peaks and the sun lighting the wild gardens, but storms can blow in with wind, thunder, and lightning. August is the best time for flower color, but different species bloom throughout the short summer growth.

Lewis monkeyflowers are numerous along the wildflower trail at Castle Crest in Crater Lake National Park.

Geology

Spanning a period of half a million years of volcanic activity, Mount Mazama slowly built up to an estimated height of 12,000 feet before climatic eruptions (42 times those of the recent Mount St. Helens explosions) so emptied the magma chamber beneath the peak that caused Mazama to collapse, leaving a huge depression, or caldera, approximately 7,700 years ago. The surrounding landscape was blanketed with frothy pale pumice lava and volcanic ash. The Modoc Indians of southwestern Oregon witnessed this catastrophic event and passed down the legend of the mountain that "shook and crumbled." One is not surprised that the place became sacred to the Indians and has since been avoided by them. Eventually, the 4,000-foot-deep hole filled to a depth of almost 2,000 feet with the waters of Crater Lake.

Today, the lake is surrounded by wild beauty. From a past of geological upheaval, when plants and animals were erased, new life slowly emerged. The forests and wildflower gardens are an example of how nature recovers over time.

Plants and Wildlife

Soaking up the sunshine, yellow fawn lilies bloom immediately after the snowmelt. The meadows produce a profusion of rose-colored Lewis monkeyflower, purple lupine, white American bistort, buttercup, scarlet paintbrush, and shooting star flowers. In drier areas, grasses, sulfur eriogonum, skyrocket gilia, rabbitbrush goldenweed, and cascade aster proliferate. The wetter places nourish mosses, sedges, horsetails, and false hellebore (corn lily). Other blossoms include white penstemon, phlox, forget-me-not, Pacific bleeding heart, pearly everlasting, blue stickseed, and mountain violet. Foxtail barley dons seed heads in the early autumn and groundsel adds a touch of yellow. Willows compete for sunlight and water as they encroach upon the meadow herbs.

The sound of the creek accompanies the hiker—a soft song in the wilderness—and it also lures wildlife, though often it is only their tracks that we see. Look for the signatures of visiting animals in the soft mud. The water ouzel (or dipper bird) is not so secretive and a joy to watch as it dives and dips into the creek, even swimming underwater or walking along the creek bed in search of caddisfly larvae and other insects to eat. Pikas forage for flowering plants and shrubs during the summer, which they store away in burrows for their winter food supply. Aquatic mosses attach to rock surfaces within the creek and provide food and shelter for numerous small animals. Yellow-bellied marmot, golden-mantled squirrel, red fox, mule deer, and black bear find food in the gardens.

Red crossbills and dark-eyed juncos are the park's most prolific breeding birds. Clark's nutcrackers, ruffled grouse, horned larks, robins, Swainson's thrushes, evening grosbeaks, Cassin's finches, pine siskins, and various sparrows feed on the ground in search of insects, fruits, berries, and conifer seeds. Watch for rufous humming-birds among the nectar-filled flowers. Peregrine falcons sometimes nest successfully in an eyrie in the park—as late as 1994 at the time of this writing. Nine pairs of northern spotted owls have been documented in the park; some are known to breed here.

Rocks, driftwood, and lush growths of monkey-flowers border Annie Creek.

Activities

Annie Creek Trail

Accessed from the amphitheater at Mazama Campground, this outstanding 1.7-mile loop descends 200 feet from the 6,000-foot-elevation canyon rim, past pinnacles that are remnants of ancient belching fumaroles, and follows a stream carved through pumice left by Mount Mazama's violent eruptions. Wildflowers are thick near the water. This creek is named after Annie Gaines, the first woman to descend the caldera walls of Crater Lake.

Castle Crest Trail

An easier and shorter trail, the 0.4-mile Castle Crest Trail is equally fine, yet different, with its thick growth of flowering plants showcasing a streamside meadow community surrounded by a mountain hemlock forest community at 6,400 feet to 6,500 feet elevation. Rocks serve as stepping stones in certain areas. Located near the South Rim, this trail is accessed at the end of the Rim Drive or across the road from the park headquarters parking area.

The Rim area is currently undergoing a redevelopment program that will not only address concerns for the natural environment but will also make the park a more pleasant place to visit year-round. Crater Lake Lodge was reopened following rehabilitation in the spring of 1995, but work on Rim Village may not be completed until 1999. The phasing of this construction will permit visitor use throughout this period.

Mirror Lake
Scenic Byway,
Uinta Mountains
Utah

Utah Travel Council
Council Hill/Capitol Hill
Salt Lake City, Utah 84114-1396
(800) 200-1160

Attractions: Scenic drive, challenging bicycling, nature study, geology, photography, hiking, backpacking, horsepacking, fishing, boating, waterfalls

Hours/Season: Overnight; summer for wildflowers (road open only for snowmobile traffic and cross-country skiing in winter)

Fees: Only for campgrounds

Picnicking: Available at all listed campgrounds

Campgrounds: Forest camps at Trial Lake, Lily Lake, Lost Creek, Mirror Lake, Moosehorn, and Butterfly are all near meadows at high elevations (9,500 to 10,400 feet elevation).

Access: Byway is 65-mile tour on UT 150 from Kamas to Wyoming border.

For some easy-to-reach viewing of mountain wildflowers and amazing high-mountain scenery via a good paved road, drive Utah's Mirror Lake Scenic Byway. The highway climbs east and then north through the Wasatch Cache National Forest into the Uinta Mountains. The road follows the Provo River for a considerable time, passing the terraced cascades of the Upper Provo River Falls at 24 miles. The high-elevation lakes offer prime fishing and there are so many of them that one can simply move on if the angler is not pulling in the fish.

The high point of the byway is Bald Mountain Pass at 10,687 feet elevation. The high-elevation lakes and their campgrounds are extremely popular, particularly Mirror Lake. In summer, notice the thick carpet of wildflowers that bloom at high elevations, particularly near the road where they are watered by runoff from the highway. A delightful area in summer, when it is 90 degrees at Provo and 80 at Heber City, it is probably 65 degrees at Mirror Lake.

Geology

Utah's highest mountains, the Uintas, are the largest east-west trending mountain range in the Western Hemisphere and part of the Rocky Mountain Province. This range is broad and gently arched, a folded anticline that contains Precambrian rocks 600 million years old. Hundreds of rock-rimmed, high-elevation lakes were left by glaciers. It is in these mountains that several major rivers have their headwaters—the Bear, Weber, and Provo. The sediments carried downstream are vital to what agriculture exists today in the rocky state of Utah.

Plants and Wildlife

Jacob's ladder, bluebell, elephants head, western bistort, explorer gentian, asters, alpine paintbrush, yellow heartleaf arnica, alpine phlox, and alpine clover are some of the flower species. Besides the meadow flowers, grasses, sedges, and small shrubs, the lakes have yellow pond lilies. Near treeline, note the small, crooked conifers, called *krummolz* (the German word for "crooked wood") that are shaped by the wind and harsh conditions.

The north side of the Uinta Mountains is home for a large population of moose. Mule deer, black bear, and elk reside here, and a short hike across a rock-slide trail leads to mountain goat habitat on Bald Mountain (11,943 feet elevation). At Mirror Lake, a viewscope is sometimes helpful for spotting these elusive mountain climbers. Grouse, cottontail and snowshoe rabbit, mountain lion, bobcat, pika, and Clark's nutcracker prefer these high altitudes. The many lakes are stocked with trout and the Provo River has good fly fishing.

Activities

In the midst of mountain peaks, Mirror Lake (31.5 miles from Kamas) offers streams, colorful meadows, lake fishing, and trails for short excursions or for taking off into the backcountry either by hiking or horseback. One trail heads east into the High Uintas Wilderness. Others head west to follow both the Weber River and its Middle Fork. Trail choices are many, whether by foot, horse, or llama. Check with the Kamas Ranger Station for maps of trails near the byway and in the national forest. For some quite scenic short hikes (great views of lakes and mountains), obtain the "4 Great Day Hikes" brochure with trails that vary from 3 to 4 miles round-trip. Some of these connect with longer trails for backpacking expeditions.

Ecotouring and Safety Concerns

Take your time traveling this scenic byway to enjoy the views and attractions, pulling over along the way rather than holding up traffic.

Broken Top Mountain, a volcano in the Cascade Mountains in the Green Lakes/Three Sisters Wilderness Area.

7

Estuaries

West

Can anything significant be happening here? That might be a question on a first visit to an estuary, a place where the freshwater of a river merges with the saltwater of the sea and tidewaters advance and retreat twice daily. At high tide, this meeting place seems simply a widening place of the sea; at low tide, it is a expanse of mudflats, seemingly lifeless. But look more closely. Why is that blue heron silhouetted so motionless against the early sun? And what are those many tracks upon this quishy mud? Maybe it is not just nothingness if it attracts wild things.

Temperatures bounce around as the sun shines on exposed soil and then glistens on shallow water as the tide turns and channels of seawater flow inland. The salinity changes gradually upriver as the gravity-fed freshwater mixes its load of minerals and detritus with the nutrient-rich soup swept in from the salty sea.

What living things can adapt to such varied conditions? What happens with all these comings and goings is an explosion of the basic energies of life. Microscopic plants known as phytoplankton thrive in the full sun and shallow water as their photosynthetic equipment harvests photons and shuttles them along enzyme pathways. Though only 10 percent of the plant material in the estuary is consumed directly, the remaining 90 percent becomes available to other organisms as nutrients recycling from detritus—dead organic material decomposed by microscopic bacteria.

Plankton and detritus are the bases of a complicated food web that supports both plants and animals in this protected, peaceful environment between flowing streams and surf-pounded seashores. Fish hatch and feed in this protected "nursery of the sea." Great blue herons, crabs, clams, oysters, bald eagles, and small mammals help harvest these biological riches.

The estuary turns out to be one of the most productive pieces of acreage on Earth, ten times more productive than nearby coastal waters, as it harvests five times the plant material of a comparable-sized cornfield. Who would have imagined that by just looking?

And always, the sea washes inland and flushes out the estuary, harvesting some of this rich garden into the ocean and connecting young fish with the wide Pacific. Humans then walk on the exposed mudflats to scavenge for clams and oysters, recalling the mud-pie days of their youth as they dig in the sticky, smelly—but oh so rich—fine-grained mix of seawater, organisms, and sediments.

Nisqually National Wildlife Refuge
WASHINGTON

Nisqually National
Wildlife Refuge
100 Brown Farm Road
Olympia, WA 98506
(360) 753-9467

Attractions: Hiking, bird watching, fishing, paddling, boating, clamming, photography, photo blinds, observation decks and tower, nature study, exhibit information, Twin Barns Education Center (open on weekends, 10 A.M. to 3 P.M.), Information Kiosk
Hours/Season: Day use; year-round
Fees: Nominal charge per family
Picnicking: Picnic tables are adjacent to the Twin Barns Education Center.
Camping: No camping is allowed within the refuge, but a private campground is accessed by turning right after taking Exit 114.
Access: Take Exit 114 off I-5 and go back under the freeway and then turn right to the refuge entrance.

Weaving waterways, grasslands, woodlands, wetlands, salt marshes, and tidal mudflats form a mosaic between the southern end of Puget Sound and the hum of traffic on I-5. This, the Nisqually National Wildlife Refuge, is one of the largest undisturbed estuaries in Washington. The freshwaters of the Nisqually River, McAllister Creek, and Red Salmon Creek widen and split into multiple channels as they merge with the tidal surge of saltwater and flow into Puget Sound. The sum total is the biologically-rich Nisqually river delta that is now protected, an important stopover for birds on the Pacific Flyway and habitat for many other organisms.

Easy, flat trails access sightings for bird-watchers, fishing areas, and good exercise for any one who can walk. At low tides, mudflats entice clammers and always the refuge is for quiet recreation. A five-mile-long dike separates saltwater habitats from freshwater habitats.

Geology

Initially fed by the Nisqually Glacier on the slopes of Mount Rainier, in Washington's Cascade Mountains, the Nisqually River flows downhill to its mouth in the saltwater of Puget Sound. The basin of this vast inland sea that connects with the Pacific Ocean was scooped out during the Pleistocene Era by a piedmont glacier that was 3,000 feet thick. It rounded the contours of the low country during the ice ages, and then filled with water.

Plants and Wildlife

Arrivals in fall and winter include 20,000 widgeon, mallard, green-winged teal, and other ducks. Short-eared owls, and perhaps a peregrine falcon, arrrive in November to hunt for mice and voles in the fields. Goldfinches, warblers, and tree swallows come in the spring to nest. Insects, including mosquitos, provide food for some of these birds. Woodpeckers, chickadees, and brown creepers move into the cavities of trees. Red-winged blackbirds perch among the marsh vegetation of cattails and sedges. Blue herons nest in trees; bald eagles and osprey patrol the area. Salmon and steelhead enter the delta to spawn upstream. Near the saltwater mouth of the estuary are clams, crabs, worms, and shrimps.

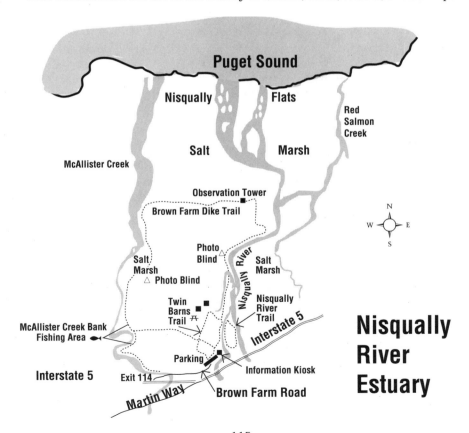

Nisqually River Estuary

Cottonwood trees, bigleaf maples, horsetails, skunk cabbage, tree frogs, and squirrels may be spotted along the river trail. Up to 300 species of birds, mammals, reptiles, amphibians, and fish inhabit this refuge. A wildlife species checklist is available.

Activities

Nisqually River Trail

A wooden bridge, sometimes slippery, accesses this 0.5-mile loop along the first part of the dike trail. A brochure is keyed to numbered markers as one wanders through a riparian woodland.

Twin Barns Trail

A 1-mile loop trail accesses the Twin Barns Observation Deck and Education Center—where there are a couple of picnic tables and a memorial tree grove. The hike traverses forest, slough, and grassland habitat areas.

Brown Farm Dike Trail

This wide, easy 5.5-mile loop trail passes through six distinct habitats of the refuge and accesses the photo blinds, fishing areas, observation deck and tower, and the Nisqually River Overlook.

Boating and Fishing

Boating is only allowed outside the Brown Farm Dike; the nearest boat ramp is located outside the refuge at nearby Luhr Beach. Fishing inside the refuge is only permitted at the designated Nisqually River and McAllister Creek bank fishing areas, following Washington state regulations.

Ecotouring and Safety Concerns

Do bring binoculars, spotting scopes, and telephoto lenses so you will not need to approach the wildlife too closely. Visitors are asked to stay on trails. Jogging, frisbee throwing, bicycling, kite flying, and jet skiing are not activities that are compatible with a wildlife refuge. Canoeists and kayakers should be aware of hazardous tides, shallow waters, and wind and weather conditions around the Nisqually Delta.

Yaquina Bay Estuary
OREGON

Hatfield Marine Science Center
2030 South Marine Science Drive
Newport, OR 07365
(541) 867-0226

Attractions: Nature trail, clamming, crabbing, fishing, boating, bird watching, photography, wildlife viewing, docent-led estuary walk, dock walk, windsurfing
Hours/Season: Day use; year-round
Fees: Free; entrance fee for Oregon Coast Aquarium, none for public wing of Hatfield Marine Science Center (HMSC)
Picnicking: Picnic areas at Yaquina Bay State Park (oceanfront just north of Yaquina Bay Bridge) and at South Beach State Park (1 miles south of Bridge)
Camping: Nearby South Beach State Park has campsites with hookups and restrooms with showers.
Access: Off US 101, just south of the Yaquina Bay Bridge in Newport

The key to the nonnative settlement of Newport was the delicious oysters found growing naturally in the estuary of the Yaquina River by Lieutenant Talbot, from Fort Vancouver, in 1849. When a ship from San Francisco entered Yaquina Bay in 1856 and spread the word, the race was on to harvest the oysters—then classified as farm animals—and ship them to San Francisco. Today, oysters are grown commercially in the estuary and eating them is one good reason for visiting.

Oyster farming in Yaquina River Estuary.

Out of Oregon's fifteen estuaries, 4,200-acre Yaquina Bay is the fourth largest, with 2,500 acres classified as tidelands. Both the public wing of the Hatfield Marine Science Center and the Oregon Coast Aquarium are situated near the mudflats and provide an excellent way to more closely view the flora and fauna of this estuary. Dredging in Yaquina Bay has produced one of three deep-draft shipping ports—on the north side of the bay—on the Oregon coast.

Geology

The estuary of the Yaquina River is one of the drowned river mouths that formed after the last glaciation, when the melting of glaciers flooded the river valleys. During the ice age, the shoreline was considerably farther out into the Pacific Ocean.

The Hatfield Marine Science Center area was an island back in 1860, but dredging spoils—to deepen the bay channel for boats—were later piled up where the marina and the Oregon Coast Aquarium were later constructed.

Plants and Wildlife

The primary producers of the estuary include phytoplankton, sea grasses, and salt marsh plants such as pickleweed, but detritus drives the food chain and a shovelful of mud teems with worms, clams, mud shrimp, and various isopods. Some clams and cockles use their syphons to filter detritus from the water. Eelgrass is found in the transition area between mudflats and open water and provides protection, trapped food, and spawning habitat for crabs, Pacific herring, and juvenile fish. Yaquina Bay fisheries include sole, flounder, perch, salmon, crab, shrimp, and clams. The only herring fishery in Oregon is found within this estuary. Sturgeon are found in deep holes. Sea lions, seals, and even killer whales can be seen in the open water of the bay.

Waterfowl and a variety of gulls feed on herring eggs. Migratory brants overwinter in the estuary and a great blue heron rookery is nearby so they can make quick fishing trips to the estuary to feed their young. Shorebirds feed on the crustaceans and bivalves at low tide.

The native oyster spawns first as a male, then as a female, and alternates between the sexes. The more recently harvested Japanese oyster also switches sexes but begins as a male for a couple of years.

Upland plants are varied and include yarrow, bush lupine, willow, Scotch broom, red clover, foxglove, and blackberries.

Activities

Yaquina Bay Estuary Walk

Starting just east of Hatfield Marine Science Center (HMSC), a 1-mile-round-trip paved walk (with wheelchair access) borders the mudflats, with exhibit information posted along the way. (This walk is in the process of being expanded.) At low tide, it is only a few steps to the mudflats and this presents an excellent opportunity to explore this broad expanse, whether digging for clams or using a sieve to see what tiny organisms inhabit the mud. This walk is also a great way to discover the salt marsh plant life, wildflowers, and other upland plants. Volunteers from the science center lead walks during the summer.

Clamming and Crabbing

If the season and timing is right, your visit can include some delicious meals of self-caught crabs or clams. Species of clams found in the estuary are gaper, littleneck, butter, cockle, softshell, piddock, and razor. A copy of the Yaquina Bay Public Access Guide pinpoints areas for digging these clams. Obtain a crab pot and you can throw it—with some bait inside—into the water from a dock and wait for Dungeness crabs to crawl into the pot before you pull it up. Many people crab from boats in the bay.

Fishing and Boating

A marina with a sport boat launch is adjacent to the Hatfield Marine Science Center. During the right season, the salmon fishing is often good right near the marina—do check the regulations. At other times of the year, boating is popular in the bay, with sailboat races at times, and a slow cruise a few miles up the river is particularly enjoyable. The bay spreads out into a wide circle past the science center and then narrows again upriver, yet maintaining adequate depth for boating. Boat rentals are available. Check with the HMSC if you are interested in taking a Dock Walk to learn about the various commercial fishing boats and what they do.

Hatfield Marine Science Center

After 30 years of providing quality educational experiences for more than nine million visitors, a remodeled public wing went under construction in 1995 and should reopen sometime early in 1997. Emphasis will be on marine research in general and particularly at HMSC (affiliated with Oregon State University). The theme, "Searching for Patterns in a Complex World," will include how marine research affects our lives, and features many live organisms in aquarium exhibits. If you've ever wondered about the tracking of whales, underwater hot springs, oyster culturing, what it's like to do commercial fishing, or how research on marine organisms helps identify and prevent disease and even sheds light on how nerves work, do visit. As in the past, a live octopus will be featured. The Seatauqua program offers more than 100 workshops and treks related to the marine environment.

Oregon Coast Aquarium

This is a world-class interpretive center that includes a 40,000 square-foot building, where four galleries are filled with the lifes and sounds of sandy shores, rocky shores, coastal waters, and wetlands, as well as a Whale Theater. Outdoor exhibits are set in forest, cliffs, bluffs, and beaches where you will find a trout-filled mountain stream, a sea otter pool, an octopus in its cave, seals and sea lions, a wave-raked tidepool, and a vast walk-through outdoor seabird aviary. This is a place of underwater camera views, of machine-generated waves, of feedings and movement, of lab demonstrations, of research, and of education about coastal ecosystems.

Ecotouring and Safety Concerns

Before crabbing or clamming, check with Oregon Department of Fish and Wildlife harvesting regulations. Their office is adjacent to the Hatfield Marine Science Center.

South Slough National Estuarine Reserve

OREGON

South Slough
National Estuarine Reserve
P.O. Box 5417
Charleston, OR 97420
(541) 888-5558

Attractions: Canoeing, hiking, bird watching, wildlife viewing, nature study, clamming, fishing, photography, summer workshops
Hours/Season: Day use; year-round
Fees: Free
Interpretive Center: Exhibits on estuarine ecology, slide and film presentations, publications, information; open September through May from 8:30 A.M. to 4:30 P.M. Monday through Friday, except holidays; open the same hours June through August, seven days a week
Picnicking: Choose a spot along a trail—and leave no evidence—or drive to picnic areas at the three state parks on Cape Arago Highway.
Camping: No camping allowed in the reserve; a campground is nearby at Sunset Bay State Park (hookups and restrooms with showers) southwest of Charleston off Cape Arago Highway.
Access: The Visitor Center is off Seven Devils Road, 4 miles south of Charleston via Cape Arago Highway, 16 miles south of Coos Bay.

On your way to the South Slough Visitor Center and estuary wanderings, cross the Charleston Bridge during a minus tide and you'll find scads of people digging clams in the sparkle of early morning. Long before people discovered the riches of this estuary, the Kakoosh Indians (later called the Coos by whites) wisely selected sites near the marshes for their homes. Archaeologists keep digging up sites of these early coastal people who fished, trapped, hunted, ate shellfish, and made ornaments of purple and white shells.

White settlers of the South Slough area attempted to alter the estuary system to fit their needs, building dikes to sever nature's interconnections and filling tidelands to run cattle in the watershed. A logging railroad carried cut timber while Valino Island held a casino and saloon during the logging days of the early 1900s. Ninety percent of the marshlands in the Coos Bay area have been filled to provide land for agriculture, housing, and shopping centers, and the impact on the ecology was not good. Fortunately, this impact has decreased in the last 30 years and the South Slough area survives, part of the 384,000-acre Coos Estuary.

Under the Coastal Zone Management Act of 1972, the 4,400-acre South Slough Estuarine Sanctuary became, in 1974, the first such system in the country to be set aside primarily as a national outdoor field laboratory for estuarine research and to study its importance to offshore waters.

Returning to "pristine" in the South Slough area, this ecosystem is a fine place for observation while canoeing or walking. The lovely solitude of the surroundings belies the ecological happenings.

Geology

Back in the Miocene, pressures created the South Slough Syncline, forming a basin which received sediments in a tropical environment. The region was uplifted above sea level during the Pliocene, followed by sea level fluctuations during the Pleistocene. As the glaciers to the north melted, the river mouth of the Coos River was drowned, alluviated river valleys formed, and the estuary was created.

Estuaries trap much of the sediments flowing down rivers to the sea and thus control the flow of land sediments to the offshore continental shelves. Estuaries are ephemeral geologic features that could be filled within several thousand years if the sea level and rate of sedimentation remain stable. Deltas would then be more prominent coastal features.

Plants and Wildlife

The open water of the shallows is rich with plankton and extensive eelgrass beds that lure migrating waterfowl. Kingfishers find good fishing here and great blue herons have established a rookery. Near the shoreline are barnacles, dungeness crab, sculpin, ghost shrimp, and bullrush. Tideflats provide habitat for cockle, mud shrimp, smelt, starry flounder, pipefish, and pink, softshell, and bent-nosed clams. The channels of water harbor larger animals that include sponge, snail, jellyfish, salmon, sea bass, perch, trout, and steelhead. Deer, elk, raccoons, bobcats, and beavers fringe the area in the upland forests where Port Orford cedar, Sitka spruce, Douglas fir, and western hemlock grow.

This estuary protects some 22 species of commercially important fish and shellfish for part of their lives. Marsh hawks, voles, leafhoppers, ladybugs, marsh wrens, shrews and short-eared owls are just a few

Skunk cabbage along Estuary Study Trail at South Slough.

of the animals that link their lifelines to the basic food sources of these wetlands. Tiny things do nourish the Earth.

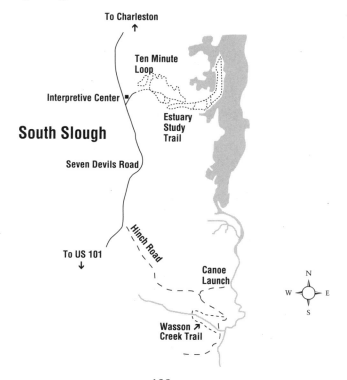

Ten-Minute Loop

Activities   A short introductory walk begins next to the Interpretive Center and gives an overview of the slough with information on patterns of change, wetlands and watersheds, plant and animal adaptations, communities, and includes a view of the estuary.

Estuary Study Trail

From the Interpretive Center, a moderately difficult, 3-mile-round-trip series of loops descends to the shore of South Slough and passes through upland forest, salt marshes, tideflats, a small stream, and open water zones for a great overview of the estuary ecosystem. (A lower parking area eliminates hiking the upper part of the trail system.) A boardwalk traverses a bog of skunk cabbage with alder trees sometimes clawed by bobcats. A lookout offers a panoramic view of the open water and surrounding environment where pilings in the water reveal the remains of the a logging train trestle. Notice the golden-brown coating of plant plankton called diatoms on the mudflats. On your return trip, look carefully for the rare insect-eating sundew plant. Mobility-impaired visitors can take advantage of the fully accessible, lower portion of the trail by vehicle; obtain a gate key at the Interpretive Center.

Wasson Creek Trail

Accessed via Hinch Road, about a mile south of the Interpretive Center, the 0.75-mile Wasson Creek Trail loops through the rolling terrain of open meadows, crosses Wasson Creek, and then travels through a grove of Sitka spruce and western hemlock. Look for wildflowers, beaver dams near favorite foods such as red alder, and a streamside hatchbox for salmon and trout management. Juvenile Coho salmon can sometimes be seen in pools of the creek before they migrate to the ocean in their second year. Mallards and great blue herons hide among the marsh plants as they stalk fish. Go quietly; I startled a herd of Roosevelt elk, though we had time to exchange a few tentative inquisitive glances before they disappeared into upland forest.

Canoeing South Slough

One of the best ways to experience the estuary is by paddling the waters quietly in a canoe. The canoe launch is just east of the Charleston Bridge at Hanson's Landing (fee charged). Plan your trip around the tides; go south and up the slough at, or shortly after, low tide, and return at, or shortly after, the high tide. At the south end of the slough another canoe launch is located at the Hinch Road Bridge (free). A leisurely paddle of the slough takes at least two hours (four hours round-trip), though winds—which are gustier in the afternoon—should be taken into consideration, from the northwest in spring and summer, with southwest winds in fall and winter often indicating an approaching storm. Stay in channels where the water is deepest and do not leave the canoe or you may get stuck in deep mud.

Ecotouring and Safety Concerns

Paddlers on the slough should carry a map; Coast Guard regulations require at least one approved flotation device per occupant.

Trip Tips

See Dungeness National Wildlife Refuge in Chapter 10 for another estuary to visit.

Overlook at South Slough National Estuarine Reserve.

8

RED ROCK COUNTRY

On the Colorado Plateau, geology dominates in a visual and exhilarating way with so many diverse and colorful rock formations that national parks are scattered about like balls on a pool table, yet the land is so rocky and uninhabitable by modern humans that there are few towns and little development. It is a landscape of harsh, cold (in winter), high desert, yet magical red rock vistas run through a video storyline that includes arches, mesas, natural bridges, pinnacles, fins, balanced rocks, crumbly spires, monoliths that look like giant mittens, and red slickrock that swirls upward gently urging feet to climb it.

Red rock canyonlands capture the light and seem to glow at sunrise and sunset, a backdrop for brilliant flowers of cacti that grab at what little moisture the soil can hold. It is a place where one can look at the geology of red rock sandstone up close and discover the scrawlings of the weather in its punctured indentations, striations, knobs, and curving lines dotted occasionally by the mingling of hardy lichens. It is a terrain that animals find harsh, yet those that inhabit it are well adapted to the life, even with lighter coloring to better camouflage them.

Though it is mostly an arid desert, the landscapes were much carved by strident rivers—the Colorado, Green, San Juan, Virgin, and Escalante—responding to gravity upon the somewhat soft sandstone layers. Explorers have ridden the often violent rapids of these rivers to see what this country was like and to chart it for the future.

It is a landscape where solitude is a short walk away, a place where one could get lost if that was desired. A young man named Everett Ruess—a writer, artist, and savvy foot traveler—did that back in 1931–1934 when he wandered in the wilderness canyons of the southeast corner of Utah. He disappeared and though skilled Navajo trackers and others searched long and hard for him, they found only his abandoned burros and the word "nemo" scrawled on a couple of canyon walls—no tracks even. His destiny remains a mystery, yet we know that he was after beauty, adventure, and freedom, perhaps in the mold of John Muir.

This is the landscape where the Anasazi Indians built directly into the Earth's uplifted warm-colored rock formations. Though older shelters were dug into the ground and called pit houses, the Anasazi and Fremont Indians graduated to these carved dwellings in red rock cliffs. They did not choose their sites based purely on the right overhangs, slopes, or desirability of the cliffs, but located their homes where water and good growing soil for their crops would permit them to stay in one place, to stop wandering with the seasons. I am often overwhelmed by the physical agility required for such a life, climbing up into these lofty homes via only tiny handholds and footsteps.

The red rock also provided the stone tablets for art and messages as early as 4,000 years ago when archaic hunters and gatherers roamed the land and etched or painted enigmatic figures on the rock walls that alone provide a stimulus for exploring this country. What does it all mean? It is not difficult to understand the images of bighorn sheep stalked by hunters, but what do the circles, dots, and lines signify?

Though much of the rock art of the Anasazi and Fremont Indians was chipped or etched into the rock, painters used charcoal for black, hematite or red ochre for red, white clay, and sometimes minerals that imparted green, blue, and purple to their art. These pigments were mixed with water, oil from beans, blood, egg white, and other binders. Yucca leaves or fingers simulated a brush, or the paint was sprayed on through a straw.

Calf Creek Recreation Area
Utah

BLM Escalante Resource Area
P.O. Box 225
Escalante, UT 84726
(801) 826-4291

Attractions: Hiking, wildlife viewing, geology, rock art and Indian history, photography, waterfall
Hours/Season: Overnight; year-round
Fees: Fee for camping
Picnicking: Picnic area by Calf Creek at beginning of recreation area
Camping: Recreation area has 14 campsites, with restrooms in the adjacent picnic area. This popular campground fills up quickly. If full, try nearby Escalante State Park (see Chapter 15).
Access: Travel 16 miles northeast of Escalante on UT Scenic Byway 12 to entrance to recreation area.

Stunning red rock scenery along the scenic byway—whether approaching from the north or south—curves and winds on the shoulder of the Aquarius Plateau along the way to Calf Creek Recreation Area. Early explorer/geologist Clarence Dutton wrote that the Aquarius Plateau "should be described in blank verse and illustrated upon canvas."

The original road, now paved, was built by the Civilian Conservation Corps (CCC) in 1938. Before then, mail was carried through here by mules and pack horses, and Boulder is said to be the last town in the U.S. to have had mule-train mail delivery; the area is still sparsely populated.

Whether you just stop at the day-use area for a picnic and stick your feet in the water, or find a campsite, or take the trail to Calf Creek Falls, you'll be delighted with this BLM recreation area. Calf Creek is an integral part of all three choices, a year-round waterway that slides in soft riffles over red slickrock through the picnic and campground area.

The headwaters of the creek lie 7 miles to the north. Between the falls and the campground is a strip of bottomland nestled between red rock walls of Navajo Sandstone that is an excellent example of the part wetlands played in the choosing of sites by prehistoric Indians.

Calf Creek Falls is the quintessential trail destination, complete with an inviting pool.

Both Fremont and Anasazi Indians visited this area, so it has not yet been firmly established which Indians settled this canyon, though the rock art seems typically Fremont in appearance. Both cultures were knowledgeable about the use of available plants and animals for survival. Squawbush branches were used in weaving baskets, which were waterproofed with resin from the pinyon pine trees. The same resin cemented turquoise stones into jewelry pieces. Rabbitbrush flowers provided a yellow dye and its inner bark a green dye. The nut of the pinyon pine and the red berries of squawbush were both food for the Indians. Ricegrass provided a cereal. Squash, corn, and beans were planted in the canyon bottoms; animal protein was hunted.

Later, the canyon bottom served as a natural pasture where pioneer settlers kept weaned calves, which obviously explains the name of the creek. One local farmer used Calf Creek water to grow excellent melons.

Geology

The Aquarius Plateau (on the northwest) is one of the seven Southern High Plateaus in what Utah geologist William Lee Stokes calls the Basin and Range–Colorado Transition Province. This high plateau, which reaches an elevation of 10,306 feet at Lookout Peak, is capped with extrusive igneous rock (lava rock) that was glaciated during the ice ages. To the southeast lies the Kaiparowits Plateau (from the Paiute Indian words meaning "the mountain home of these people"), part of the Colorado Plateau Province. The Escalante River flows from the edge of the Aquarius Plateau east to join the Colorado River.

The walls of Calf Creek Canyon are of Navajo Sandstone, with cream- to red-colored walls that are streaked and discolored by rain. The sandstone was formed, over time, from sand dunes. At the falls, look for volcanic rocks washed down from the Aquarius Plateau.

Plants and Wildlife

Cattails are abundant in the wetlands bordering Calf Creek. Trees species include pinyon pine, box elder, Gambel oak (with acorns that provide food for deer, birds, and other wildlife), dogwood, and Utah juniper. Four-winged saltbush and rabbitbrush are a couple of the shrubs. Horsetail or "scouring rush," was used by pioneers for cleaning pots and pans. Squawbush, ricegrass, buffalo berry, holly grape, and prickly pear cactus are also found here, along with cheatgrass—an exotic from Europe that, unfortunately, is a fire hazard.

Watch for deer tracks on the sandy trail. Fish are easy to spot in the clear water of the creek. Wildlife eat the seeds of Utah juniper, and rodents and birds eat pinyon pine nuts. About halfway along the trail, look for beaver ponds in riparian areas. Do stop and listen for birds in this productive wetland ecosystem—hummingbird, downy woodpecker, golden eagle, mourning dove, western bluebird, and common crow. Evidence of porcupine can be found in the scars on pinyon pine where they have scratched to get to the tender inner bark.

Calf Creek Falls Trail

Activities

At the northwest corner of the road entering the campground, access the trailhead and obtain an interpretive brochure. This very special 5.5-mile-round-trip trail leads to a very special waterfall. Begin your hike without any distractions so you can absorb the historical perspective of the Indians who once inhabited this canyon, the smashing walk between cliffs of Navajo Sandstone, and the unexpected wetlands and wildlife. The trail gains little overall elevation, with the first half of the hike more open and sandy—before the canyon narrows—which can be strenuous in hot weather and too hot for a dog's paws. The second half involves considerable ups and downs, though easy ones. The last part of the hike has more shade and is often cool and pleasant. The path follows the creek the entire way and is surprising verdant.

Though all waterfalls fit under the definition of a steep fall of water from a height, individual ones are all different, unimaginable destinations. Sometimes waterfalls are so inaccessible that one can hardly even get a photo, but not this one. Approach Lower Calf Creek Falls in the right light, particularly after a rain when the wet brown, gold, and mossy green colors on the rock gleam in the sunlight as the water falls from a 126-foot height, and it will grab at your emotions. This complex waterfall begins at a notch high in sandstone where water first catches on a wide ledge and then plunges into a shallow, sandy pool. Some of the water swirls about a dome on the lower area and complements the main falls with several rivulets. The pool is enchanting and inviting on a hot day.

Trail markers point out granaries (ancient storage structure) that were built 800 to 1,000 years ago; one is adjacent to the remains of ancient Indian living quarters. These granaries are high, dry, and rodent-proof. An east wall in the canyon has four large red figures of rock art that are visible from the trail, more clearly with binoculars.

Ecotouring and Safety Concerns

Historical and archeological sites are protected by federal law. Please report any vandalism to the Bureau of Land Management (BLM) or the local sheriff.

Kodachrome Basin
State Park
UTAH

Kodachrome Basin State Park
P.O. Box 238
Cannonville, UT 84718-1238
(801) 679-8562;
Trail Head Station: (801) 679-8536

Attractions: Hiking, mountain biking, horseback riding, guided trail rides (both horse and stagecoach tours—good for the handicapped, elderly, and young), photography, geology study, rock arch, wildlife viewing, concessionaire (Trail Head Station)
Hours/Season: Overnight; year-round
Fees: Charge for day use or for campground
Picnicking: Picnic tables in group area
Camping: Park has 37 campsites and restrooms with showers, plus a group campground.
Access: From Cannonville on UT Scenic Byway 12, go 7 miles south on Cottonwood Canyon Road.

Perhaps too many people have already discovered nearby Bryce Canyon—though it is certainly spectacular and one of my favorites—but fewer have discovered the allure of colorful Kodachrome Basin State Park. With their acknowledged ability to discover and photograph what is worthwhile, the National Geographic Society appropriately named the park when they visited it back in 1949.

Long a favorite picnic stop for locals, it now has a campground so one can stay long enough to explore its unique geology and many trails. Except for holiday weekends, it offers the quiet and solitude of remote country.

Kodachrome is a place where visitors can visualize a time when cowboys rode into the sunset. Campers today hope for a full moon rising above the kaleidoscopic colors that range from gray and white to several shades of red and orange. Swirling layers of slickrock invite scrambling explorations near the campground. When temperatures at higher elevations become cold, this southern desert location at 5,800 feet elevation is warm in both early spring and late fall.

Geology

Located on the northern edge of the Colorado Plateau, many layers of geological formations are seen in the strata of the park. And it is a place of extra geological fascination with its unique sand pipes, monolithic spires often called chimneys.

According to a popular geologic theory, this area once had underground springs and geysers, a southern Yellowstone-type area. Over time and with the accompanying geological changes, the spring channels dried up and filled with sediment which then solidified. The softer Entrada Sandstone surrounding this core eroded away and left the filled-in springs, or sand pipes, standing. Sixty-seven of these rare chimneys of various sizes and shapes have been identified in the park. They range from two to fifty-two meters high, with some serving as excellent navigation points.

The Entrada Sandstone of the park includes both the solid red hills and the gray-white Cannonville member. The iron oxides that contribute many of the vivid colors is sometimes so rich in the soil that it shows up as a purple layer.

Plants and Wildlife

Juniper trees are sometimes utilized by deer and other animals for medicinal purposes. Pinyon pines provide nutritious nuts with as many as 100 calories per nut. Along the nature trail, notice how the lichens on the soil form pedestals called "peds" when water erodes the soil around them. Yucca is a common plant that the

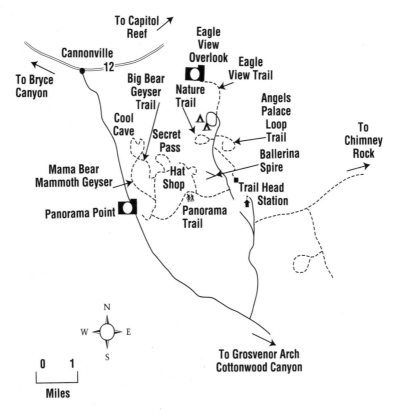

Kodachrome Basin State Park

Navajos used parts of for food, weaving, and even soap. Other plants include sagebrush (winter food for deer and rabbits), buffalo berry, rabbitbrush, Indian ricegrass, false buckwheat, four-winged saltbush, holly grape, serviceberry, snake weed, princess plume with its lemon-colored flowers, and rattleweed milkvetch (or "locoweed," since it absorbs the toxic mineral selenium).

Chukars are often busy around the campsites, trying to find shade and scooping out nests to cool off in the dirt under trees. These birds have adjusted well to people in the vicinity. Red ant colonies are seen along the nature trail. Deer, black-tailed jackrabbit, and desert cottontail rabbit are frequently seen in the park.

Activities

Nature Trail

Access this easy 0.4-mile trail near the campground area and pick up a brochure at the trailhead, which is helpful in identifying many of the desert plants and informative as to their interconnections with the ecosystem, even after they die. Both a large and a small chimney can be seen along the trail, as well as striated rock layers.

Panorama Trail

This 3-mile loop is also an easy hike and mountain bikes are allowed, except for on the steep spur to Panorama Point. The trailhead is located on the park road south of the campground, with the path beginning on an old wagon road and first traversing flat desert punctuated with numerous hardy plants.

Another trail then turns north to access some intriguing rock formations. The Hat Shop Trail is a 0.25-mile side trip near Ballerina Spire, a sand pipe. The next side trail is the Secret Pass, a narrow path between red rock walls after skirting slickrock and a cone-shaped rock.

A moon is seen above one of the unique sand pipes at Kodachrome Basin State Park.

Shortly after returning to the main trail, the turnoff to the optional 2-mile Big Bear Geyser Trail jogs off to the southeast. This trail loops around past Big Bear and Mamma Bear, a cool cave, and Mammoth Geyser before returning to the Panorama Trail and heading south on it. A spur path soon climbs steeply to Panorama Point.

From here, the return loop is through yellow-green stands of grasses with darker green junipers. Some microbiotic crust is visible (see Dead Horse Point State Park) along this section of the loop as well as lots of rose-colored finely powdered soil, soft and crumbly erosional material slightly resembling hardened mud sculptures.

Angels Palace Loop Trail

Though not long, this 1-mile loop is accessed across from the group camping area and involves a bit of strenuous maneuvering on both rocky terrain and a hardened mud-like soil.

Grand Parade Trail

Just south of the Angels Palace Loop Trail, on the same side of the park road, this new 1-mile trail wanders easily toward and past Trail Head Station, with chimneys and rock formations along the way.

Eagle View Trail

Across from the campground, a strenuous and treacherous 1-mile trail leads to the top of a white sandstone cliff. It starts out as a mild, uphill climb on a wide open path, but then it jogs left up the sheer face of the cliff. You can see the dirt trail as it ascends all the way up to a break in the cliff rim. One needs to be sure-footed and energetic to reach the Eagle View Overlook on the top. It is difficult to imagine that until 1977 cattle were driven from the cliff top down to the basin below. But then again, maybe it was once a wider affair.

Shakespeare Arch Nature Trail

Park manager Tom Shakespeare discovered this arch rather recently while trying to find a coyote den. The 0.25-mile nature loop to the arch is moderately strenuous as it passes plant communities and a distant view of Chimney Rock. To reach the trailhead, take the rutted dirt road that branches off to the east just before reaching the ranger station.

Guided Horseback and Horse-Drawn Stage Coach Tours

The cowboys of yesterday in this area are no more, but Bob and MiraLoy Ott operate Scenic Safaris out of Trail Head Station. Bob will take you on any of a variety of guided horseback tours ranging from one to four hours long while pointing out the highlights of the park. Physically impaired or senior travelers might prefer the horse-drawn stagecoach, a one-hour trip. Bob helped lay out the Big Bear Geyser Trail, which was recently opened to hikers.

Ecotouring and Safety Concerns

If you must hike alone, do let someone know where you are going and when you expect to return. Check dirt road conditions, especially after a rain, if exploring in the backcountry near Kodachrome Basin.

Valley of Fire State Park
NEVADA

Valley of Fire State Park
P.O. Box 515
Overton, NV 89040
(702) 397-2088

Attractions: Scenic drives, hiking, orienteering, rock art, prehistory, nature study, photography, geology
Hours/Season: Overnight; year-round
Fees: Day-use fee or camping fee
Visitor Center: Exhibits on geology, ecology, prehistory, park and area history, and dried plants for identification purposes; books, postcards, slides, and film for sale; open daily, 8:30 A.M. to 4:30 P.M.
Picnicking: The Cabins, Seven Sisters, Mouse's Tank Trailhead, and Atlatl Rock
Camping: 51 sites in two park campground areas, one with showers in the restrooms; 3 group areas available by reservation for camping and picnicking
Access: 55 miles northeast of Las Vegas via I-15 to NV 169, or 15 miles southwest of Overton via NV 169

Though Valley of Fire was Nevada's first state park, a place of about 46,000 acres today and established in 1935, it is off the beaten path; an incredible find for those who enjoy exploring a varied red rock landscape with all its wrinkled, fractured, etched, swirled, angled, and scoured components. One magnificent arch stands out in particular. Other rock formations resemble a poodle, a duck, an elephant, and some seven rocks are called "The Sisters," though they do seem rather like blobs. Though a few developed trails exist, the visitor can easily make jaunts across the desert expanses to view the geology and discover wildflowers popping up out of rose-colored sand.

A significant representation of the geological attractions can be observed by simply stopping your vehicle along NV 169 as it passes through the park. The Beehives reveal a solidified story of the erosion forces of wind and water. Two interpretive trails feature petrified logs and stumps washed into the area from an ancient forest about 225 million years ago. Rainbow Vista is an excellent site to photograph multicolored sandstone. Cabins of native sandstone were constructed by the Civilian Conservation Corps in the 1930s as shelters for travelers along the Arrowhead Trail—the first road through the Valley.

Though a harsh landscape for year-round living, the prehistoric Basketmaker people came to this area to hunt bighorn sheep with the notched stick called the *atlatl*, and to gather plants, many of which were used in their basketry. The Anasazi came later, with their occupation of the valley spanning the time from about 300 B.C. to A.D. 1150, though humans may have known this region for as long as 15,000 years. Pottery making followed basketry skills.

The sites in the two campground areas provide intriguing temporary homes for today's travelers, fitted into the red rock formations. And if you search about on foot, you might find a cave. Let your mind wander to that faraway time when life was closely woven into the natural world.

The climate is that of a typical low desert, with an average four inches of annual rainfall arriving in the form of both light winter showers and heavy summer thunderstorms. Winters are mild with anywhere from freezing to 75 degree temperatures. Summer highs usually exceed 100 degrees and may reach 120; spring and fall are ideal times to visit.

Geology

An expansive, deep sea covered this area some 600 million years ago, with vast numbers of living marine organisms that eventually died to form layers of carbonate sediments several miles thick. These are exposed today in the Muddy Mountains south of the Visitor Center. About 200 million years ago, the sea floor was uplifted and muds washed over the area. These subsequently cracked and rains dimpled the surface. Sand was brought to the area via deposits by sluggish streams. The resulting geology includes sand, gravel, and mud components variously layered in rock formations.

Some of the most dramatic formations in the park are of fiery red Aztec Sandstone formed from great shifting sand dunes during the age of dinosaurs, about 150 million years ago. Complex uplifting, thrust faulting, and fracturing occurred, followed by erosion, which continues to add to the shaping of this landscape today with its chemical, wind, climate, compression, and particularly water components—both rain and ground water.

Plants and Wildlife

Part of the Mojave Desert that formed 10,000 years ago, leafy plants dominate, with more than 125 species of shrubs, annuals, and grasses and abundant creosote bush, burrobush, and brittlebush. Some cactus species have adapted to the extreme range of temperatures and these include beavertail and cholla. Given enough rainfall, these cactus bloom in mid-April, roughly corresponding to the peak wildflower bloom, when desert marigold, indigo bush, datura, desert rhubarb, desert primrose, and desert mallow provide nice color contrasts. Yucca is found in the White Domes area.

The desert tortoise is a rare, protected species that can live for more than 100 years and has family roots that date back 175 million years ago to the age of dinosaurs. It spends much of its time underground and is most active in the spring when it forages—look for serrated teeth marks on lower cactus pads—and mates. Resident birds include raven, rock wren, canyon wren, house finch, sage sparrow, roadrunner, and many migrant birds. Pick a campsite near some wildflowers and watch for hummingbirds. Most desert animals are nocturnal. Lizards and snakes are common, as are coyote, kit fox, spotted skunk, black-tailed jackrabbit, and antelope ground squirrel.

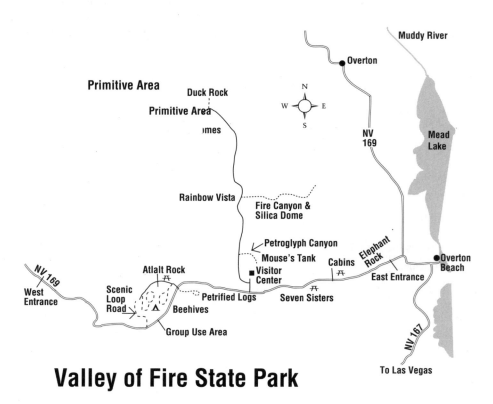

Valley of Fire State Park

Scenic Drives

A 2-mile scenic loop road begins at the turnoff to the campgrounds and continues to Atlatl Rock—where stairs lead to a fascinating petroglyph display on the deep red rock—and past the campgrounds to a final gravel section, accessing interesting formations that include Arch Rock and Piano Rock. The recently-paved, 7-mile-round-trip road to the White Domes passes rock formations of marvelous colors—purples, golds, mauves, creams, and oranges—all jumbled together in a marvelous mosaic of layers and swirls, textures and patterns, sometimes with straight raised seams of thin rock, razorback ridges that indicate joints cemented by quartz and calcite.

Petroglyph Canyon Self-Guiding Trail

Walk through a sandy canyon to Mouse's Tank—a natural rock basin of water—named for a Paiute Indian who used the area as a hideout in the 1890s. Examples of prehistoric rock art are pointed out along the 0.5-mile-round-trip trail.

Fire Canyon/Silica Dome Trail

Accessed from Rainbow Vista, this 3-mile-round-trip trail lets hikers savor the red sandstone formations and see the unique geology that produced Silica Dome.

A striking red rock arch frames a full moon at Valley of Fire State Park.

Ecotouring and Safety Concerns

If you are lucky enough to spot a desert tortoise, do not disturb it. As a human visitor to this harsh land, conserve water. Drive and park only on approved roads and shoulders. Watch for flash floods and do not enter dips in the road if these occur.

Canyon de Chelly National Monument
ARIZONA

Canyon de Chelly
National Monument
P.O. Box 588
Chinle, AZ 86503
(520) 674-5500

Attractions: Scenic drives, hiking, horseback riding, 4-wheel drive exploring (only with authorized guide), photography, geology, rock art, prehistory, visitor center

Hours/Season: Overnight; year-round

Fees: None, except for guided tours, but obtain free permit at visitor center

Picnicking: Allowed in campground

Camping: Cottonwood Campground is adjacent to the visitor center and is available free, first-come, first-served with a maximum 5-day stay. Group sites (no trailers or RVs) can be reserved; (520) 674-5500.

Access: From Chambers and US 40, take US 191 north for 74 miles to Chinle, and then proceed 2 miles east to the monument.

Canyon de Chelly National Monument (pronounced de Shay) encompasses 130 square miles of canyonlands within the Navajo Nation. From the wide mouth of Chinle Wash, canyons fan out to the east looking on a map like a slightly scattered V-formation of flying geese. The two dominant canyons are Canyon de Chelly to the east and Canyon del Muerto (Massacre Canyon) veering to the northeast.

When one looks into the canyon from the rim drives, the landscape of verdant green vegetation, the twisting waters of Chinle Wash, and red rock canyons is an appealing one. The sculpted canyon walls glow a rich salmon hue in early or late light as shadows and sun-washed shapes mingle and change, but appear a pale pink and tan closer to midday. To see the canyon under a full moon is inspiring.

These canyons are one of the awesome sites chosen by the Anasazi Indians, so unlike our paved and skyscrapered cities. From the early Basketmakers until the later Anasazi built apartment-type dwellings high in the cliff walls, human occupation here has spanned more than 2,000 years. The original hunter-gatherers who discovered the canyon area found that springs ran with cold, clear water even in the driest of years. The name "de Chelly" comes from the Navajo word for "where the water comes out of the rock."

The number of Anasazi inhabitants grew to 800 or so by the 13th century as they raised dogs and turkeys, wove cotton textiles, and decorated fine pottery with intricate designs. The last timber for a roof beam was cut in 1264 and became part of the Tower. The Anasazi were gone soon after that, mystifying historians as to what really happened. They left varied rock art—concentric circles, figures holding hands, humans with horns, a life-sized standing cow, and Spanish soldiers on horseback.

Spectacular views of Canyon del Muerto are seen from the North Rim Drive at Canyon de Chelly.

The canyon was quiet and uninhabited until the Navajos, who had moved down from Canada, found refuge in the latter part of the 18th century, or perhaps earlier. Today approximately 450 Navajo Indians go into the bottomlands of the canyons during spring and summer to plant and harvest corn, beans, squash, melons, alfalfa, and small orchards of peach and other fruit trees, living in a primitive manner in hogans with their horses, roosters, sheep, dogs, and goats nearby. In winter, they leave and return to nearby homes.

The traditional Navajo considers the canyon a holy place, the place where the mythological Holy People taught the Navajos how to live. It was on a visit to the White House Ruin that author Tony Hillerman decided to devote his writings to the Navajo and their sacred land.

Geology

After the sea retreated from this area, swirling sand dunes were compressed into Red de Chelly Sandstone 200 million years ago. Above the thick layer of this sandstone is a layer of pinkish rocks of the Shinarump Conglomerate, stream sediments deposited 170 million years ago during the

Triassic Period. A 30-million-year gap in geologic history exists between these two layers. The vividly colored Chinle Formation once topped the Shinarump Conglomerate, but it has been completly eroded away from most of the rim. A little of it remains near the Visitor Center and the first overlook on the South Rim Drive.

The canyons are a recent geological development, less than 3 million years old, the result of uplift in this region. As the Defiance Plateau slowly rose, streams flowing out of the Chuska Mountains that once meandered over plains, picked up energy and the rapid flow, along with the sediments and rocks carried by the waters, cut the canyons during the uplift.

Plants and Wildlife

The canyon rim and talus slope community of plants is that of the high desert with pinyon pine, juniper, alderleaf mountain mahogany, and scrub oak along with cholla and prickly pear cactus. Bright green snakeweed and blue-green rabbitbrush are evidence of overgrazing of the native grasses. On the canyon floor, phreatophytes (waterhogs) are a result of the high water table. Fremont cottonwood provides green color in spring and summer, and golden hues in October. Coyote willows are native, with Russian olive and tamarisk exotics.

One doesn't see much wildlife, though packrats undoubtedly inhabit rock cavities and small mammals scurry about unseen. Overhead sightings include ravens and hawks. The Pinyon jay is closely tied to the natural history of the pinyon pine tree.

Activities

Canyon Tours

Except for the White House Trail into the canyon, rangers or authorized Navajo guides must accompany visitors into the canyon. With a permit, these guides will accompany you on foot or on 4-wheel drive tours, with you furnishing a vehicle (fees are charged). Or you can go on tours offered by the Thunderbird Lodge, who will supply the vehicle. Horseback tours must be accompanied by National Park Service horse operators. Horse rentals are available in the area.

White House Trail

This 2.5-mile-round-trip trail descends 600 feet into the canyon and aims toward the White House Ruin (Kini-na-akai), your only chance to savor Canyon de Chelly on your own. The trail starts about 150 yards to the right of the parking lot on the South Rim Drive. If the weather is hot, it is best either to hike early or late in the day, and remember that coming out of the canyon is all uphill. On the canyon floor, you will wade across Chinle Wash, which is usually quite shallow. Sheep, and perhaps a dog moving them, as well as a corral, might be seen. Listen for the tinkling bells of goats and imagine a time when humpbacked Kokopelli—seen often in rock art—filled the canyons with the sounds of his flute. Notice the interesting pictographs between the two levels of these cliff structures that had perhaps 80 rooms and were occupied by 10 to 12 families. Do not wander off the trail. Free guided hikes are scheduled.

South Rim Drive

The White House Trail at Canyon de Chelly National Monument traverses wonderful red rock formations.

From the Visitor Center and campground, head southeasterly to the first pullout at mile 2.1 where the canyon is about 275 feet deep. At 2.5 miles, from the Tsegi Overlook, a farm and many-sided Navajo home (called a "hogan") can be seen. These dirt-floor structures were made of logs or stone chinked with mud. At Junction Overlook (3.9 miles), both Junction Ruin and First Ruin (the first Anasazi pueblo described by archeologist Cosmos Mindeleff when he visited in 1882) are in view. At mile 5.7 is the turnoff to White House Overlook, where hikers can descend into the canyon on a good trail (see description above). The scenic drive continues to Sliding Rock Overlook at mile 12.9, and then finally to the last stop at Spider Rock Overlook (21.8 miles), where a 600-foot path accesses the overlook. The canyon is now 1,000 feet deep and here Monument Canyon joins Canyon de Chelly. Spider Rock is 800 feet high and located at the junction of the two canyons. With binoculars, several ruins can be spotted in this area. Return via the same road.

North Rim Drive

From the Visitor Center, cross Chinle Wash and head 5.4 miles northeast along Canyon del Muerto to the first turnoff to Ledge Ruin. A path leads to two viewpoints: Ledge Ruin and Dekaa Kiva. Besides being used for ceremonies, evidence points to the use of the kiva for weaving—a masculine occupation. Antelope House (mile 8.2) is named for the fine antelope painting attributed to Navajo artist Dibe Yazhi. Anasazi pictographs are also found here. Several structures show occupation in this area from A.D. 693. Across the wash from Antelope House is the Tomb of the Weaver, where a well-preserved body of an apparently highly respected individual was wrapped in a blanket made of golden eagle feathers. An isolated, high red stone butte across the canyon is called Navajo Fortress. Mummy Cave (mile 17.5) was a continuously occupied site of the Anasazi from A.D. 300 to approximately A.D. 1300. The last stop is at Massacre Cave (mile 21), a place where Navajos took refuge but were massacred by Spanish forces. Detailed information is included in the guide to this drive.

Ecotouring and Safety Concerns

Be aware that stray dogs, cats, and panhandlers can be a problem in the campground. At all times, respect the fact that the Navajos are allowing you to visit their land. Do not photograph Navajo people or their personal property without permission; a fee is usually required even then.

Trip Tips

As part of the Navajo Nation, this monument goes on daylight saving time, while the rest of Arizona observes standard time year-round. The Navajos also make and enforce their own laws—it is advisable to be aware of these.

9

GEYSERS, FUMAROLES, HOT SPRINGS, AND MUD POTS

Photographer and columnist Dewitt Jones wrote of his emotional response to one of Yellowstone's geysers: "… a moonlit apparition of wonder and enchantment" that inspired seven rolls of film, but more importantly helped him see again "how beautiful this planet is!"

How can one wander ever so slowly and quietly among that landscape on foot and not feel the powerful tug at the senses of the artist, the writer, the geologist, the adventurer, the poet, the naturalist—even the magician— within us.

Our eyes need time to take in the exquisite emerald pools rimmed with undulating curves of golds and oranges, the marbled tapestry of thin crusted mineral deposits, the river steaming at its limestone edges, the exuberance of erupting geysers, bubbling pots of silvery mud, and animals coming in winter to warm themselves and be nourished by the green grasses that mock the cold. The nose is perhaps not so joyous as it detects the sulfur in the air, but the ears listen to the happy sound of a mountain bluebird on a whitened tree snag.

For touch, we need to visit hot springs that are so accommodating to the human body, and these are spread throughout the West. The "deep heat" within the Earth that triggers the catastrophic eruptions of volcanoes and uplifts mountain ranges is a source of energy that is retained long after after the event. Hot water many emerge near fault lines and yield water that has never before been at the surface, or it may be water from rain or snow that has descended to underground heated rocks or steam and then returned to the surface. Unless the heat of underground magma is entirely dissipated, it is always trying to reach equilibrium with its sur- roundings, passing on its energy. The Earth is dynamic because of constant

143

change, its geothermal energy a resource involved in both recreational and scientific pursuits that may be tapped and diminished by industrial exploitation.

Many developed hot springs are commercial soaking pools today—though others heat homes and industries—but the real magic of soaks is found in primitive hot springs found in natural terrain. Some are widely known, others are not difficult to discover, and a few are a long hike into the wilderness; one has a choice to suit the temperament.

Yellowstone National Park WYOMING

Yellowstone National Park
Superintendent
WY 82190-0168
(307) 344-7381
TDD (307) 344-2386

Attractions: Photography, hiking, hot springs, geysers, mud pots, fumaroles, fishing, bicycling, interpretive programs, ranger-led activities, winter activities at Mammoth Hot Springs

Hours/Season: Overnight; year-round

Fees: Entry charge per vehicle and for campsites

Picnicking: Picnic areas at Madison, Mammoth Hot Springs, Norris, along Firehole River, Mud Volcano, and just north of Midway Geyser area

Camping: Campsites near geysers and hot springs are at Madison Campground (reservations via (307) 344-733) and first-come, first-served at Mammoth Hot Springs.

Access: East entrance to Yellowstone National Park is 53 miles west of Cody, Wyoming, via US 14-16-20. South entrance is 64 miles north of Jackson, Wyoming, via US 89-91-287. West entrance is just east of West Yellowstone, Montana, via US 20. North entrance is just south of Gardiner, Montana, via US 89. The park road from the north entrance to Cooke City is open all year.

As you explore the spectacular thermal landscapes of Yellowstone, you may think you are dreaming of science fiction plots set on a distant planet or perhaps you have traveled into the future and wandered off the spaceship that has spun you into an alien world.

Is that figure you see in a mist of steam rising from a pool an alien being? Pull out your wrinkled map and find names like Cyclops Spring, Comet, Druid Peak, Firehole Falls, Mustard Spring, Sizzling Basin, and Dragon's Mouth. These don't exactly solve your dilemma, but go cautiously and be rewarded with the dazzle of colors, textures, patterns, and mystical vistas of emerald pools and exploding geysers that are totally natural, yet so artistic, that your wandering is slow and concentrated. Wildlife viewing is an awesome accompaniment to visiting the thermal features of Yellowstone, a place unparalleled in the lower 48 states.

Yellowstone is magical. You will never see anything else like it in this world. The "deep heat" of the park is best seen in the 50 miles from Mammoth Hot springs past Norris Geyser Basin to the Old Faithful area. Some say Old Faithful is the essence of the park, but look for your own candidate.

Established as the country's first national park in 1872, the thermal features are especially significant because they are the unaltered clues to understanding this unique landscape. Elsewhere, geothermal activity is so often quickly harnessed for human use and then altered.

Geology

A dramatic volcanic past has given Yellowstone the world's largest concentration of geysers and hot springs—some 10,000 thermal features including 200 to 250 geysers. Magmatic heat continues to power surface activity.

Geysers are the visible results of a mostly invisible process: surface water from rain and snow seeps down into porous rock layers, is heated under pressure, and then reemerges periodically above ground. The pressure accompanying this superheated water is released near the surface and it flashes into the steam of a geyser. Hot springs result if the water is not superheated or under pressure. Fumaroles, lacking enough moisture to flow, vent steam. When acid gases decompose rocks into mud and clay above fumaroles, mud pots are formed.

The travertine terraces at Mammoth Hot Springs are formed when acidic hot water—which dissolves limestone—reaches the surface and carbon dioxide escapes, causing the limestone to be deposited in these crystalline cascades. Most new rock from these geysers is called geyserite, a noncrystalline mineral chemically similar to glass.

Plants and Wildlife

Large mammals wander amongst the park protected and easily seen. In fact, drivers must yield to bison (which now number some 4,000 in the park) that frequently cross the road. The bison sometimes soak in the less dangerous hot springs. In winter, the animals keep warm by staying close to thermal areas, though these hot spots with thin crusts are dangerous and can take their toll.

Though bears are not as often sighted as in the easy food-acquiring past of the park, both black and grizzly bears, requiring vigilance from visitors, find plenty of suitable habitat here. Elk, moose, mule deer, bighorn sheep, coyote, and pronghorn are not difficult to find. The numerous populations of Uinta ground squirrels seem curious about human behavior. Birding is rewarding, too; watch for trumpeter swans, white pelicans, Canada geese with their young, green-winged teal, osprey, and mountain bluebird flying from dead snags in thermal areas. I saw one Canada goose join a herd of doe elk.

Roadside forests consist mostly of lodgepole pine, with dead snags observed frequently in thermal areas. The most intriguing plants found in the thermal areas are the algae that add enhancing hues to pools and hot springs. Some live in water as hot as 167 degrees Fahrenheit, where

Bison soak in hot springs at Yellowstone National Park.

they are yellow. Slightly cooler water is inhabited by orange, red, or brown algae. Other colors are specific for the temperature. Bacteria grow in even hotter water and form yellow or pink strands. Algae and bacteria nurture small flies, which in turn feed larger insects and birds.

Activities

Mammoth Hot Springs Terraces

Pick up a booklet and wander up and down the walkways of the Lower Terraces where Minerva Spring forms outstanding sparkling terraces. A one-way drive—a narrow road with sharp curves on which motorhomes longer than 25 feet are prohibited—accesses the Upper Terraces with excellent views of the Lower Terraces. Because this is an area of rapid change and scalding water, walking off the road or straying from designated pullouts is not allowed.

Travertine terraces of Minerva Spring at Mammoth Hot Spring in Yellowstone.

Norris Geyser Basin

Norris contains Steamboat Geyser—the world's largest—which is irregular in erupting, ranging from days to years, and seen in the Back Basin of Norris, as is the more predictable Echinus Geyser, which erupts regularly about once an hour. Across the road, Porcelain Basin is Yellowstone's hottest exposed area. Well-maintained trails access both of these basins.

Upper Geyser Basin

Stop at the Old Faithful Visitor Center for orientation and maps. Eruptions of Old Faithful vary with earthquake activity and are presently occurring every 75 minutes. South of the park road in this area, photogenic highlights at Black Sand Basin include Emerald Pool and Sunset Lake.

Emerald Pool is one of the highlights at Black Sand Basin, near Old Faithful.

Mud Volcano Trail

Six miles north of Fishing Bridge, this 0.67-mile loop starts at Mud Caldron and passes Black Dragon's Caldron, Sour Lake, Grizzly Fumarole, hillsides of trees cooked by steam, strange odors, and other seemingly unworldly hot spots.

Human Soaks

According to the park public affairs office, soaking is allowed in two hot spring areas: in an area along Firehole Canyon Drive, just south from Madison Campground, and at Boiling River, just north of Mammoth. The latter empties into the Yellowstone River and is only safe at certain water levels.

In the past, I have joined others soaking in a year-round ditch of natural mineral water on the north bank of the Madison River near the Madison Campground. Reach this hot water by taking a short trail south from Loop H near Site #292. This spring results from underground water that bubbles up through a mudflat and is retained by a small sod dam so that 100-degree Fahrenheit water accumulates to about 18 inches—a nice depth for a short soak. This area along the Madison River is excellent bison-viewing territory. These monstrous mammals frequently wade across the river and roll around on the ground afterward.

Bicycling

Some trails allow bicycles. A good one to try is the walkway that heads southwest from the Old Faithful area and roughly follows the Firehole River and a varied assortment of thermal features. Do check for up-to-date regulations on bicycles.

Ecotouring and Safety Concerns

Check with a ranger before soaking in any of the thermal areas since regulations do change. In most areas, this is prohibited.

Yellowstone is so loved that only strict regulations will help it to remain a great place to visit. Obey the "do not approach wildlife" regulations. Contrary to observations, the animals are unpredictable and dangerous, especially bison and bears. If you cause the animal to move, you are too close. Bison can sprint 30 miles per hour. Campers at Madison Campground should be aware that bison find the grass in that area tantalizing, so watch out for them. (I awoke one night as one was chewing under the window of my camper.) Food and odors attract bears—even cosmetics, toiletries, pet food and water containers. (Read the detailed written set of cautions that the park distributes regarding bear encounters.) Feeding any of the wildlife is unlawful.

While driving, be alert for sudden stops by others who are observing wildlife. From the 1988 fire, trees that were killed and became snags continue to fall unpredictably, so use caution in such areas. And please do not throw coins or other objects in thermal pools. (A once-favored destination, water debris that had collected in Morning Glory Pool was part of the

Steam from underground heat rolls along the edge of Firehole River in Yellowstone National Park.

reason for a some loss of its thermal activity.) Always stay on walkways in thermal areas since nearby thin crusts are hot and dangerous. Protect cameras, lenses, and glasses from spray or mist as they contain dissolved minerals. No pets are allowed on trails.

Trip Tips

The mentioned thermal features are highlights; there are many more that will entice you to make frequent road stops.

Hot Springs State Park
WYOMING

Hot Springs State Park
220 Park Street
Thermopolis, WY 82443
(307) 864-2176

Attractions: Hot springs, mineral water bathing and slides (both public and concessionaire), buffalo drive, Rainbow Terrace, walking paths, river fishing, photography
Hours/Season: Day use; year-round
Fees: Free except for concessionaires
Picnicking: Excellent facilities on spacious park grounds
Camping: No camping in the park, but several private campgrounds and motels are nearby, a few with mineral water pools
Access: At the north end of Thermopolis, off US 20 at Park Street

---

Billed as the world's largest single mineral hot spring, Hot Springs State Park is a fun place to visit, possibly even therapeutic. Certainly, soothing hot-water soaks make one feel good.

Originally part of the Shoshone Indian Reservation of 1868, 10 square miles—including the hot springs with its "health-giving properties"—was deeded to the U.S. government in 1896 for $60,000, with the stipulation of free use of the hot springs. An annual Gift of the Gods Pageant in August in Thermopolis commemorates the original deeding.

Millions of gallons of mineral water exit the spring every 24 hours at a present temperature of 127 degrees Fahrenheit. It is so hot that cooling pools must be used before water is diverted to the soaking pools. Excess water flows over Rainbow Terrace and into the nearby Big Horn River where cascades of cooling water leave glittering salt deposits.

Do take note of the rich ochre shades of the adjacent Owl Creek Mountains east of Big Horn River as they literally glow when hit by the setting sun. Geology buffs will appreciate the intriguing swirls of gray rock seen at the East River Road Viewpoint.

Geology

The Thermopolis hot springs are believed to flow underground from the Owl Creek Mountains. Rain falling on these mountains soaks through porous rock and slowly filters down through various underground formations. Heat and chemicals are derived from rock and subterranean volcanic gases as water is forced up through crevices in the rock in the hot spring areas.

Created over a span of thousands of years, the travertine of Rainbow Terrace has been formed primarily from calcite and gypsum that has crystallized out of solution as the water from the hot springs cools and loses carbon dioxide, decreasing the solubility of these salts. Analysis of the mineral waters here shows 27 different minerals, with 2,373 dissolved solid parts per million.

Plants and Wildlife

A small herd of bison numbering approximately 10 to 20 head is free roaming throughout most of the year. In May and June, the bison are confined to the corral area to allow for pasture rejuvenation. When I visited in July, three calves were easily viewed near this area. During the cold months, supplementary feeding is provided and visitors can view this activity from their vehicles.

State Park Bath House

Activities

Free inside and outside mineral pools at 104 degrees Fahrenheit offer relaxing soaks. Private tubs are also available where cold water can be added to control the temperature if desired. Suit rentals are available. The park staff monitors the length of the soaks since it is recommended that these be 20 minutes long. Hours are 8 A.M. to 6 P.M. from Monday through Saturday; 12:00 P.M. to 6 P.M. on Sunday and some holidays; closed on Sundays on winter holidays.

Concessionaire Facilities

The Star Plunge was built in 1900 and has been used by such personalities as Buffalo Bill Cody and Butch Cassidy. It features the all-weather Blue Thunder 300 Slide, the outdoor Super Star 500 slide, and a 60-foot slide for kids and seniors. Other offerings include a hillside steam cave, indoor and outdoor pools, Jacuzzi, game arcade, exercise room, and suit rental.

The Hot Springs Water Park offers a 272-foot outdoor water slide, a 162-foot indoor all-weather slide, soaking pools of various temperatures, steam room, game room, sauna, massage therapist, and suit rental.

Buffalo Drive

Drive north on Big Spring Drive to access the Buffalo Pasture Road, which soon turns south past the corral area and an overlook point.

Nature Trails and Walkway Destinations

At the south end of the park, near East Arapahoe Road, is the River Walkway. It heads north past the Holiday Inn, crosses Park Street, passes the Plaza Hotel, crosses Pioneer Street, heads east to Rainbow Terrace, and then continues to a Big Horn River overlook.

From the Big Horn Spring parking lot, view the main spring with its bubbling pool and green moss and then take the paved walkway that heads northeast to the "Swinging Bridge" over the river—with its unique vantage point of the river, cooling ponds, and terrace. Other paths connect here and lead past the cooling pools, Rainbow Terrace, and south to the State Park Bath House.

One can also walk the official 10K Volksmarch (6.2 miles) that goes through the state park and other areas of Thermopolis. Pick up a map of the route at the Bath House and follow the brown and yellow Volksmarch signs.

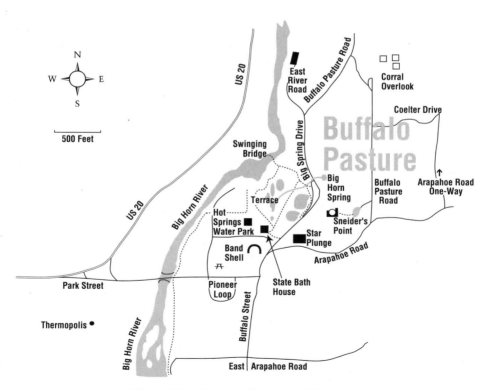

Hot Springs State Park

For obvious ecological reasons, no soap or shampoo usage is allowed in the mineral pools. Soaking and wading in mineral pools is restricted to facilities designed for such use. Use caution along the buffalo drive. Bicycles are restricted on the roadways.

Hot Springs on the Rio Grande, Big Bend National Park

TEXAS

Big Bend National Park
Rio Grande
TX 79834
(915) 477-2251

Attractions: Soaking in hot springs, hiking, wildlife viewing, history, photography

Hours/Season: Overnight; year-round

Fees: Vehicle entry fee to park; extra charge for developed campgrounds

Picnicking: Nearby Daniels Ranch and Rio Grande Village picnic areas

Camping: The park's Rio Grande Village Campground does not have hook-ups, but a concession trailer park near Rio Grande Village Store does. Both are first-come, first-served, and very popular.

Access: North entrance at Persimmon Gap is 42 miles south of Marathon on US 385. West entrance is 82 miles south of Alpine on TX 118.

Along the great curve of the Rio Grande River on the Mexican border that is Big Bend National Park today, J.O. Langford and his family homesteaded the Hot Springs area in 1909. He chose this spot because he hoped to regain his health after suffering with malaria bouts in Mississippi. A health resort was constructed that included a post office/trading post and motel units for frequent guests since this became a popular place.

Before his arrival, Indians soaked in a chiseled-out cavity in sedimentary rock where hot water poured off a lip in a rock. Over this area and its 105-degree Fahrenheit water, Langford built a bathhouse out of limestone blocks. He attributed both the hot springs—soaks and drinking the water— and the relaxed peacefulness of the area to his health recovery.

In 1942, the property was sold to the state of Texas and it eventually became a national park. Hot Springs is now on the National Register of

Historic Places. The bathhouse is no longer intact, but its foundation serves as a location guide and tub for soaks. River floods occasionally inundate the hot springs rendering them inaccessible.

A zillion good reasons should lure you to the vast varied and wild terrain of Big Bend National Park; just don't miss a soak in the hot springs along the river.

Geology

As the Cretaceous seas of the Big Bend area grew shallower, lime mud deposits formed layers that are now exposed in the flagstone formations visible at the Hot Springs. Notice the artistic swirls and textures of rose and cream colors in the rocks by the bathing area.

Hot Springs is the largest of several hot springs on this section of Rio Grande River. In 1936, it was claimed that 250,000 gallons per day of hot water poured out of the rocks. Research indicates the hot water arises from a pocket of "fossil water" deposited at least 20,000 years ago that is not being replaced. This water is heated geothermally by igneous rocks under water. The rocks of the area are thin-bedded limestone and shale.

Plants and Wildlife

Of this country's national parks, the most bird species—more than 430—have been recorded at Big Bend, and the Hot Springs area is a good sighting place adjacent to riparian floodplain with its green slash in the Chihuahuan Desert. Watch for vermilion flycatcher, scarlet tanager, warblers, and pyrrhuloxia among the mesquite thickets and cottonwood trees and painted bunting amidst waving grasses. Listen for white-winged doves and keep an eye out for fleeting roadrunners.

It is not difficult to discover javelinas or collared peccaries, and some scouting will find horned toads and the Texas tortoise. Although it is unlikely you will see one, be aware that the shy mountain lion considers Big Bend a valuable solitary habitat. And a sprinkling of the four endangered cats—jaguar, jaguarundi, ocelot, and margay—range the brushland.

Trails to the Hot Springs

Activities

A choice of two trails access the Hot Springs. Check with a ranger for road and trail conditions. The easy 2-mile Hot Springs Historic Walk (a booklet is available for this loop) is reached via a 2-mile primitive dirt road situated 1 mile below the Lower Tornillo Creek Bridge on the road to Rio Grande Village. On the hike you will pass the buildings of the resort and pictographs on the limestone cliffs just beyond the motel.

Or one can hike the slightly more strenuous primitive trail (about 2-miles-round-trip) that begins just past the Daniels Ranch site west of Rio Grande Village. This trail offers a wonderful perspective of the river, its floodplain, and the adjacent low rock formations. Take time to discover mortar holes used by Indians for grinding mesquite beans and seeds. Continue on past the hot springs to view the resort remains.

Ecotouring and Safety Concerns

As a visitor to this desert floodplain, your impact lasts a long time. So go gentle, don't litter, and do not use soap in the hot springs or the river. Respect others by restraining from nude bathing. The river itself is a deceptive danger, with strong currents and quicksand that warn off swimmers.

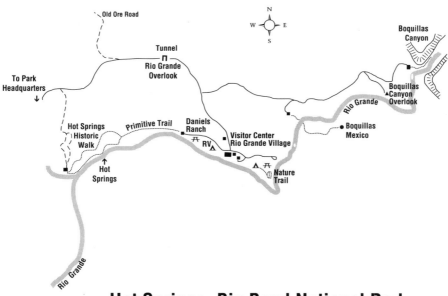

Hot Springs, Big Bend National Park

10

WILDLIFE PRESERVES

West

Have you ever sat around a campfire and reminisced about some of your favorite experiences? You might find that many of them revolve around the magic of wetland areas. I recall the time I explored a watery inlet that branched off from Tillamook Bay in the quiet of a cruising kayak. The fluid movement was such that ducks were undisturbed in their swimming and a bald eagle didn't fly away from its nearby perch. Never had I been able to bird watch and paddle with a feeling of such total immersion in nature.

Or perhaps you have found that great private camping spot amidst lush wetlands bordering a lake where you spent a week relaxing, windsurfing, swimming, fishing and watching sunsets, your tent snug amongst shady trees overlooking a private cove where you tied up a small boat.

Many natural areas and most refuges are almost synonymous with the word wetlands, though federally designated wildlife refuges usually do not allow camping since wildlife has first priority. As some of the most productive areas of the world, wetlands produce a bounty of natural products usable by people—fish and shellfish, game, timber, cranberries, and blueberries. But the existence of many animals depends on wetlands. If we have any concern for the natural world, it is important that we save both the dull stuff such as snails, reeds, frogs, and beetles as well as several rare and endangered species that would not survive without these moist places. And biodiversity is best found where habitats merge and species must be vigorous and strong to survive.

By saving wetlands, humans also benefit in several ways other than the above mentioned economic ones. Wetland plants absorb toxic materials from the water and convert them to harmless molecules—nature's water purification system working free for us. Some towns are beginning to utilize natural and human-made marshes as part of their water treatment systems. Wetlands also aid in flood control by serving as sponges when rivers overflow, and later releasing the water downstream, saving homes and crops from destruction. Wetland vegetation also binds the soil and prevents erosion.

Because wetlands make good nesting places, with vegetation for both food and protective cover, they are much sought after by wildlife, especially birds. But humans want to grow crops where water is available so the use of these lands is furiously debated at times. It seems somewhat strange that hunting—via programs like duck stamps, Ducks Unlimited, and "Adopt a Pothole"—has provided funds that will save wetland habitat for wildlife, though as a photographer it is rather disheartening to try to photograph birds after they have been spooked during hunting season on the refuge, a place Webster defines as "shelter or protection from danger, difficulty, ..." Saving habitat is the positive result, though, and that in itself is a commendable achievement that gives hope for the survival of much wildlife.

Though hunting, shellfish harvesting, and fishing are traditional pursuits in wetlands, a recent focus includes outdoor recreation. It makes good emotional sense besides being food for the curious mind. It is difficult to put a price tag on the benefits of wetlands for recreation, tourism, and aesthetics. Whether seen through the eyes of hikers, boaters, bird watchers, fishermen, artists, or photographers, this watery habitat is a wonderland of vistas and wildlife. Be thankful that the U.S. Fish and Wildlife Service manages more than 500 refuges encompassing almost 92 million acres of lands and waters.

Dungeness National Wildlife Refuge
WASHINGTON

Dungeness National
Wildlife Refuge
c/o Washington Coastal
Refuges Office
33 South Barr Road
Port Angeles, WA 98362
(360) 457-8451

Attractions: Hiking, wildlife viewing, beachcombing, photography, crabbing, oysters, fishing, boating, paddling, educational programs
Hours/Season: Day use only; best wildlife viewing in spring, fall, and winter
Fees: Entry charge per family
Picnicking: No facilities on refuge, but in adjacent recreation area
Camping: Campsites adjacent to refuge at Dungeness Recreation Area (not affiliated with refuge, county operated)
Access: From US 101 west of Sequim, go 3 miles north on Kitchen Road, then right on Lotzgesell Road. Drive through the Dungeness Recreation Area to the dead end at the refuge parking lot.

On the Strait of Juan de Fuca, a long spit of land studded with driftwood and beachgrass stretches northeast to the New Dungeness Lighthouse. More than halfway along this narrow arm, the Graveyard Spit curves south while Cline Spit extends north from the coastline, leaving a small opening that prevents New Dungeness Harbor from being completely enclosed. East of this water entry point is the mouth of the Dungeness River, where seawater and freshwater mingle in this estuary. A small boat mounted with a crabbing hoist moves slowly offshore, picking up crab pots to see what harvest they contain. A kayak easily maneuvers through the mild surf of the strait and a rubber raft cruises the sheltered bay. Across the strait is Vancouver Island, mountains topping the land.

Most of this area—a mix of rich habitats—is Dungeness National Wildlife Refuge, an enticing magnet for visiting and resident bird life, bird watchers with binoculars, beach walkers, and clammers who find vast mudflats at a good low tide.

The spit was named by explorer Vancouver because it reminded him of the spit and tidelands of Dungeness, England. From the 1880s to after the turn of the century, the harbor here was a busy shipping place, with a steady flow of such goods as eggs, potatoes, rhubarb, baled hay, and cows transported by water to Port Townsend and Port Crescent. Farmlands still occupy part of the coast here, though development—particularly retirement homes—is increasing.

Geology

The Dungeness Spit is a classic example of a coastal spit formed by eroding soil, wind, and water currents. Accretion of land also occurs here; old photos show a long wharf ending in a building that is now approximately a mile inland.

Clallam Indian legend says that two sandspits—in Port Angeles and at Dungeness—were once one long spit until mythical hero Kakyhuck, tired of portaging across or paddling around the lengthy affair, split them apart. Could there be any prehistoric truth behind such a legend?

Plants and Wildlife

Offshore, harbor seals sometimes haul out onto the beach amidst a variety of seabirds. The estuary of the Dungeness River behind the spit has a rich food web that is bottomed with microorganisms that nourish waterfowl, seabirds, as well as anadromous and ocean fish.

Salmon spawn in the river and use the estuary as a nursery for about a year before swimming out to sea. The tide flats are rich with crabs, clams, oysters, and other shellfish.

As many as 30,000 migratory waterfowl—scoters, widgeon, bufflehead, grebes, dunlin, and plovers—stop briefly in autumn and up to 15,000 birds spend the winter here, with good numbers of eelgrass-feeding black brant. Other winter residents include cormorants, loons, and harlequin ducks. In summer, the bird population diminishes, but cormorants, great blue herons, and loons are still around. Bald eagles are sometimes spotted on the driftwood.

Brown pelicans scan the ocean for fish along the coast near Dungeness.

Hiking Trails

Activities

A 0.5-mile trail traverses coastal forest—where black-tailed deer wander early and late in the day—to a panoramic viewpoint above the spit. This path continues downhill to the spit, where one can either walk along the beach or skirt the inland waters. Exploring is varied depending on the tides and the expanse of exposed tide flats. The New Dungeness Lighthouse is a 5.5-mile excursion (11 miles round-trip), but involves easy, flat walking.

A trail also exists along the bluffs in Dungeness Recreation Area that offers splendid water views, frequent picnic tables, and a connecting path to the refuge trail.

Boating

Boaters and paddlers can enjoy the quiet waters either behind the spit or on the strait side. Clamming and fishing are permitted, according to Washington State regulations, but oysters are privately owned and cannot be collected. They must be purchased at the nearby oyster farms.

Equestrian Trails

A 0.75-mile horse trail accesses the refuge from Dungeness Recreation Area. This winds through the refuge forest area on a separate path from the hiking trail before they merge shortly before the downhill to the spit. The horse trail within the refuge is open daily from October 16 through April 14, and weekdays only (except for holidays) from April 15 through October 15.

Horseback riders will find more trails—through upland meadows and near cattail and pond wetland marshes—in the adjacent Dungeness Recreation Area.

Ecotouring and Safety Concerns

Do remember that the refuge is not a park; you must respect the rights of wildlife. Metal detectors are not allowed, nor are pets, bicycles, or firearms. Also prohibited are jogging, kite flying, windsurfing, and jet skiing.

Lower Klamath and Tule Lake National Wildlife Refuges
OREGON AND CALIFORNIA

Lower Kamath/Tule Lake NWR
Refuge Manager
Route 1, Box 74
Tulelake, CA 96134
(916) 667-2231

Attractions: Auto tours, bird-watching, wildlife observation, paddling, fishing, hunting, photography, nature study
Hours/Season: Day use; year-round
Fees: None
Visitor Center: Exhibits, information, maps, road conditions, upcoming events; open Monday through Friday, 8:00 A.M. to 4:30 P.M., weekends and holidays, 8:00 A.M. to 4:00 P.M. (except Christmas and New Year's Day)
Picnicking: No facilities on refuges, although one can certainly have lunch while using the car as a blind.
Camping: No camping on the refuges
Access: Located on the Oregon-California border, 24 miles south of Klamath Falls, Oregon, the refuge has several entrances. Check at the headquarters for the refuge on Hill Road, 5 miles west of Tulelake, CA, 4 miles south of the border.

At dusk the air is thick with the honking sounds of Canada geese as they fly into the Lower Klamath National Wildlife Refuge. A muskrat swims across the tangerine-colored water at sunset looking for cattails, rushes, and pond weeds to eat. White pelicans turn in front of a rising full moon and then dip down to land in the water. The time is fall and nearly a million birds will stop at this feeding ground on their way south for the winter. In the shadow of majestic Mt. Shasta, I have found this one of the most exciting places to watch birds.

This refuge near the border between Oregon and California was our country's first waterfowl refuge, established by President Theodore Roosevelt in 1908 when some people were beginning to understand the importance of wetlands. Today, only 25 percent of the original wetland acres remain, as the rest were converted to agricultural land by government and private efforts. But four out of five birds migrating through the Pacific Flyway stop in the Klamath Basin.

The U.S. Fish and Wildlife Service manages the 53,598 acres of Lower Klamath and the neighboring 39,116 acres of Tule Lake National Wildlife Refuge, a landscape of open water, marsh, grassy meadows, sagebrush and juniper grasslands, conifer forests, agricultural land, and cliffs and rocky slopes. For continued high numbers of waterfowl, concerned management must address problem areas involving water usage, habitat, pollution, and even water temperature.

Geology

Approximately 10,000 years ago, this region of southern Oregon was covered with huge Pleistocene lakes that arose when the final major period of glacial resurgence ended and waters melted. In more recent historic times, the Klamath Basin was dominated by approximately 185,000 acres of shallow lakes and extensive marshes, which attracted over 6 million waterfowl.

Plants and Wildlife

Much of the water here is shallow marsh with vegetation that grows in and along its edges. Tule (large hard-stem bulrushes) and cattail in the permanent marsh is prime nesting habitat. Periodic draining—waterfowl eat the exposed vegetation—allows oxygen to reach bottom soils, promotes the release of nutrients, and stimulates plant growth when reflooded. Keeping the exposed bottomland dry in summer controls diseases such as botulism. Waterways are kept full in winter.

Fall migration begins in late August and September with the arrival of pintails, white-fronted geese, duck and geese numbers peaking about early-November. Major species are tundra swan, mallard, widgeon, green-winged teal, and snow, Ross, and Canada geese. August and September are good times to see marsh birds: pelicans, cormorants, egrets, herons, gulls, terns, and grebes.

Bald eagles are the big attraction from December through February when more than 500 of these raptors use the refuges as a food source. In the spring, the refuges are teeming with birds stopping on their way north to fatten up, along with the thousands of birds and waterfowl that nest in the basin's marshlands. Nesting species include gadwall, mallard, cinnamon teal, pintail, ruddy duck, and Canada geese.

From May through August, auto tours reveal large numbers of young birds, about 45,000 ducks and 2,600 Canada geese. Lower Klamath is one of three remaining white pelican nesting colonies in the West. Other sightings in summer can include cormorants, herons, egrets, terns, white-faced ibis, grebes, gulls, avocets, black-necked stilts, and killdeer.

Pheasants dash across roads open to public driving. Hawks sweep low looking for rodents in the grass. Deer and coyotes wander through the vegetation, and otters play in the water pumped through the wetlands. A total of 411 wildlife species have been observed on the refuges.

Many Canada geese visit Lower Klamath and Tule Lake Wildlife Refuges.

Auto Tour Routes

Activities

Both Lower Klamath and Tule Lake have marked one-way auto routes that are improved dike roads where one can take time to observe, while leaving room for other vehicles to pass. At certain times, various areas are closed, so observe the signs. Lower Klamath encompasses many varied units while Tule Lake is primarily composed of two large open water areas. A limited number of photography blinds are available for use with advance reservations.

Although not part of the auto routes, lots of good bird sightings are seen while driving along the upper edge of Lower Klamath on CA 161. This route, however, has truck traffic, so one should be extremely cautious. It is not a route to traverse leisurely, though one can find a few places to pull over and get out of the way.

Canoe Trail

A self-guiding canoe trail is located in the northwestern open water area of Tule Lake and may be paddled from July through September when visitors do not spook the nesting birds. The marked trail route follows marsh canals and open water edges, with excellent birding opportunities for viewing both waterfowl and songbirds. Access is 5 miles west of the town of Tulelake on East-West Road.

Hiking Trails

A steep 0.3-mile trail near the Tule Lake Refuge Visitor Center leads to a spectacular view 150 feet above the Klamath Basin; obtain a brochure at the Center. In addition, a Discovery Marsh Trail complete with exhibits is being developed by the visitor center.

Ecotouring and Safety Concerns

Respect areas when the refuge is closed to visitors, as these do vary with conditions. The best bird viewing is done by using your vehicle as a blind and staying inside it. Do not disturb nesting birds.

Snake River Birds of Prey National Conservation Area

IDAHO

Bureau of Land Management
Boise District Office
3948 Development Avenue
Boise, ID 83705
(208) 384-3300

Attractions: Bird-watching, geology, nature study, hiking, boating, fishing, exhibits
Hours/Season: Overnight; year-round
Fees: None
Picnicking: Swan Falls Dam, Celebration Park
Camping: The only developed campground within the National Conservation Area (NCA) is the Cove Recreation Site on C.J. Reservoir, south of Grand View, on the south side of the Snake River. Primitive camping is permitted throughout the NCA. Also on the south side of the river, Bruneau Dunes State Park offers 48 nice shady campsites and restrooms with showers.
Access: From Kuna, ID (8 miles south of I-84 via Exit 44), travel 3 miles south on Swan Falls Road to the entrance of the NCA. The western portion of the NCA is 7 miles from Melba. The eastern portion is near Grand View and Bruneau. All of these access roads are paved. See access map. Boaters and hikers should contact BLM for more detailed maps.

What makes the Snake River Birds of Prey National Conservation Area (NCA) special? It supports the densest nesting concentration of birds of prey in North America, maybe even the world. The NCA includes 483,000 acres of public land adjacent to 80 miles of the Snake River in southwest Idaho, a place where the river is often hidden in its rocky canyon as it winds it way north and west.

These cliffs rise to 700 feet and provide the necessary ledges and crevices raptors require for nesting habitat. From these aeries, they launch themselves into the air and soar taking advantage of the lift that the canyon provides.

This is definitely a place of predator and prey as the raptors hunt the surrounding plateau. The best way to spot these birds and discover their nesting places is by boat or by hiking next to the river. As the BLM warns, be self-sufficient in this area as you're pretty much on your own, but that's what makes it a good nature experience.

Geology

Lava was spread across southern Idaho by volcanic forces one to two million years ago. From one million years ago to the present, the Snake River carved a canyon through basalt and sedimentary deposits. Lake Bonneville reached into southern Idaho 15,000 years ago and floodwater spilled through the canyon creating ledges and cavities which today are used as nesting spots by raptors.

Plants and Wildlife

The small riparian unit by the river nourishes willow, rushes, and other water-oriented plants. Beyond this, the desert winds have deposited a deep layer of fine soil on the north side of the Snake River that supports a hardy vegetation base of native grasses and shrubs for the small animals residing here—sagebrush, cheatgrass, needle and thread grass, and bottle-brush squirreltail.

In spring, more than 800 pairs of falcons, eagles, hawks, and owls gather here to mate and raise their young. This works well because the surrounding plateau supports large populations of ground squirrels and jackrabbits, the main prey of the raptors. The 15 nesting raptor species found here are golden eagle, prairie falcon, red-tailed hawk, ferruginous hawk, Swainson's hawk, northern harrier, American kestrel, turkey vulture, barn owl, great horned owl, western screech owl, burrowing owl, long-eared owl, short-eared owl, and northern saw-whet owl. The raptors who use the area during migrations include the bald eagle, osprey, peregrine falcon, merlin, northern goshawk, sharp-shinned hawk, Cooper's hawk, rough-legged hawk, and gyrofalcon. Other animals found in the area are the gopher snake, desert woodrat, rubber boa, rattlesnake, tiger salamander, scorpion, whipsnake, collared lizard, and horned lizard.

Driving Loop Tour

Activities

A 56-mile driving tour begins by heading south from Kuna on Swan Falls Road and following the access map arrows. This drive will give travelers a fine overview of the wildlife, and cultural and scenic resources. Begin birding immediately upon starting the drive as raptors are plentiful in spring on the sagebrush flats.

Stop 1. 8 miles. A survey marker at Initial Point designates the geographic reference point for legal descriptions in Idaho. A short, steep trail accesses the marker at the summit of a prominent lava butte to the east.

Stop 2. 15.5 miles. Do stop at Dedication Point and walk the 0.5-mile-loop trail that includes a good view of the Snake River Canyon. In spring, watch for birds of prey.

Stop 3. 20 miles. A steep, winding road descends to Swan Falls Dam, the first hydroelectric dam on the Snake River, built in 1901. A restful picnicking site is available and a boat tour of birds of prey launches from this area.

Stop 4. 39 miles. Adjacent to the NCA is Celebration Park, with a boat launch, restrooms, and picnic area. Check with park staff members for information on the archaeology and cultural history of this Snake River area. A short hiking trail accesses rock art, and a hiking and bicycling trail accesses Halverson Lake, nestled against a canyon wall. More energetic hikers (no motorized travel allowed) should consider the 10-mile trail upstream to Swan Falls Dam. Guffy Bridge, a short hike away from Celebration Park accesses the south side of the river.

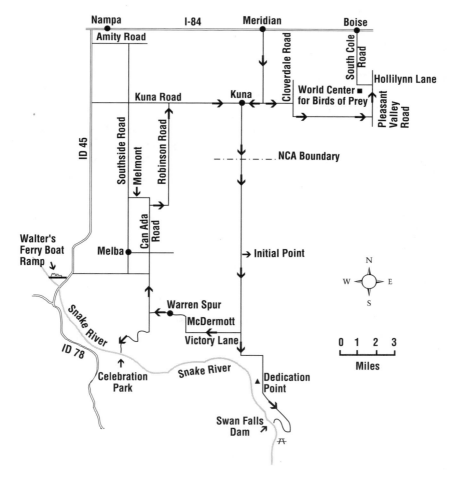

Snake River Birds of Prey National Conservation Area

Boating

Experienced boaters with motorized craft can travel with caution above Swan Falls Dam and below Celebration Park, although hazardous conditions can occur due to of variable winds, fluctuating water levels, and shifting sand and gravel bars. Between these two areas, the river is quite rocky and treacherous for motorboats. Float boats can run the river from Black Butte to Swan Falls, which can be portaged. The 10-mile river stretch from Swan Falls has two Class II rapids along the way to Celebration Park, an exhilarating day trip for rafters or experienced canoeists. For a bird watching boat trip from Swan Falls, call Steve Guinn at (208) 922-5285.

Fishing

Good fishing has been reported between Swan Falls and Walter's Ferry, but not between Grand View and Swan Falls. An Idaho state fishing license is required.

World Center for Birds of Prey

Visiting the Velma Morrison Interpretive Center at the World Center for Birds of Prey is a great way to complement a field trip to the NCA. This center is headquarters for the Peregrine Fund, a research and educational organization dedicated to raptor conservation. Some birds of prey—bateleur eagle, ornate hawk, bald eagle, and golden eagle—are on exhibit outdoors and a peregrine falcon is walked about in the Visitor Center to acquaint visitors with this endangered bird that is so symbolic of wildness in the outdoors. Visitors get a chance to peek in tropical raptor rooms, housed breeding projects that will allow rare birds of prey to be released in the wild. The center has been involved in projects with the peregrine falcon, California condor, northern aplomado falcon, bald eagle, harpy eagle, and Hawaiian forest birds. Three multimedia shows and many exhibits are quite informative and worthwhile. And a small exhibit displays live tropical species. The Center is reached from I-84 by taking Exit 50 south from Boise and following the signs to South Cole Road. Continue south on this road about 6 miles and up the hill to the interpretive area. Or one can travel from the NCA using the paved roads shown on the access map; (208) 362-3716.

Ecotouring and Safety Concerns

Cliff areas along the river are composed of crumbling, unstable rock, so stay back from edge. And do watch for rattlesnakes, scorpions, and poison ivy. Though canyon exploring via boats and climbing is a good way to getting closer to raptors, do not disturb nesting birds.

National Bison Range

MONTANA

National Bison Range
Range Manager
Moiese, MT 59824
(406) 644-2211

Attractions: Wildlife viewing, refuge drives, hiking, fishing, photography
Hours/Season: Dawn to dusk; year-round
Visitor Center: Educational film, three-dimensional model of refuge, exhibits
Fees: Entry charge per vehicle
Picnicking: A large picnic area is located near the entrance by Mission Creek and fishing access is available.
Camping: No camping on the refuge; ask at the Visitor Center for a map of area campgrounds.
Access: From Missoula, travel 37 miles north on US 93/MT 200, then about 6 miles northwest on MT 200, and another 5 miles northeast on MT 212 to the refuge entrance. Be aware that you are bordering the refuge after turning off US 93.

Visit the National Bison Range in the scenic Flathead Valley of northwestern Montana and see what this landscape looked like a couple of centuries ago, when bison thrived on the harsh climate of the prairie as they still do today. One of the country's oldest national wildlife refuges, heavy woven-wire fence surrounds 18,541 acres that include steeply rolling hills, segments of the Jocko River along its southern boundary, and extend north to include Mission Creek. Elevations of this bison recovery preserve vary between 2,585 and 4,885 feet.

To get some idea of the drama of bison rutting and the annual bison roundup, don't miss the film at the Visitor Center. Some bison are sold at auction in the fall to maintain a fairly constant herd number of 370 bison after reaching about 450 following spring calving.

Geology

The Flathead Valley is situated between the Rocky Mountain ranges of Mission and Flathead to the east and the Bitterroot to the West.

Plants and Wildlife

The plant habitats of the refuge comprise palouse prairie (wheatgrass-fescue mixture), montane forest (Douglas fir-ponderosa pine mixture), riparian vegetation that includes Rocky Mountain juniper and black cottonwood, and wetland plants that lure turtles and birds.

Naturally, the bison is the featured animal of the park, with bulls that weigh up to 2,500 pounds; cows are smaller at 800 to 1,000 pounds. Both sexes have a single set of hollow, curved horns. Contrary to their appearance, bison are quite agile, move with considerable speed, and can find footing on mountain summits. Calves are born in April and May, with sharp-tempered rutting taking place in summer.

Besides bison, the refuge has considerable numbers of other animals that include mule and white-tailed deer, cougar, badger, bobcat, mountain goat, bighorn sheep at high elevations, large pronghorn on the bottom-land, black bear, bald eagle, gray partridge, black-billed magpie, ring-necked pheasant, American kestrel, red-tailed hawk, northern harrier, golden eagle, mourning dove, meadowlark, and quite a few prairie rattlesnakes.

Activities

Wheelchair-Accessible Nature Trail

An easy walking loop is accessed shortly inside the refuge entrance. This is a peaceful place replete with birds singing, grasses, chipmunks, a murmuring creek, stagnant ponds with frogs and cattails, deer sometimes moving about quietly, nearby cottonwood trees, and wildflowers that include fuller teasel, yarrow, thistles, daisies, and asters. A dirt path provides access to a fishing deck over the creek.

Refuge Drives

A short one-way-loop drive originates adjacent to the Visitor Center, where elk and deer can be seen. Another short, introductory tour is the two-way Buffalo Prairie Drive that extends past the picnic area, with a spur that reaches the Visitor Center. The Red Sheep Mountain Drive is a one-way, 19-mile dirt road that is steep in places with switchbacks. It is closed in winter except for a portion of the lower area, where two-way traffic is extended from Buffalo Prairie Drive. No trailers are allowed and large motorhomes are not a good idea. Photographers should consider a mounted tripod for their vehicles. Scan for blue grouse near the High Point on Red Sleep Mountain Drive. This drive should be started by 7 P.M. No motorcycles or bicycles are allowed on this drive. Professional photographers might be interested in getting a key to the service-road gates for $25 for access to some secluded photography. These limited permits must be acquired in advance.

Ecotouring and Safety Concerns

Allow plenty of time for the Red Sheep Drive; wildlife viewing requires time, patience, and a peaceful attitude. Visitors on the drives are required to remain at their cars and on the road at all times, a caution issued to prevent bison gorings and encounters with rattlesnakes.

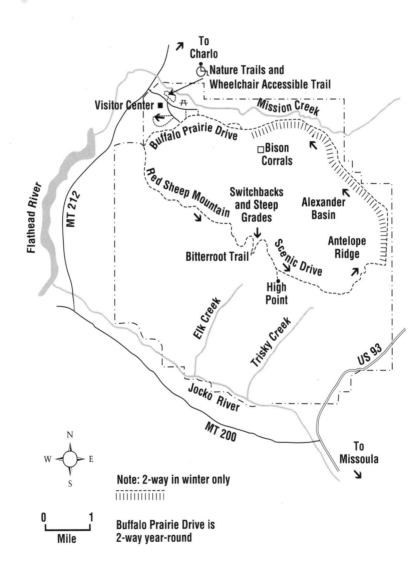

Note: 2-way in winter only

Buffalo Prairie Drive is 2-way year-round

0 — 1 Mile

National Bison Range

Trip Tips

For two other national wildlife refuge destinations, see Nisqually National Wildlife Refuge in Chapter 7 and Bear River Migratory Bird Refuge in Chapter 14. Another natural area is that of Yaquina Head Outstanding Natural Area, described in Chapter 5. The Mono Lake Tufa Natural Reserve, Chapter 14, is also a designated natural area.

11

LAVA ROCK AND VOLCANIC AREAS

Billions of years ago, some remote chunks of rock and metal, ice, and organic molecules fell together to create a place called Earth, which has been continually changing ever since then. Of all the dynamic processes shaping Earth's landscapes, volcanic events seem the most dramatic and the most devastating over time. Only a few humans have witnessed such catastrophic happenings at close hand and have lived to tell about them.

It seems as if we stand on a solid Earth, but in fact our land is the upper crust on top of the round body, and underneath us is a vast area of slightly molten, hot rock called magma that is fluid and continually heated by the radioactive decay of certain elements. Some of the heat results from the buried energy of Earth's formation. At the center of Earth is a core of iron.

A volcano is an aperture to this underground realm. During an eruption, liquid rock under great pressure and high temperatures is released as lava. It emerges from a hole or fissure in Earth's crust with enormous force and energy, then cools and solidifies and generates a volcano that often involves successive eruptions. It is exposed to erosive factors and perhaps more eruptions.

The explosive belching of hot magma and gases—including sulfuric acid—from the bowels of our hot-centered Earth has resulted in the uplifting of spectacular mountains and various lava evidence left strewn about the geography of the American West.

We understand a little more about how these eruptions happen with the geological theory of plate tectonics that has been around since the early 1960s, though Alfred Wegener proposed the theory earlier in the century. Several tectonic plates, which are rigid, make up the Earth's crust, and they move separately. Our ideas of the permanency of landforms, even continents, have changed considerably.

Most of Pacific Coast is newly acquired terrain that came not from the North American continent but from somewhere else in the Pacific Ocean. Volcanos of the Pacific Northwest are part of the "Circle of Fire" that rims the Pacific Ocean.

Mount St. Helens National Volcanic Monument

WASHINGTON

Mount St. Helens National
Volcanic Monument
42218 Northeast Yale Bridge Road
Amboy, WA 98601
(360) 750-3900

Attractions: Hiking, geology, photography, nature study, fishing, interpretive walks, visitor centers
Hours/Season: Day use; year-round depending on road conditions; visitor centers open only during summer season
Fees: None for park entry
Picnicking: Smith Creek, Bear Meadow, Iron Creek, Coldwater Ridge, Lahar
Camping: No campgrounds are in the park at this time. The closest forest camps are at Iron Creek (northeast on FR 25), Swift (southeast on FR 90), and Beaver Bay and Cougar (southwest on FR 90).
Access: From FR 24 on the east side of the mountain, take the 17-mile road (FR 99) to the new Windy Ridge Viewpoint. Coldwater Ridge Visitor Center (west side) is reached via WA 504.

How often do we get the chance to watch nature recover from volcanic eruptions? For an unusual opportunity to see the slow healing of such a landscape and to witness the steps in vegetation regrowth and the return of wildlife—some even surviving the blast—visit the Windy Ridge Viewpoint (elevation 4,000 feet) in Mount St. Helens National Volcanic Monument. It is now 16 years since the mountain's major volcanic explosion on May 18, 1980, after which it was no longer called the Mount Fuji of the West.

The Windy Ridge Viewpoint is within five miles of the volcano and on the side where the cone that is currently building is best observed. This paved road is a winding one, though relatively new. The drive initially travels through forest until the sharp line of devastation shocks you. The view is open now and trees are still sprawled helter-skelter on the slopes. Viewpoints along the drive show the starkness surrounding Spirit Lake.

While near Mount St. Helens, travel the Spirit Lake Memorial Highway (accessed from the west side), past the debris-filled Toutle River Valley, to the new, futuristic-looking Coldwater Ridge Visitor Center to learn about the volcano and its history. Hikers will find short trails in the area.

Geology

Mount St. Helens was a young volcano of 9,677 feet when it blew in 1980, though an ancestral volcano preceded its formation. Its entire visible cone—the most perfect composite cone in the high Cascades before this eruption—is thought to have been constructed during the last millennium. This cone building was witnessed by Indians and pioneers settling the Pacific Northwest.

The Juan de Fuca Plate (this micro-plate is what remains of what was once the large ocean Farallon Plate) caused the uplift of the Cascade Mountains as it moved slowly northeast and was forced beneath the North American Plate. The 1980 explosion was another subduction of the heavier Juan de Fuca Plate beneath the West Coast. Eventually, this plate will be completely consumed beneath the continent.

The recent explosion started with a series of earthquakes on March 20 and led to the devastation on May 18, 1980, after a dormant period of 123 years.

The hiking trail to Butte Camp, on the south side of Mount St. Helens, passes lava chunks.

Now, 16 years later, new dome building is progressing, with obvious vents of steam that you will be able to see on this excursion. In 1982, 110,000 acres were designated to be a national volcanic monument and research is being conducted in the area.

Plants and Wildlife

It is a little startling to still see so many downed trees and so much devastation, but in plant succession, small things—both tiny organisms and pioneer plants—slowly prepare the way for shrubs, and then trees, until finally a new climax forest grows. Right now, vegetation is somewhere along that process, with small conifers—silver firs, in particular—mixed in with small plants and wildflowers. Wind-dispersed seeds of red fireweed, followed by lupine (which fix nitrogen), aster, penstemon, avalanche lily, bleeding heart, vanilla leaf, bunchberry, beadlily, foamflower, and various grasses are colonizing the ash-covered landscape. Huckleberry popped up when its snow cover melted, as did trillium and other plants whose roots and bulbs survived underground. The fireweed is quite widespread and looks quite striking in the summer.

Look for a great blue heron in the wetland area near Meta Lake, and if you're alert, you might see a myriad of ever-so-tiny frogs at the edge of the water. Fish, frogs, salamanders, crayfish, snakes, and water insects survived the blast beneath the snow- and ice-covered lakes. Some underground squirrels survived as well. There are signs that beaver have returned to the blast area. Insects and chipmunks have returned, as have mule deer, coyote, elk, and bear, as deduced from the proliferation of their tracks after the blast. Bear droppings left seeds that have spouted. Mountain bluebird and rufous hummingbirds have also been sighted.

Fishing

Activities

Anglers can fish (with a valid Washington license) in both Meta Lake and Coldwater Lake (adjacent to the new Visitor Center). Artificial flies or lures with single, barbless hooks are allowed, but not bait.

Meta Lake Trail

At the junction of FR 26 and FR 99, take the short, barrier-free path (wheelchairs welcome) to Meta Lake and marvel at the riot of wildflower color in the area. Look carefully for evidence of nature's recovery.

Independence Pass Trail

Don't miss a stop at this trailhead (#227), located a couple of miles past Meta Lake on the drive to Windy Ridge Viewpoint. This trail can be hiked for 3.5 strenuous miles, but you'll discover a superb view of Spirit Lake and the dome building within Mount St. Helens in less than a mile. And you'll be standing in the midst of a wonderful stand of wildflowers amidst fallen trees and new green growth.

Harmony Trail

The only access trail to the edge of Spirit Lake is the Harmony Trail (#224), which descends in 1 mile with a drop of 600 feet to the water. Do note trail restrictions in this research area. The trailhead is 3.5 miles west of the 26/99 road junction.

Windy Ridge Viewpoint

This viewpoint is situated at road's end. If you're energetic, climb the 361 steps for a better view of the still-steaming volcano.

Climbers

Those climbers wanting to access the rim of the volcano need permits from May 15 through October 31, which are available at Jack's Restaurant and Store on WA 503, 5 miles west of Cougar. The most popular route is the Ptarmigan Trail (#216A) on the south side of the mountain. The 27-mile Loowit Trail (not an easy hike, and of varying difficulty) goes around the mountain near the rim of the crater, and is accessed from several trails. According to legend, Loowit was the name a lovely maiden who long ago was turned into Mount St. Helens.

Good views of Mount St. Helens and its developing dome are seen along the Independence Pass Trail.

Birth of a Lake Trail

Adjacent to Coldwater Lake, take this 0.25-mile, barrier-free paved path to better understand how this lake came to be and how it nourishes life-forms.

Ecotouring and Safety Concerns

The park staff would like visitors to remember: "Plants grow by the inch but die by the foot." The blast area is a fragile place of struggling new life.

Trip Tips

This monument is huge, with miles and miles of trails and activities. I've concentrated on some recently developed areas that are very informative and interesting. Do get a map at one of several visitor and information centers that circle the mountain.

Newberry National Volcanic Monument

OREGON

Newberry National Volcanic Monument
Lava Lands Visitor Center
58201 S. Highway 97
Bend, OR 97707
(541) 593-2421

Attractions: Newberry Crater, Lava Cast Forest, Lava River Cave, Lava Lands Visitor Center, interpretive displays, waterfall, caldera lakes, hiking, horseback riding, fishing, boating, campfire programs, photography, snowmobiling, skiing, archaeology, stargazing

Hours/Season: Overnight (campgrounds open in summer; Paulina Lake Lodge is open all year, phone: (503) 536-2240); Lava Lands Visitor Center is open May to September; snowmobiling area in winter

Fees: Fee for camping

Picnicking: Lava Lands Visitor Center, Lava River Cave, Paulina Peak, and Benham Falls

Camping: Campgrounds in the monument are Paulina Lake, Little Crater, East Lake, Cinder Hill, and Hot Springs. North Cove and Warm Springs are accessible by boat or trail only. Both Newberry Group Camp (reserve by calling 1-800-280-CAMP) and Chief Paulina Horse Camp are available to groups.

Access: Travel 11 miles south of Bend on US 97 to the Visitor Center. Most of the monument is to the southeast reached by driving 13 miles east of US 97 on FR 21 (6 miles north of La Pine), but a portion is located northwest of the Visitor Center.

Not many people are aware of the newest national volcanic monument—Newberry—established in late 1990. The central feature is a 500-square-mile caldera that has two lakes inside it—Paulina Lake and East Lake. On the crater rim, overlooking the lakes, is Paulina Peak (7,985 feet), a good vantage point for getting an overall perspective of the terrain that includes the monument, the Oregon Cascades, and the High Desert.

Now protected as a scenic jewel of volcanic wonders not often seen in one locale, the monument contains a mile-wide, 700-foot-high Central Pumice Cone, Lava Butte, glassy fields of obsidian, ash flows, a waterfall, hot springs, and more than 150 miles of trails.

Human history dates back to 10,000 years ago, when Native Americans lived near the active volcano, hunted with obsidian arrowheads, and traded the valuable obsidian with faraway tribes. Paulina Lake was named for Paiute Indian Chief Paulina.

Obsidian later played a vital role in modern history when Astronaut R. Walter Cunningham, accompanied by scientists and engineers from America's Manned Spacecraft Center in Texas, came to Newberry Crater in 1964 to test the mobility of moon-suited workers on the shattered black volcanic glass and stark pumice surfaces.

Geology

A shield volcano that may have been 10,000 feet high at one time, Newberry Volcano lost its summit many years ago, but that does not mean it is no longer active. Recent studies show that a chamber of magma lies about two miles under East Lake. Over the last half million years, Newberry has erupted thousands of times.

Twelve basaltic lava flows, dated 7,000 years ago, were relatively quiet eruptions (typical of shield volcanos) and produced cinders cones—Lava Butte is one of them—and lava in the Lava Cast Forest area, as well as in other areas. Other eruptions during this general time period in Newberry Crater were more violent rhyolitic ones that began with pumice and ash showers and ended with obsidian flows. These occurred 7,300, 7,200, 7,100, 3,500, and 1,300 years ago, this last one being the Big Obsidian Flow—the youngest known lava flow in Oregon—which poured out of a high vent on a crater wall.

If one looks at these happenings and speculates, the possibility of another eruption soon is not far-fetched. Significant geothermal energy is being generated in the vicinity of the monument and hot springs feed East Lake from its depths.

Paulina Creek flows out of Paulina Lake, on the west side, but East Lake has no outlet and is approximately 40 feet higher than Paulina Lake.

Plants and Wildlife

Pumice grape fern is a plant found only in the monument and on Mount Bachelor. It grows in ash deposited by the eruption of Mount Mazama some 7,000 years ago. Except in areas of recent lava flows, the monument is densely forested. Ponderosa pine has reestablished itself in the Lava Cast Forest area, and wild currant, rock penstemon, and Indian paintbrush provide bright color in early summer. In the crater, the pine is lodgepole, and mountain hemlock and whitebark pine grow near the lakes.

Golden-mantled squirrels and yellow-pine chipmunks attract attention with their friendly antics. Bald eagles nest near East Lake within the Newberry Caldera Wildlife Refuge, which occupies the entire crater area. Osprey, migrating ducks, geese, and tundra swans are seen around the high lakes. Bats in the caldera are busy catching mosquitos (up to 600 per hour). Mammals include the pine marten, badgers, deer, elk, and bear.

Activities

Fishing

Anglers will find boat launches available to access rainbow trout, brown trout, and kokanee salmon fishing in Paulina Lake. East Lake also has these fisheries plus the recently planted Atlantic salmon.

Snowmobiling

The monument is very popular with snowmobilers. Many of the trails are used by these motorized vehicles and by cross-country skiers during the popular winter recreation season. The few riders who attempt a trip up Paulina Peak are rewarded with views of graceful, snow-covered trees and a winter wonderland scene of the lakes and forest below. During winter, 10 miles of FR 21 are plowed to the Sno-Park area (permits required).

Trail of the Whispering Pines

This 0.25-mile, wheelchair-accessible, paved, level path is adjacent to the Visitor Center. The brochure and numbered signposts provide useful information on the surrounding area.

Lava Butte

At the beginning of Trail of the Whispering Pines, the paved Trail of the Molten Land wanders a short distance on the slope of this cinder cone. In summer, a shuttle bus travels to the fire lookout stationed atop the butte.

Obsidian Flow Trail

A 1-mile interpretive loop (#58A) offers an unusual opportunity to walk on black shattered glass. Do walk with caution.

Paulina Falls Trail

A 0.3-mile trail (#54) leads to a dramatic waterfall. I saw this via snowmobile in March and it was quite a spectacle. Hikers only are permitted on this trail during the rest of the year.

Paulina Lake Shore Loop

This hikers-only trail (#55) circles the edge of the lake in 7.5 miles. It crosses a rhyolite flow on the east side of the lake, and accesses the two walk-in campgrounds.

Newberry Crater Rim Trail

Energetic hikers can tackle this 21-mile trail (#57) that circles the entire crater rim. Snow is still present on this high trail until July.

Peter Skene Ogden Trail

From Paulina Lake, this 8.6-mile trail follows Pamelia Creek west out of the monument to Ogden Group Camp.

Lava River Cave

Located on the east side of US 97, 1 mile south of the Visitor Center, is the longest uncollapsed "lava tube" in Oregon. A nominal entrance fee is required and lanterns are available for rent. Using lanterns, one can explore a mile of underground cavern that runs downhill in a northwesterly direction toward the Deschutes River. The mouth of the cave drops suddenly over volcanic rocks bridged by stairs. Explore very cautiously wearing good shoes and warm clothing (the temperature remains about 40 degrees year-round). Watch for ice and carry two light sources; be sure the batteries are fresh.

Lava Cast Forest

Located 9 miles east of US 97 via FR 9720, a 1-mile paved, interpretive trail features a fine collection of tree molds and smooth-textured pahoehoe lava.

Ecotouring and Safety Concerns

If you find obsidian arrowheads and flakes in the monument, pick them up and hold them if you wish, but put them back in place for others to see and touch. And please do not feed the squirrels and chipmunks. They must retain their natural ability to survive through the winter.

McKenzie Pass Tour
OREGON

Willamette National Forest
McKenzie Ranger District
McKenzie Bridge, OR 97413
(541) 822-3381

Deschutes National Forest
Sisters Ranger District
P.O. Box 248
Sisters, OR 97759
(541) 549-2111

Attractions: Geology, hiking, backpacking, waterfalls, photography, wildlife viewing, nature study, Craig Monument
Hours/Season: Overnight (summer only); the pass is usually open between July and October, sometimes longer, depending on snow. In winter, there are closed gates across the highway, 9 miles from the pass on both sides.
Fees: Fee for some forest camps
Picnicking: Alder Springs
Camping: West to east, forest camps are Limberlost (fee), Frog Camp, Scott Lake, and Lava Camp Lake (fee).
Access: OR 242 goes west out of Sisters, or travel east from OR 126, 4 miles east of the town of McKenzie Bridge (OR 242 is not suitable for trailers).

This 37-mile highway is a slow, winding tour with hairpin turns as it ascends to McKenzie Pass (5,325 feet) and then descends more easily and quickly to Sisters. It offers impressive views of volcanic activity and a panoramic view of the crest of the high Cascades from Mount Hood to Three Sisters. At the pass, 75 square miles of broken, rugged lava flows invite exploring on a paved path. Bonsaied trees have sunk deep roots into the harsh terrain and bleached dead trees look like skeletons upon the dark lava.

Around 1871, a courageous man named John Craig built a wagon road over the pass about 1871 for a mail route, chipping and leveling the lava roadbed. During the winter he carried the contracted mail on skis. In an 1877 storm, he froze to death in a cabin at Craig Lake. Each April, as a memorial, a John Templeton Craig Ski Tour and Race carries specially marked mail on the 18-mile route over McKenzie Pass.

Today's pass road splits two wilderness areas, the Mount Washington Wilderness to the north, and the Three Sisters Wilderness to the south, so backcountry exploring possibilities are many.

Geology

The area of the high Cascade Range seen from McKenzie Pass was built starting about 3 million years ago by volcanic action as part of the "Circle of Fire" that rims the Pacific Ocean. Most of the peaks, however, are less than 70,000 years old, with considerable eruptive action occurring in recent times, particular the formation of cinder cones and lava flows. McKenzie Pass lies nearly in the center of the high Cascades volcanic chain, which extends from Lassen Peak in California to Manning Park in Canada.

The observatory was built on the western edge of the Yapoah lava flow—which in general is block lava, or a'a lava—characterized by rough, jagged, clinkery surfaces. It contains little gas and is very viscous.

Plants and Wildlife

One drives through lush rain forests at the western end of OR 242, with Douglas fir and western hemlock. Limberlost Campground has much of the vegetation nourished by abundant rainfall along Lost Creek, and there is even some subtle autumn color and some brilliant red vine maples. Nearer the pass, mountain hemlock, and true fir are seen. Wildflowers, rhododendrons, and bear grass grow along the Proxy Falls Trail. The barren lava fields at the pass are punctuated by an occasional dwarf tree—fir, pine, and juniper—that complement photo compositions. Though short and stunted, these trees are old and well rooted. Notice the sharp transition in flora on the drier east side of the pass as one descends through lodgepole and ponderosa trees.

Mule deer summer in the valleys near Mount Washington. Pikas (also called whistling hares) are of the same order as rabbits and hares and have adapted to the lava rock area between Mount Jefferson and the Sisters. They live under and amongst the rocks, and gather plants for winter food, which they stack in haystacks to dry in the sun before storing them in their dens below the rocks.

Activities

Proxy Falls Trail

From the west end of OR 242, drive 9,7 miles to the hiker symbol for this trail. Short trails lead to both the upper and lower falls, both spectacular 200-foot plunges.

Some lava is seen along the way, but the area is predominantly rain forest with green moss edging the falls. This is a great place for a bag lunch while sitting on a fallen log.

Benson Lake Trail

From Scott Lake, a 1.4-mile trail climbs 400 feet to a deep, blue lake. Other trails continue on and offer solitude and access to other lakes. Those interested in orienteering should bring a compass and try some cross-country exploring.

Hand Lake Shelter

A popular day hike is the 0.5-mile trail through wildflower meadows to Hand Lake Shelter, about a mile north of the turnoff to Scott Lake. Hand Lake is a short distance to the north.

Dee Wright Observatory

This stone tower has 11 windows for identifying various mountain peaks of the Cascade Range.

Lava River Nature Trail

Don't miss this 0.5-mile excursion through lava fields adjacent to the Dee Wright Observatory. Molten lava gushed from numerous vents in this area of the Yapoah Lava Flow, and one can see lava gutters, pressure ridges, levees, and crevasses.

Pacific Crest Trail

At McKenzie Pass, the Pacific Crest Trail crosses the highway. To the north, this trail continues from the Lava River Nature Trail to Belknap Crater and then on past Mount Washington. To the south, the Pacific Crest Trail offers a pleasant day hike from the Lava Camp Lake Campground to South Matthieu Lake. Return via the abandoned Skyline Trail back past North Matthieu Lake (or return on the same trail)—a 6-mile loop through both lava and forest areas. Or continue past South Matthieu Lake to Scott Pass and on to Yapoah Crater for a longer day trip with some great scenery and discoveries.

Ecotouring and Safety Concerns

Trails are cleared of snow from mid-June through mid-October. Day hikers need only register at trailheads, but backpackers must obtain a permit from a ranger station or outdoor store in advance.

Craters of the Moon National Monument
IDAHO

Craters of the Moon
National Monument
Highway 93
P.O. Box 29
Arco, ID 83213
(208) 527-3257

Attractions: Hiking, backpacking, geology, nature study, photography, conducted walks, evening programs, skiing
Hours/Season: Overnight; year-round
Fees: Fee for camping
Visitor Center: Geology and history video, information, publications for sale; open year-round except for holidays in winter. The Loop Road is open to vehicle traffic from late April to mid-November.
Picnicking: At the visitor center, caves area, and available tables in campground
Camping: 51 sites with restrooms, available from May to October
Access: Off US 93, 20 miles southwest of Arco and 24 miles northeast of Carey

---

If one approaches the monument from the east, it is a rather startling sight after miles and miles of flat sagebrush desert terrain, though one sees the snow-peaked Sawtooths as a sharp demarcation in the distance and knows that the landscape will change.

Within the 83-square-mile monument are stories written on the surface of dynamic events that happened in the hot belly of Earth, now cooled and rigid in a lava rock scenario punctuated with cinder cones. Visit in early June when creamy, pink-edged bitterroot flowers pop up through cracks in the lava and a carpet of rose-colored dwarf monkeyflowers intermingles with bleached fragments of wood.

The park was established after these rugged lava beds were encountered on a 28-mile expedition by Robert Limbert in 1920, with W. L. Cole and a dog. Cole's feet blistered and the dog's paws were cut so badly that it had to be carried; it was not easy to find water.

The campground is situated on tree-speckled lava terrain. Surface temperatures in the summer can reach 150 degrees Fahrenheit. Surfaces that sizzle in summer blister with snow and cold in winter. Expect afternoon winds in summer.

Geology

Craters of the Moon Monument straddles the "Great Rift," a weak spot in the Earth's crust in Idaho where lava has poured forth from cracks eight times in the last 15,000 years. Some lava emerged as gas-filled lava erupting hundreds of feet into the air and showering down to form cinder cones. Scatter cones are lava bubbles that were belched up with a little gas and landed a few feet from a vent. This material came from almost 37 miles below the surface. Sometimes the lava just flowed out in sheets and rivers. Under the right conditions, as the lava crust cooled, the hot lava beneath tugged at the surface to form folds resembling coils of rope—like poured hot fudge—called pahoehoe lava. Cooler, thicker a'a lava twisted and shattered into masses of jagged rocks. "Bombs" are ejected lava blobs.

Lava tubes formed caves under complex conditions when lava flowed in channels and a crust hardened to form the roof and floor while most of the hot lava flowed through. Stalactites sometimes hung from the roof where hot lava dripped and then hardened. The monument caves formed during the Blue Dragon Flow, which was named for the iridescent blue color caused by titanium magnetite crystals suspended in the glassy rock surfaces.

Plants and Wildlife

Look for wildflowers growing in lava crevices—cinquefoil, penstemon, fleabane, rock spiraea, and bush tansy—along the North Crater Flow Trail. Devils Orchard Trail has limber pine trees and rabbit brush. Antelope brittlebush, dwarf buckwheat, wild onion, mock orange, and dwarf buckwheat are other discoveries. Peak wildflower blooms are in early June. More than 300 plant species grow around the monument.

The animal species include some 2,000 insects (some blind ones dwell in the caves), 148 birds, 47 mammals, 8 reptiles, and a lone amphibian—the western toad. Pikas, golden-mantled squirrels, and yellow-pine chipmunks find habitat in crevices among the lava rocks. Weasels, prairie falcons, and great-horned owls hunt the smaller mammals. Other bird sightings are rock wren, Clark's nutcracker, mourning dove, mountain bluebird, and the violet-green swallow. Bobcats are secretive and rarely seen. More easily spotted are yellow-bellied marmots along the drive. Mule deer trails criss-cross the hillside near the Tree Molds Trail spur road turnoff. Look for pronghorns along the entry roads.

Loop Road

Activities

A 7-mile drive begins at the Visitor Center and accesses the park's attractions. (This road is available for skiing in winter.) After passing Paisley Cone, the one-way loop begins, with a spur road to the Tree Molds Trail, Trench Mortar Flats, and the Craters of the Moon Wilderness area. One sees lava cascades and the Big Sink along this route. The following trailheads are passed in sequence.

North Crater Flow Trail

This 0.25-mile interpretive trail, through an area of sparse vegetation and a 2,100-year-old lava flow, offers an opportunity to distinguish between a'a (ah-ah) and ropy pahoehoe (pay-hoy-hoy) lavas. Notice the lava squeeze ups, large chunky crater fragments, pressure ridges, and the 1,350-year-old Triple Twist Tree. The varied, but strenuous, 1.5-mile-one-way North Crater Trail begins nearby. This trail drops into the crater mouth, continues to the rim of Big Craters, and then descends to the Spatter Cones.

Devils Orchard Trail

This barrier-free, paved 0.33-mile trail traverses a weird-looking area of trees and scattered fragments of the North Crater wall.

Infernal Cone

A short, steep walk up fine lava rock will take you up this cinder cone, where an expansive view of the chain of cinder cones along the Great Rift is seen to the south. One of the largest, purely basaltic cones in the world, 6,515-foot Big Cinder Butte is visible in the distant wilderness area.

Big Craters and Spatter Cones Area

A moderate, paved 0.5-mile trail from this viewpoint accesses Big Craters more easily. Several interesting spatter cones are nearby and one can peer into a snow vent. Hikers can be picked up from the North Crater Trail here.

Tree Molds Trail and Craters of the Moon Wilderness Trail

From the parking area at the end of the spur road to this area, the moderate 3-mile-round-trip Tree Molds Trail accesses the edge of the Blue

Dragon Flow and good examples of what happens when a lava flow ignites and knocks down trees in its path. The Trailhead to Echo Crater is 75 yards from the parking lot back along the road and takes you into a wilderness area offering plenty of solitude on a moderate 6-mile-round-trip trail over Broken Top cinder cone and through Trench Mortar Flat. Lava trees are also seen along this trail.

Cave Area

When the ice melts, several cool caves—lava tubes—can be accessed in this area via a trail system. (Boy Scout Cave has an ice floor even in the summer.) The largest and easiest of these to visit is Indian Tunnel, which has enough sunlight to view without a flashlight. One-half mile from the parking lot, Indian Tunnel is a 800-foot-long collapsed lava tube with a stairway leading down into it. Other trails access Dewdrop, Beauty, Surprise, and Boy Scout caves, which are pitch black inside. One needs to carry an artificial light and to be physically capable of maneuvering around sharp rocks, low ceilings, and uneven floors. Wear a hat, long pants, and good hiking boots. A detailed brochure is available at the visitor center.

Ecotouring and Safety Concerns

Remember that a'a means "rough on the feet" in Hawaiian. No running water is available on the Loop Road, and lava gets very hot in midsummer. A backcountry camping permit is required for the wilderness area. Be prepared for exploring lava tubes.

Snow Canyon
State Park
UTAH

Snow Canyon State Park
P.O. Box 140
Santa Clara, UT 84765-0140
(801) 628-2255

Attractions: Hiking, backpacking, horseback riding, wildlife viewing, photography, geology, petroglyphs, rock climbing, sand dunes, lava caves, nature trail
Hours/Season: Overnight; year-round
Fees: Day-use and camping fees
Picnicking: Both individual and group picnicking, separately located near the campground
Camping: Shivwits Campground, in the middle of park, has 36 campsites (some with electrical hookups) and restrooms with showers. Reservations are available in person or by phone: (801) 322-3770 or (800) 322-3770.
Access: Travel 11 miles north of St. George off UT 18 and take the signed road southwest to park; or enter park from the south by going through St. George, then west through Santa Clara, and follow signs north to park for a total of 7 miles from St. George.

Red rock formations and basalt lava juxtaposed. This combination is symbolic of one of Utah's most popular state parks, Snow Canyon, which has warm weather year-round (Utah's Dixie) with scenery and recreational possibilities that are varied, interesting, and extensive. Huge monoliths of red sandstone rise in various shapes and textures above a lava-studded canvas of lava that is interspersed with desert plants. The geological saga of sand to sandstone, with concomitant swirling and cross-bedding caused by wind, is frequently illustrated in the park.

Cultural artifacts have been found left by nomadic tribes who camped and traveled in the Snow Canyon area. The Shivwit Indians used this place as a hunting preserve until a century ago. Later, Lorenzo and Erastus Snow hunted for lost cattle in the canyon, hence the name of the canyon. Real snow would be difficult to find here.

The campground is very inviting with its swirled rock formations that edge right up to some of the sites. These sandstone attractions can be climbed with caution to do some exploring. Other campsites offer spectacular views of the canyon landscape. The group site has a volleyball area and is lit at night.

Geology

The terrain in this area of Utah was much different 130 million years ago when it was a desert covered with sand dunes. Time, pressure, and a cement of iron oxides, lime, and clay substances turned these dunes into layers of Navajo sandstone, which are again being exposed to wind and erosion. A small area of sand dunes is seen along the road where the wind has piled up erosion grains against rock formations.

Snow Canyon is part of the St. George Basin, which has experienced at least two dozen individual lava flows that average slightly more than two million years old and include a dozen cinder cones. Two classic examples of these cones are easily viewed near the north end of the park. The recent lava flows in the canyon came from these cones.

You will notice lava at various elevations in the park. The older flows are seen on the highest ridges, the youngest lava is on the canyon floor. The flow above the campground is thought to have occurred about one million years ago. The basaltic lava formations are varied, with lava tubes in some places. Lava is found in many areas and tells the story of uneven cooling and the gas bubbles it entrapped.

Plants and Wildlife

The desert terrain along the hikes has many plant species including prickly pear, purple torch cactus, creosote bush, Indian paintbrush, sacred datura, brittlebush, Mojave aster, Eaton's penstemon, narrow-leaf yucca, long-leaved phlox, desert marigold, yucca, and western peppergrass. Cliffrose—that favorite of Edward Abbey—and Mormon tea, the plant used by Mormon pioneers for colds and allergies, are both found along the Hidden Pinyon Trail. Notice the symbiotic clusters of lichens that add color to the sandstone and lava rocks. The usual sagebrush is around, along with Utah juniper and pinyon pine, the most prevalent tree of the Southwest.

Crickets are vocal at night amidst the vegetation. Gambel quail are numerous at campsites next to Gambel oak trees where there are acorns. Squirrels also find these nuts and rush around with full mouths. One squirrel was a puzzle, however. It had climbed to the top of a sandstone formation behind my campsite to a perch on the edge of the rock about fifty feet up and started chirping loudly. This went on for some time and I wondered what it meant. Was it exercising some territorial signaling?

Desert cottontail rabbits are numerous, especially on the well-watered grass of the picnic area. Much rarer is the endangered desert tortoise, which does inhabit the canyon area, along with the toxic Gila monster, the chuckwalla lizard, banded gecko, and the sidewinder rattlesnake. Bird life includes eagles, owls, scrub jays, black-chinned hummingbirds, ravens, and hawks. Butterflies are seen flitting among the flowering desert plants.

In the backcountry, energetic hikers can find ponds and waterholes inhabited by opportunistic tadpoles and algae living in rock formations formed by rain runoff. Knowledge of the whereabouts of these pools was often crucial to Indian and pioneer survival, though they are no longer potable.

Lava rock and red rock at Snow Canyon State Park.

Activities

A short drive from UT 18 (before turning left into the park) leads to Panorama Point Overlook where the visitor can get a good overall view of the old and new lava flows. Ask a park ranger for directions to ancient Indian rock art found on the sandstone walls of the canyon. Rock climbers will find a vertical rock to climb on the road south of the campground.

Hidden Pinyon Trail

This 1.5-mile-round-trip hike is a joy. Obtain a brochure at the entry station of the park which explains the numbered posts along the hike, with varied vegetation of the open desert at the beginning of the trail. Then the trail meanders through slickrock slots and to viewpoints of more distant geology.

Johnson Arch Trail

Walk 0.75 mile into a small canyon at the south end of the park road and you'll find Johnson Arch high up on a rock formation. It was named after Maude Johnson, a pioneer. Afternoon is the best time for photography if you want some light on the arch.

West Canyon Trail

For a longer hike into more isolated country, or a horseback trip, try the 3.5-mile-one-way trail into West Canyon, accessed a short distance south of the campground.

Lava Caves Trail

A 0.75-mile hike from the road north of the campground leads to a couple of lava caves, which were sometimes occupied by Indians in the past. Be alert for these caves. One looks like a sheer drop into a black hole. The trail has moderate ups and downs, with lots of chunky lava, so wear

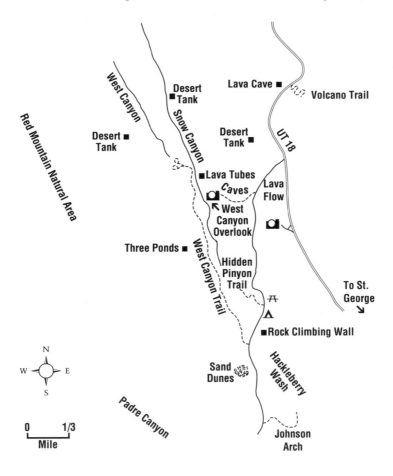

Snow Canyon State Park

good boots to cushion your feet. Another 0.25 mile of trail ends at the West Canyon Overlook, a wondrous place to wander about among stairstep slickrock and lava hills. Take a close-up or macro lens and spend time noticing the striated and swirling sandstone with its varied patterns. The view of the old road down in the canyon and the panoramic surroundings are full of geological discoveries and beauty.

Cinder Cone Trail

A short, but steep trail leads straight uphill to the rim of a cinder cone where there is a view of a volcanic dike on the interior of the cone. Continue north on UT 18, past the spur road to the park, to access this trail at the side of the road.

Ecotouring and Safety Concerns

Though many of the plants in the park were used by ancient Indians for religious and other internal or external purposes, do not experiment and try them. It can be quite dangerous. And do not chisel or carve on rock formations. For some reason, today's rock graffiti does not simulate the artistic, historical value of ancient rock art. Use caution around lava caves.

Trip Tips

For another lava landscape tour, see the Upper Rogue River trip in Chapter 1.

12

CAVES

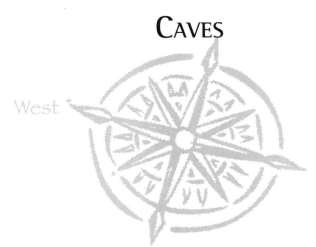

West

Caves once sheltered humans from rain, wind, and diverse temperatures, places to circle around a fire—rather than television—and communicate. Though it is possible that a few lone individuals still find them admirable as homes or temporary shelters, many animals certainly still use them today—bats being a notable example—but larger mammals. such as cougars and coyotes, value them as excellent hideouts.

I remember a time when I was with a group of horseback riders high in the Rocky Mountains and we took refuge in a small cave during a sudden thunderstorm. Another time, I visited a camper in Valley of Fire State Park who invited us into his cave one night where a fire served as our only light. And there is no doubt that some larger caves have been developed as recreation destinations.

Caves come in all shapes, sizes, and dimensions, some so massive that they have their own barometric pressure. Their varied formations can be found in all types of terrain, and in almost all the countries of the world.

Unusual geological happenings formed around open space where rock formations have collapsed caves are often of limestone character, but other rocks such as gypsum and alabaster may be important components.

The ecosystem of the cave environment—fairly constant temperature and humidity and darkness—attracts cave mammals where the developed attributes of smell, hearing, touch, and memory are an advantage. Bats have evolved to fill an underpopulated niche in caves, undisturbed by predators, as they hibernate or raise their young. These unique mammals— the only ones capable of true flight—have an unearned reputation for terror thanks to stories of Count Dracula and vampire bats. Though they have perfectly good eyesight, many bats are extraordinarily efficient predators of night-flying insects using echolocation to locate them—living insecticides without the toxic environmental effects.

Caves and their inhabitants are an exciting source of undiscovered scientific information for biologists that adds to our knowledge of evolution, provides us with archeological artifacts from the past—if undisturbed—and contributes to our medical drug resources. A family of mold-like bacteria called actinomycetes has already produced a variety of antibiotics. What other miracle medicines await discovery?

Though most well-known commercial caves are easily viewed during tours led by guides, wild cave explorations require lanterns, candles, climbing ropes, and venturing into the unknown geography of sheer drops, narrow ledges, and narrow passageways, with route-finding always a challenge. Serious spelunkers have a strict code for exploring and preserving newfound caves.

Wild caves are easily damaged by the amateur explorer, who is also in danger in unmapped terrain that invites injury unless great caution is exercised; lights can only project short distances. And vandalism—including painting on or carving rocks—is reprehensible. To protect both the undiscovered information to be learned from the cave—and the spelunker—contact the National Speleological Society for the best procedures for adventuring in these caves.

Lewis & Clark
Caverns State Park
MONTANA

Lewis & Clark Caverns State Park
Box 949
Three Forks, MT 59652
(406) 287-3541

Attractions: Limestone caverns (tours), hiking, fishing, wildlife viewing, geology, photography, interpretive programs, exhibits, Tourism Information Center, concession with food service
Hours/Season: Overnight; year-round
Fees: Charge for day use, cave tours (reduced price for campers), and camping
Picnicking: Picnic tables at two wooded areas along drive to caverns
Visitor Center: Located at the caverns' tour site, obtain tickets and view historical, geological exhibits, and interesting old photos
Camping: Park has 44 campsites (no hookups) and restrooms with showers.
Access: 19 miles west of Three Forks on MT 2

Montana's first and best-known state park, Lewis and Clark Caverns, has intrigued more than 2.5 million visitors since the discovery of the caverns, and recently lured National Geographic writers and photographers to include this attraction in a book.

Though prehistoric Indians left artifacts in this area 10,000 years ago, no evidence indicates they had any knowledge of the caverns. The first recorded explorations of this cave in the side of Cave Mountain occurred when two ranchers—Tom Williams and Bert Pannell—discovered the cave in 1892. They noticed "smoke" rising near the entrance (really steam in winter from the warmer interior temperature) and observed that no snow existed at this spot.

Stalactites at Lewis & Clark Caverns State Park.

A period followed when entrepreneur Dan Morrison offered tours, advertised widely, and built 2,000 steps and a famous spiral staircase until it was proved that ownership belonged to Northern Pacific Railroad, who then deeded the caverns to the federal government. By 1908, the caverns were so famous that Theodore Roosevelt preserved them as the 12th National Monument. Lack of funding for development resulted in turning the caverns over to Montana in 1937, followed by the construction of the road, Visitor Center, and trails by the Civilian Conservation Corps.

The 3,000-acre park includes flat terrain near the Jefferson River, contrasting canyonlands surrounded by the London Hills, and fascinating limestone caverns 1,400 feet above the river that scientists call a "maze cave." Though the caverns are named after Lewis and Clark, these explorers breakfasted nearby along the river but never mentioned the caverns in their journals.

Geology

Hundreds of millions of years ago, a sea rich in shellfish organisms covered this area. As these marine animals died, layers of calcium carbonate accumulated and gradually compressed and hardened into limestone sedimentary rock. Sand, mud, and rocks were deposited on top of this, followed by erosion and geological activity.

About 80 million years ago, as part of the Rocky Mountains, the Tobacco Root Mountains were uplifted. Another major geological event took place 3 million years ago when limestone was brought to the surface and exposed. Rainwater—with its dissolved carbon dioxide—dissolved minerals in the limestone and percolated through crevices, which in time caused weakened rock formations to collapse and leave caverns.

At about the same time, the nearby Jefferson River began carving Jefferson Canyon, which lowered the water table and drained the caverns. Circulating acid water carried calcite through fissures in the rock and deposited three types of cave formations (speleothems) in the caverns— dripstones, flowstones, and erratics. Stalagmites (on the cave floor), stalactites (on the cave ceiling), and columns are types of dripstones. Ribbons and sheets of limestone are examples of flowstones. Erratics are observed as clusterites or cave popcorn formed by slow, widespread seepage. When hydrostatic pressure from very slow seepage overcomes gravity, growth of erratics called helictites occurs upward or sideways.

Plants and Wildlife

The cave ecosystem is an unusual one with cave soil composed of pigeon, pack rat, and bat droppings, or guano, that provides nutrients for bacteria and fungi that have the ability to grow in darkness.

Feeding on this lower ring of the food web are springtails and mites, which are then fed upon by harvestmen and spiders. Many "true cave dwellers" have adapted to darkness, with loss of sight and color pigmentation.

Some mammals move back and forth from the caves to the outdoors. Bushytail wood rats do this often while making their nests in these caverns. The western big-eared bat supports an annual nursery colony of 150 to 200 females and young in Lewis and Clark Caverns between April and September. The males are solitary and live in nearby caves.

Outdoors in the park is habitat for mule deer, wild turkey, black bear, and numerous birds with an occasional golden eagle sighted. The nature trails have representative wetland plants, trees, and animals.

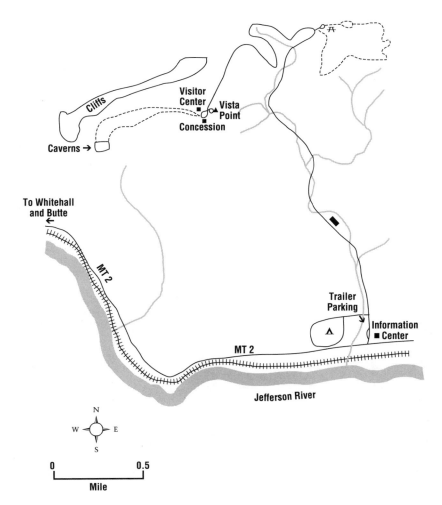

Lewis & Clark Caverns State Park

Caverns Tour

Activities

A winding, fairly step 3.2-mile paved road leads to the Visitor Center and access to the caves. (A trailer/ motorhome parking lot is available at the beginning of the drive.) Stop at Vista Point for incredible views of Greer Gulch, the Jefferson River, and the distant Madison and Gallatin mountain ranges, perhaps taking time to do some patient wildlife viewing.

The walking tour led by park rangers (a 2-hour affair) begins with a 0.75-mile hike to the cave entrance at 5,600 feet elevation (300-foot gain), followed by a 0.75-mile cave walk that involves descending some 600 steps along with various bending and stooping in some passageways. Another 0.5-mile trail returns to the Visitor Center. The caverns are naturally air-conditioned, electrically lighted, and when visited with caution, a safe place to visit.

Highlights of the caverns are the Cathedral Room, Paradise Room, Brown Waterfall, Atlas Column, Garden of the Gods Room, Bacon Room, Glow Room, and Grand Canyon Room.

Nature Trails

Two interpretive trails are accessed from the upper picnic area on the caverns drive. One is a short 0.25-mile loop through the woods with creeks,

View of campground and Jefferson River at Lewis & Clark Caverns State Park from cave location.

while the other is a longer loop from the same trailhead that is 2 miles and offers views of the countryside.

Fishing

Fishing access in the park is located across the highway on the Jefferson River with species including mountain whitefish and brown and rainbow trout. The river is popular with fly-fishing anglers, but bait fishers do well in spring, and spin fishers consistently take fish in both summer and fall.

Ecotouring and Safety Concerns   The fragile underground environment of caves should not be polluted with trash nor the water contaminated, often a problem associated with the large numbers of cave visitors on commercial tours. Exercise caution so that damage to the intriguing formations does not occur. To tour the cave, wear rubber-soled walking shoes and bring a sweater for the 50-degree Fahrenheit temperature. Avoid contact with the bats, but be aware that less than 0.5 percent of bats carry rabies.

Campground at Lewis & Clark Caverns State Park

Alabaster Caverns
State Park
OKLAHOMA

Alabaster Caverns State Park
Route 1
Freedom, OK 73842
(405) 621-3381

Attractions: Alabaster cave (tours), hiking, nature study, geology, photography, guided tours, outdoor swimming pool (open Wednesday through Sunday during the summer season), Interpretive Center, gift shop
Hours/Season: Overnight; year-round
Fees: Charge for camping
Picnicking: Picnic tables and shelters in park
Camping: Campsites in the park include 12 primitive sites and 10 semi-modern RV hookup sites.
Access: 6 miles south of Freedom on OK 50, then 1 mile east to park on OK 50A

The underground centerpiece of this 200-acre park is billed as the world's largest gypsum cave open to the public. This cave has three surveyed levels for a total of 6,146 feet of passageways, with the central layer of 2,300 feet open for tours a comfortable walk-through. The other levels are not walkable and are often just a jumble of rocks. Twelve openings are discernible in the main cavern, though only half of these are humanly accessible.

Besides the hydrous calcium sulfate (gypsum) formations in the cave, there are formations of alabaster (anhydrous calcium sulfate) and selenite (the crystalline form of gypsum). It is believed that this black alabaster deposit is the only one documented in North America. A sample from here is displayed at the Smithsonian Institution; only three caves worldwide have this type of rock formation.

With the energy of moving water continuously at work, change is constant in the cave. Formations are different here from those found in limestone caves due to the solubility of gypsum.

Besides the main cavern, five other caves are found in the park; the Ice Stalactite, Bear, Hoe Handle, and the Water Caves. These range from 221 feet to 1,615 feet long.

If you are visiting the cave near the third week in August, consider attending the nearby Freedom Rodeo, billed as the "Biggest Open Rodeo in the West."

Geology

Geologists believe that these alabaster caverns started forming some 200 to 270 million years ago when this area was covered by the Permian Sea. When the sea receded and evaporated, mineral deposits were left behind. Upheavals and erosion followed. During the course of these events, mineral deposits were brought to the surface where they dried and hardened. Cracks formed and water slowly seeped through these holes and formed the caverns. A perennial stream flowing through the caves is fed by various arterial tunnels and by seepage from the roof. What is now a tiny brook was once a roaring river that geologists say was capable of completely fill the main cave. Sinkholes on the surface become domes in the caverns.

Plants and Wildlife

The interpretive trail provides some insight into the vegetation of the park. In areas of good water drainage, wild grapes, cottonwood, smooth sumac, and soapberry are all plants that provide both food and shelter to wildlife. Bluebirds, cedar waxwings, robins, and mockingbirds eat the bluish berries of eastern red cedar, as do mice and kangaroo rats, while deer browse on its twigs and leaves. Sixty species of birds eat the white berries of poison ivy.

Along the trails, listen and watch for a variety of birds that include cardinal, Bewick's wren, bobwhite, eastern bluebird, and painted bunting. Mammals include coyote, skunk, cottontail, squirrel, opossum, and raccoon. Lizards—collared lizard is the state lizard—are seen among the rocky outcrops where they can quickly abscond into cracks if spooked or get too hot in the sun. These reptiles also do "push-ups" to cool off, raising their bodies away from the hot rock surface.

Bats, however, are the most distinctive animal residents of the park, particularly in the caves. Five species use the cave on and off during the year—cave myotis, western big-eared, eastern pipistrelle, Mexican free-tailed, and western big brown bat. Besides their unusual proficiency in natural sonar, they "swim" through the air, rather than actually flying. Tiger salamanders and a cave-dwelling crayfish are also found in the caverns.

Cave Tour

Activities

Wear good walking shoes and a light jacket for the 50-degree temperature and take the one-hour guided tour down the 330 steps of the cave. After entering the large natural opening, one descends about 40 feet on a stairway to the lowest point of the tour. The Nescatunga gypsum ceiling in this first area, called the collapsed section, looms 50 feet overhead. Continuing, walk past the selenite mouse and sandwich rock, followed by black alabaster, and then by the stream that formed the cave. After seeing the encampment room, the selenite boulder (680 tons of gypsum), and the total darkness room, enter the hand-carved walkway to the second or dome section of the cave, where nine major domes include the Cathedral, Sweetheart, and Keyhole domes. The third or channel section is the best place to observe the abrasive action of water. A small waterfall is found here along with the only stalactite included in the tour, though it is only 0.75 inch in length since gypsum ones are extremely slow in forming. This one is probably 30,000 years old. Tours are offered from 8:00 A.M. to 5:00 P.M. from May 1 to September 30, and 8:00 A.M. to 4 P.M. from October 1 to April 30. A shuttle returns people to the entrance area after the approximately 0.75-mile walk.

Cedar Canyon Interpretative Trail

A 0.5-mile path leads down into Cedar Canyon and up the other side where a natural bridge of gypsum rock once stood; it crumbled in 1992. The presence of gypsum rock—a soft, easily scratched rock—in this landscape was once covered with water. A small stream flows in the canyon bottom.

Wild Caving

The other five caves have been surveyed, mapped, and are open to the public, if you are equipped with the proper caving gear.

Ecotouring and Safety Concerns

The cave tour is not recommended for those who get claustrophobic or have respiratory or heart problems. Watch for poison ivy along the trails.

Trip Tips

For more cave excursions, read about the caves of Craters of the Moon National Monument listed in Chapter 11.

13

OPEN RIVERINE HABITAT

West

Imagine you are a Canada goose migrating north in springtime to nest. High above the land, your keen eye picks out the wide sweep of a major river bordered by lots of green. You drop down for a landing to feast on the bounty of food to fatten you in order to produce healthy progeny. If you are human, the same landscape will attract you, though not by flying, unless you are a pilot of small planes.

In the West, rivers must often find their way amongst uplifting rocky terrain, in many cases the only water in an arid desert. As Wallace Stegner so aptly wrote, water availability has dominated the settling of the West. For plants and animals, water has a lot to do with the adaptations that fit them to certain habitats. Humans, as well, must meet the challenge of finding water to sustain them.

Given that vital need, it is no wonder that the more accessible rivers, surrounded by stretches of rich bottomland in open country, were woven so tightly into the fabric of land settling. Consider the influence of the Willamette River and its lush valley of good farmland for growing crops. Pioneers on the Oregon Trail endured much hardship to relocate in that fabled place where the soil was rich beyond comparison and the land was not yet crowded with people.

Though the Willamette River is located in a land of frequent and plenteous rainfall, the lower Rio Grande carries water through a more arid landscape; yet it nourishes vegetation and farmlands along miles and miles of open country on its way to the Gulf of Mexico.

With good wetland soil rather than canyon walls as river neighbors, the exuberance of vegetation is a powerful lure to wildlife. It is no wonder that most of our national wildlife refuges border such waterways or that

201

development by humans is aimed like an arrow at them. Fortunately, many states have chosen to preserve choice locations edging these rivers as recreational sites so that people can fish, hike, paddle, and observe the wildlife.

I often remember the words of Loren Eiseley when he floated on his back in the shallow waters of the Platte River, "Once in a lifetime, if one is lucky, one so merges with sunlight and air and running water that whole eons, the eons that mountains and deserts know, might pass in a single afternoon without discomfort." Perhaps you will experience your own connection with nature at one of these rivers—though it is best to paddle a canoe—where the sound of flowing water is enough to calm you.

Willamette River Greenway
OREGON

Oregon State Parks
and Recreation Department
525 Trade Street SE
Salem, OR 97310
(503) 378-6305

Oregon Tourism Division
775 Summer Street NE
Salem, OR 97310
(800) 547-7842

Attractions: Paddling, hiking, bicycling, boating, fishing, photography, nature study, bird watching, wildlife viewing, waterskiing, exhibits

Hours/Season: Overnight; year-round

Fees: Day-use fee in summer for Willamette Mission State Park and Champoeg State Park; charge for camping at Champoeg

Picnicking: Willamette Mission State Park, Champoeg State Park, Elijah Bristow State Park, Molalla River State Park, and Mary S. Young State Park; plus many county and city parks with picnic areas

Camping: Champoeg State Park has 48 electrical and 6 tent sites, plus group tenting and group RV area (restrooms with showers); numerous other areas are designated as campgrounds along the Greenway.

Access (north to south): Mary S. Young State Park is off OR 43, 9 miles south of Portland; Molalla River State Park is 2 miles north of Canby on North Holly Street; Champoeg State Park is reached by taking Exit 278 from I-5 and following signs 5 miles west to the park; Willamette Mission State Park is reached by taking Exit 263 and driving 1.75 miles west on Brooklake Road, then north on Wheatland Road for 2.5 miles; Elijah Bristow State Park is off OR 58, 17 miles southeast of Eugene.

The Willamette River is birthed high on the western slopes of Oregon's Cascade Mountains, just below the spine of snow-covered peaks that trend in a north-south direction through the state. As its waters flow downhill and west, many creeks join it before it bottoms out near Eugene and continues north in a lazy meandering journey. Here, in a valley between the Cascades and the Coast Range to the west, several rivers—the McKenzie, North and South Santiam, Clackamas, Yamill, Tualatin, the Luckiamute, and others—join it before it pours over Willamette Falls and reaches the Columbia River near Portland.

It is interesting that the Lewis and Clark expedition missed finding the Willamette River until they backtracked on their return journey with Indian guides to this waterway; the Indians called it Multnomah. This is the river that nourishes the valley that lured pioneers to travel the hazards of the Oregon Trail. The beauty of the end of this arduous and hazardous trail was that the fabled stories about the richness of the land were actually true. And early on, the river was the easiest route for pioneer travel, with its many ferries and even a few sternwheelers traversing its waters and connecting people and supplies. Before their arrival, this valley was rich in beaver, but with statistics such as half a million skins handled by the Hudson's Bay Company between 1834 and 1837, their decline was rapid, though conservation efforts have now reversed that trend.

Drive through the Willamette Valley, taking numerous side trips, and you will see the bounty of vegetables, flowers, and nuts that spring from the richness of the land, many available at roadside stands and U-pick farms. Since the valley produces world-class Chardonnays and Pinot Noirs, picnic ingredients are easily assembled to take to the Willamette River Greenway in the sunny warmth of its summers.

The Willamette River Greenway covers 255 miles of the river from St. Helens in the north to Cottage Grove in the south of the valley, and includes 50,000 acres, though less than half of these are in public ownership. This program was legislated by Oregon "... to protect, conserve, enhance and maintain the natural, scenic, historical, agricultural, economic and recreational qualities of lands along the Willamette River."

The five major recreational areas are the state parks along the river, but the Oregon State Parks and Recreation Department manages 43 small Greenway public-use sites set aside for picnicking, hiking, boat launching, fishing, and primitive camping; these are supplemented by varied local parks. Three national wildlife refuges—William L. Finley, Ankeny, and Baskett Slough—are in the Willamette River floodplain west of I-5.

Geology

The Willamette Valley extends from the Portland area south to a fault at Eugene. The floor of the valley consists of sand and gravel that was deposited over lava flows from eruptions that occurred about 20 million years ago. In places, a skin of silt—with occasional boulders—was washed over the sand and gravel during the last ice age when glacial Lake Missoula drained.

Plants and Wildlife

The wildflower, camas, is found in wet meadows. It was an important food resource of the Native Americans, which they prepared by fermenting the onionlike bulb underground with hot stones and then forming it into large cakes that were baked in the sun. Wappato or duck potato—with its flowers in whorls of three—is often found standing in water; its tuber was described by Lewis and Clark as the most valuable of Indian roots and an important trading item. The reed grass of swampy areas can be converted to string by twisting its fibers. Besides providing food, willows are of value in stabilizing gravel bars which become habitat for plants and animals. The river meanders through grasslands, woodlands, and swampy areas. Tree species include cedar, alder, bigleaf maple, Douglas fir, oak, and cottonwood.

Some birds commonly sighted in this area are the tree swallow, great blue heron, common yellowthroat, green heron, and red-tailed hawk, but more than 130 species of birds can be observed at various times in the different riverine habitats throughout the year.

Activities

Sauvie Island

North of Portland, this island is adjacent to the Sauvie Island Game Management Area, an active migratory region for birds. Wappato plants are found here, a valuable food source and trading material of the Indians.

Mary S. Young State Park

This urban park provides a fun recreation area complete with forests and spacious playfields, 2.5 miles of hiking and bicycling trails, and offers access to the river.

Molalla River State Park

Surrounded by flower and vegetable farms, this developed park area is situated along the Molalla River, which joins the Willamette River inside the park. A great blue heron rookery, 0.75-mile river trail, wetlands, and water sports are featured at the park. Just past the park a ferry crosses the river.

Champoeg State Park

A Visitor Center with a splendid array of information and artifacts is the best way to orient oneself to this park and learn about its significance as the place where the first American government on the Pacific Coast was organized in 1843. In July, an outdoor pageant by the river recreates images of pioneer life in Oregon. Four miles of bicycle trails and 1.5-miles of hiking-only trails hug the river and traverse diverse habitats of woods and prairie, including one of the oldest groves of white oak trees in Oregon.

Willamette Mission State Park

Named for the first Indian Methodist Mission in the Willamette Valley—though unsuccessful—this park has a substantial stand of both filbert and walnut trees, with good numbers of nuts easily plucked off the ground. A ferry accesses the park from the west. Shortly after entering the park, a spur leads to a nature-viewing platform and wildlife blind. Wheelchair-accessible fishing piers border Mission Lake, an old channel of the river since cut off. A hikers-only trail follows the lake to the river, where a bicycling and hiking trail continues for some distance, with a final hiking spur to Windsor Island Slough. A 2-mile equestrian trail begins at the filbert grove. A short trail leads to the world's largest black cottonwood tree—155 feet tall, 26 feet in circumference, and about 260 years old. Visitors

Ferry along Willamette River Greenway by Willamette Mission State Park.

can put in a canoe at Spring Valley access, just upriver off OR 221, and paddle up Windsor Island Slough, or launch from the park boat ramp near the ferry landing and paddle downriver to a section of the park accessible only by boat.

Elijah Bristow State Park

Horseback riders, and hikers also, will find 16 miles of level trails that meander through dense woods and cross bridges over a couple of creeks in a tangle of interconnecting pieces that require a good sense of direction. Some paths are layered with wood chips, others are muddy after a rain. The river is not far off but not often viewed. Frogs are heard in the bordering wetlands and birds nest in the wooded areas. An abundance of blackberries provide summer snacking.

Ecotouring and Safety Concerns

Boaters can check for river warnings and flood information by calling (541) 249-0666. If your boat capsizes, do not try to stand or walk in fast flowing water; keep your feet up and pointed downstream; and swim ashore in calm water. Do not trespass on private land.

Trip Tips

A comprehensive map displaying all the facilities and access points along the river is available from the state parks department. Botany enthusiasts can obtain more information about native plants and field trips by writing to the Bulletin Editor, Native Plant Society of Oregon, 2584 N.W. Savier Street, Portland, OR 97210.

Lower
Rio Grande
Texas

Falcon State Recreation Area
P.O. Box 2
Falcon Heights, Texas 78545
(210) 848-5327

Bentsen-Rio Grande Valley State Park
P.O. Box 988
Mission, TX 78572
(210) 585-1107

Santa Ana National Wildlife Refuge
Route 2, Box 202A
Alamo, Texas 78516
(210) 787-3079

Attractions: Bird watching, hiking, nature study, boating, paddling, fishing, swimming, water sports, photography (Santa Ana has photography blinds.)
Hours/Season: Overnight at state parks day use at Santa Ana; year-round
Fees: Day-use and camping fee at stat
Santa Ana Visitor Center: Open 8:00 A.M. to 4:30 P.M. on weekdays, 9:00 A.M. to 4:30 P.M. on weekends, closed on federal holidays
Picnicking: Three picnic areas at Falcon; two picnic areas at Bentsen-Rio Grande Valley
Camping: Campsites with hookups plus restrooms with showers at both Falcon State Recreation Area and Bentsen–Rio Grande Valley State Park.
Access: Falcon State Recreation Area is 15 miles northwest of Roma, via US 83, FM 2098 and Park Road 46; Bentsen–Rio Grande Valley State Park is about 6 miles southwest of Mission, via US 83, FM 2062, and Park Road 43; Santa Ana National Wildlife Refuge is 7.5 miles south of Alamo, 0.4 mile east of US 81–FM 907 intersection.

Why is birding so enticing? Visit what is left of the wildlife habitat along the lower Rio Grande in its final passage of 190 miles and you'll get interesting answers. For instance, the green jay is a beautiful piece of artistic evolution flying on the wing. His black throat patch comes up to look like a costume-ball mask over his eyes. Its bright blue head stops in a line that changes to emerald green and this color flows to its long, golden-edged tail. The bird's flight is like an exquisite poem. It could star in a Walt Disney production.

Considered one of the ten most endangered of this country's rivers, the habitats bordering the Rio Grande Valley form an international crossroads for animal species arriving from every direction, an oasis in an arid land, a hot spot for bird watchers. For many of the species found here, this is the only place to see them in the United States.

Because of the fertile soil and almost year-round growing season, much of the riverine environment is now developed. Yet a string of parks and wildlife refuges offers varied recreation choices in an area where prime habitat still lures wildlife. Since 1979 and the formation of the Lower Rio Grande Valley National Wildlife Refuge, a concerted effort is being made to protect various preserve units in this valley and to add more units whenever possible to provide wildlife corridors. Small areas simply do not work in conserving species. Probably no other part of this country is so rich in biological value and yet so under threat from development as the lower Rio Grande Valley.

Geology

Though long called a valley, the Rio Grande is really bordered by a flat alluvial plain. Thousands of years of flooding and silt deposition by the Rio Grande, combined with humid gulf winds and a near year-round growing season, turned the Rio Grande Delta into one of the most fertile, species-rich habitats in the country. When the first Europeans arrived in the 16th century, they found 80 miles of impenetrable palm jungle fringing the riverbanks of the delta. As the river changed its course over time, river oxbows were cut off and became isolated ponds, freshwater resacas that can be seen on this tour. Low areas are often places where old resacas slowly filled with sediments.

Lower Rio Grande Valley

Plants and Wildlife

This unique landscape along the lower Rio Grande River is a transition area between temperate and tropical climes, called the Tamaulipan Biotic Province, which today only exists in protected pockets. Many animals must move across disturbed terrain—a manscape—to reach protected areas that nourish some 1,200 plant species.

The dominant tree of riparian woodlands is cedar elm, with hackberry usually codominant and anaqua usually present. Rio Grande ash and willow grow along the river in especially moist places. Texas persimmon, Jerusalem thorn, honey mesquite, sugarberry, Mexican leadtree, Texas ebony, sandpaper tree, bluewood, and spiny hackberry are other trees of the riparian woodland of the Rio Grande Delta topography. A remnant patch of native Sabal palm trees is watered near the mouth of the river.

Examples of plants of the brushlands called thorn-scrub—*matorral* in Spanish—are coyotillo, brasil, prickly pear, snake-eyes (with white berries with a single black seed that looks like an eye), and several kinds of vines that decorate trees.

More than 370 species of birds, including at least 30 tropical species such as olive sparrows, white-tailed hawks, and kiskadee flycatchers comprise the rich birdlife. Robins, cedar waxwings, white pelicans, sandhill cranes, and Cooper's hawks arrive from the north, and vagrants including the brown jay, ringed kingfisher, and clay-colored robin breed here.

Common visitors at bird feeders are the alta mira oriole, green jay, golden-fronted woodpecker, mockingbird, cardinal, and the large, chattering chicken-like chachalaca. These birds all form part of a colorful collage against the vegetation, accompanied by noises that resemble a tropical jungle—an audible picture. A blue bunting, tufted titmouse, or even a spectacular scissor-tailed flycatcher might fly in for breakfast. Look for great horned owl nests in tall trees and be alert for several species of hawks making kills. I was confused at first seeing goldfinch not yet wearing their bright breeding plumage, which is the way I see them up north. And the loan of a spotting scope helped to tentatively identify a pygmy owl that inhabited a box out on Pintail Lake at Santa Ana. At this refuge, the arrival of a crane hawk was causing considerable excitement among birders. The lower Rio Grande Valley is a great place for birders to expand their life list.

Though the birds are the special attraction, 145 target vertebrate species, out of a total of 700 vertebrates, draw both interest and concern for their habitat. Spotted ocelot cats hide amongst the tangled brush. Another cat (both are endangered species), the dark-colored jaguarundi, is even harder to see and to find. The armadillo—the only North American mammal with an armor of heavy, bony plates—digs for insects in the moist soil next to the river. White-tail deer, eastern fox squirrel, collared peccary, bobcat, coyote, Texas Tortoise, Texas spiny lizard, speckled racer, and indigo snake are indicator animals of the lower Rio Grande Forest.

Falcon State Recreation Area

Activities

Bird watching is excellent near campsites that front the lake; the park offers a field checklist. The 572 acres of terrain includes rolling hills covered with thickets of mesquite, huisache, ebony, wild olive, cactus, and native grasses. Serious birders may want to visit the woodlands just below the dam where birding is exceptional along the river. Look for least grebe, green kingfisher, black-bellied duck, elegant white pelican, and the ringed kingfisher, with its loud, harsh, and rattling call.

Fishing in the reservoir is first-class, with black and white bass, crappie, stripers, and huge catfish plentiful. The 60-mile-long, 87,000-acre reservoir is a joint effort between Mexico and the United States. An lighted asphalt airstrip (50 feet wide and 3,000 feet long) is located near the entrance booth of the park.

White pelicans fly overhead at Falcon Lake.

Bentsen–Rio Grande Valley State Park

The birds in this park dine out most of the time at bird feeders that campers hang up on trees, using the locally grown oranges, as well as nuts and bird seed that they bring. As if drawn by a magnet, the birds arrive, along with a certain amount of disputes and taking turns. The mesquite-prickly pear brush and river-bottom woodlands have done the initial job of providing the habitat that attracts so much wildlife to this 585-acre park. Two resaca lakes are located within the park, one quite near the campground. One can spend days just strolling around the campground roads—or simply relaxing at a campsite—searching for various species of birds and wildlife in the trees and bushes. Fox squirrels also visit the campground, quite happy to enjoy nuts on a picnic table. People tend to stay awhile in this park and it becomes a friendly place, with visitors sharing their findings. The park offers a bird checklist.

Two hiking trails help to acquaint one with the vegetation of the area, though the birds are usually out to lunch. At the south end of the park—via the park road—the 1.9-mile Rio Grande Trail is a loop with numbered stations and a spur trail that accesses the river. It is near one of the park resacas, where blue boneset, Berlandier mimosa, and cattails grow. The majority of the vegetation is thorn-scrub, often incorrectly called chaparral, and includes black willow, anacua, sweet acacia, cedar elm, and bloodberry rouge-plant, which is used as a dye in both ink and cosmetic rouge. Nuts, insects, and flowers attract butterflies and other animals, including the Texas leaf-cutter ant, sawbugs, waterfowl, and armadillos. Between the entrance station and the campground is the 1-mile Singing Chaparral Trail. Look for Texas tree snails, which glue themselves to tree trunks when they estivate, waiting for a rain that lures them to crawl around and feed. Antlions—also called doodlebugs—make conical pits and lie in wait for ants. Listen for both mourning and white-winged doves.

Santa Ana National Wildlife Refuge

This wildlife refuge consists of 2,080 acres of thick, brushy growth that is typical of the valley before agriculture changed it. An open-air, interpretive wildlife tram operates from late November to mid-April, but private vehicles can travel the mostly 7-mile-one-way Refuge Drive at other times (9:00 A.M. to 4:30 P.M.). Foot travel is allowed at any time during daylight hours.

A total of 12 miles of trails provide plenty of choices for looping through the refuge on your bird watching walks. Choose among—or combine—three self-guiding nature trails that begin at the Visitor Center. A paved 0.5-mile wheelchair-accessible Santa Ana Trail loops down to Willow Lake and back. A brochure is available with a tree quiz to take while traveling this trail that acquaints the viewer with the junglelike riparian thorn woodland terrain and many trees indigenous only to the Rio Grande Valley. The 1.6-mile Santa Ana's Communities Trail makes a bigger sweep as it accesses Willow Lake and returns. The 2-mile Wildlife Management Trail heads east and weaves around the Pintail Lake area before returning. Feeding stations let you watch the birds easily. Eight more trails—Cattail Lake, Highland, Jaguarundi, Mesquite, Owl, Resaca, Terrace, and Vireo—are accessed via the Terrace Trail or Refuge Drive. Two photography blinds can be reached along the two shorter nature trails.

Ecotouring and Safety Concerns

The Santa Ana NWR prohibits feeding the wildlife and picnicking; wildlife is the priority but you are allowed to observe quietly. Since insects, thorns, and spines are part of refuge, you should check plants before touching them; wear suitable clothing, and take along some insect repellent. Oranges for the birds are okay in the campgrounds, but please do not top them with marshmallows.

14

Salt Plains and Salt Lakes

West

What happens when a lake has no outlet and salt deposits build up from rivers washing into the lake? If the sun shines hot and evaporates water—and if humans lower the level of the basin—salt concentrations increase even more and salt flats edge the lake. Habitats change; fish cannot survive in the high salt content of the water so species that can adapt to this ecosystem move in and thrive—blue-green algae, brine flies, and brine shrimp.

Though often called "dead seas" because few animals tolerate alkali waters, the numbers of these few species are astronomical, fueled by the simple pyramidal food chain that begins with microscopic blue-green algae harvesting sunlight. In winter, this prolific growth colors some alkaline waters a pea-soup green. The algae bloom nourishes brine shrimp and the larvae of brine flies. The eggs of brine flies hatch into larvae and go through a pupa stage before emerging as adult flies. Tiny brine shrimp peak in numbers in summer, die off in winter, and repopulate the water as spring warms it. Birds enjoy the resulting menu of flies and shrimp; they fly in to eat and then move on.

Wind swirls the alkali salt flats, wringing the water out of them, grinding the particles smooth on the surface of the mineral-rich land. The flat whiteness is blinding at midday and a sweeping palette for reflecting the colors of a sunrise or sunset, a stark, inhospitable landscape with an inland sea unpalatable to humans. Where the flats are vast enough, as are those west of the Great Salt Lake, one can actually see the curvature of Earth.

Salt flats vary, however, and can arise from a deltaic river deposit—rather than at a lake's edge—with different major salts. In Oklahoma, the Great Salt Plains have large amounts of gypsum salts which crystallize out as selenite crystals. These plains are a wetter terrain, yet common salt also crusts the surface there and the landscape stretches out flat, not quite dazzling white, but a muddier color.

Great Salt Lake Area

Utah

Attractions: Bird watching, nature study, photography, boating, beaches, geology, visitor center, auto tour
Hours/Season: Overnight in state parks, day use at refuge and rest stops; spring, summer, and fall
Fees: Day-use and camping fees at state parks
Picnicking: Great Salt Lake State Park, at several locations at Antelope Island State park, and at day-use areas of Willard Bay State Park (both north and south marinas)
Camping: Campground at Antelope Island State Park and at both the north marina and the south marina of Willard Bay State Park, both have restrooms with showers; primitive camping at Great Salt Lake State Park
Access: The salt flats at Great Salt Lake State Park are 1.5 miles east of the Saltair Pavilion, off Exit 104 of I-80, 16 miles west of Salt Lake City. Highway rest stops along I-80 west of the lake are adjacent to the salt flats. The Bear River Migratory Bird Refuge is reached by traveling 15 miles west from Brigham City on Forest Road (watch for the large sign) to Bird Refuge Road.

Bear River Migratory Bird Refuge
866 South Main
Brigham City, UT 84302
(801) 723-5887

Utah Division of Parks and Recreation
1636 West North Temple, Suite 116
Salt Lake City, UT 84116
(801) 538-7220

Nothing else in the United States is comparable to the Great Salt Lake and its environs of sweeping salt flats that appear so sterile, a place of mirages and stark whiteness where one sunflower enhances the reality of it. Yet, some of these salt flats, and their adjacent marshes, attract vast numbers of birds as well as some curious humans. Edwin Way Teale called his and his wife Nellie's visit to the Bear River Migratory Bird Refuge near Great Salt Lake "our million-duck day."

For writer and naturalist Terry Tempest Williams, this landscape is also a refuge, one she knows well. In her book, *Refuge,* she chronicles the devastating rise of Great Salt Lake that flooded bird habitat. That 12-foot rise above normal—to 4,212 feet elevation—peaked in 1987. The opposite effect occurred when an earlier record low reached 4,191 feet in 1963 and the salt flats were much more extensive. Today, the refuge is recovering and is again a birding hot spot.

Once a dreaded area of travel for pioneers, the salt flats near the Nevada border are now visited by daring race drivers at the Bonneville Speedway, where record speeds of more than 600 miles per hour have been set on the smooth salt surface. In spring and winter, water sits on the surface of the salt flats until the wind irons and dries the sand into a perfectly flat raceway.

Geology

The Great Salt Lake is a remnant of ancient Lake Bonneville, a vast inland freshwater Pleistocene lake that once covered 20,000 square miles to an extreme depth of 1,100 feet. Wave cuts from Bonneville are visible today as terraces carved on the Wasatch Range to the east.

This area in Utah was a vast highland 65 million years ago before it collapsed along hundreds of faults. Erosion modified the structural blocks into the "basin and range" topography of today's Great Basin—a large, imperfect bowl of ridges and valleys.

Lying on the floor of the Great Basin, the lake has no outlet, and the salts that flow into the lake from the Bear, Jordan, and Weber rivers just accumulate in the water. Except for the Dead Sea, Great Salt Lake is the saltiest body of water in the world, varying from 5 to 27 percent depending on the amount of water it contains. Evaporation intensifies the saltiness—contributed by common sodium chloride and 15 other salts.

Plants and Wildlife

Gnatlike brine flies cluster in dense mats along the shore in July and August. The lake itself supports only three types of organisms: blue-green algae, larvae of the brine flies, and orange brine shrimp—with no fish in the main area of the lake. During the recent high waters, a tiny rainwater killifish took up temporary residence in places where warm-water springs diluted the salt concentration.

Vast numbers of migrating birds pick and choose from various habitats. White pelicans nest on barren Gunnison Island and fish where the Bear River pours freshwater into the lake. Great blue herons, snowy egrets, cattle egrets, and double-crested cormorants need trees, tall shrubs, or man-made structures for nesting. Franklin gulls, black-crowned night herons, and white-faced ibis prefer the habitat of cattails and bulrushes. American avocets, black-necked stilts, and other shorebirds need nothing more for their ground nesting than a few sticks or low-lying clumps of vegetation such as salt grass and pickleweed. The brine shrimp and swarms of brine flies are devoured by the birds. The wetland areas are also home to tiger salamanders, leopard frogs, orchids, buttercups, and rodents.

The Bear River Migratory Bird Refuge has recorded 221 species of birds, with 62 of these nesting on the refuge. Banding of birds by the refuge has shown that a pintail found dead in Ohio wore a band over 17 years old. Other bands have turned up in 31 states and five foreign countries. Large numbers of whistling swans arrive in autumn.

Activities

Sunflowers are occasionally seen on the salt flats of Great Salt Lake.

Great Salt Lake State Park

This park has three areas on the southeast edge of the lake: a marina, the developed area that includes the Saltair Pavilion, and a day-use area (primitive camping is allowed) with a beach of expansive salt flats that one walks across to reach the water. Anyone can float easily in Great Salt Lake. After swimming, bodies turn white as salt crystals dry on the skin. On Wednesdays during the summer, sailing races are scheduled on the lake.

Antelope Island State Park

The beach at Bridger Bay on Antelope Island consists of a long stretch of salt flats situated in a protected cove where one can walk and go out into the water. One accesses the island via a 7.5 mile causeway. Take Exit 335 on I-15, then west on UT 109 and UT 127.

Bear River Migratory Bird Refuge Auto Tour

Located on the delta of the Bear River, where it empties into Great Salt Lake, are 74,000 acres of marshes, uplands, and open water that comprise the Bear River Migratory Bird Refuge. A 12-mile auto-tour loop begins and ends at the old headquarters site (destroyed by high water in the 1980s) and follows a dike road around one of the large refuge impoundments—Unit 2—to allow visitors to view wildlife in marsh, mudflat, and open pool habitats; open daily from sunrise to sunset. At the beginning of the tour is a boardwalk around a natural observation pond and a picture guide that identifies 21 common birds of the refuge. Fishing is permitted only in the old headquarters area (mostly channel catfish). A wheelchair-accessible fishing pier is available. The rest of the refuge is open for fishing only to the birds.

Since the Visitor Center and other refuge buildings—in addition to many dikes—were all destroyed in 1983, efforts are underway to restore dikes and canals, acquire more land, and construct a new, year-round Education Center on the refuge offering interpretive exhibits and educational programs.

To travel around the boundary of the refuge and see more birds, travel west from Brigham City on UT 13 and then continue on US 83 to the turnoff for the Golden Spike National Monument. Then turn left at the fork in the road leading to Promontory. This is a long paved road on the eastern side of the Promontory Mountains with varied views of salt flats, farms, and bird habitat.

Bonneville Salt Flats

Off Interstate 80, near the Nevada border, one can stop at the rest stop and walk on vast expanses of salt flats near the Bonneville Speedway. Exhibits describe the speedway and its history. Most of the 44,000 acres of salt flats in this area are managed by BLM.

Ecotouring and Safety Concerns

Never dive into the Great Salt Lake as injuries will occur due to the heaviness of the water. At Bear River Migratory Bird Refuge, no snowmobiles, all-terrain vehicles, or motorized dirt bikes are allowed on the auto tour. Bicycling, however, is a great way to see the refuge.

Mono Lake
Tufa State Reserve
CALIFORNIA

Mono Lake Tufa State Reserve
P.O. Box 99
Lee Vining, CA 93541
(760) 647-6331

Attractions: Bird watching, geology, tufa towers, nature trails, paddling, photography, naturalist-led walks, evening programs, children activities
Hours/Season: Day use; year-round
Fees: Day-use fee in certain areas
Scenic Area Visitor Center: Off US 395 north of Lee Vining; exhibits on natural and human history; (760) 647-6572
Picnicking: Mono Lake County Park
Camping: Primitive camping is allowed throughout most of the scenic area, but permits are required for campfires. Numerous developed forest camps are found nearby—along Lee Vining Creek, Mill Creek, and CA 158.
Access: The reserve is east and south of the town of Lee Vining, off US 395.

The Mono Basin area is a wonderland of 13,000-foot snow-peaked mountains and glaciers rising above a sage-covered desert dotted with craters and fissures. Within this basin, Mono Lake has changed considerably since the city of Los Angeles diverted streams that flowed into the lake, causing much environmental concern. In 1941, the elevation of the lake was 6,417 feet; now it is 6,379 feet and covers some 60 square miles in area. The reserve was established in 1982 to protect the lake bed lands exposed below the 1941 elevation, which now includes about 17,000 acres bordering the water.

The lake has no outlet and has long filled with salts via freshwater springs and streams entering it from the eastern Sierras. The lake is now two and a half times as salty and eighty times as alkaline as the ocean.

A main attraction is the tufa (pronounced "toofah") towers, limestone (calcium carbonate) formations that have precipitated out of the water when calcium from the underground springs combined with the carbonates of the salty lake water. These porous spires and knobs range from six to eight feet tall, with many of them above water since the lake level has dropped. Smaller sand tufas are composed of a mix of brine-saturated sand, calcium, and carbonates.

Though a court order recently restored the flow of the streams to the lake, complex issues—including the level of the lake and the wind-blown alkali dust effect on air quality—do not offer simple solutions.

Geology

To the north and east of the Mono Basin, volcanism dates back 11 million years. The basin itself has been tilting westward and sinking with the rise of the Sierra peaks during the last three to four million years. The eruption of the 600-year-old Mono Craters—the youngest mountain range in North America—is part of this ongoing process as are the 200-year-old Mono islands. Active steam vents and hot springs in the basin confirm that volcanic activity is still present.

Mono Lake is one of the oldest lakes in the country, more than 700,000 years old. After the peak of the last Ice Age advance some 12,000 years ago, the Mono Basin filled and overflowed. Mono Lake was then five times larger than the modern lake.

The South Tufa Towers are estimated to be 200 to 900 years old, but some towers along the ancient shore could be 13,000 years old. Rain and snow continue to shape them.

Tufa towers at Mono Lake.

Plants and Wildlife

Mono Lake is highly productive biologically, but with only algae, brine shrimp, and brine flies. The female brine fly performs the strange act of walking into the lake in an air bubble to lay her eggs on rocks or tufa. The Kuzedika Paiute Indians valued the pupa stage of the brine fly as a food source and trade item. "Mono" is the Indian word for "brine fly."

Half-inch-long brine shrimp (probably a unique species here) also feed on the vast quantities of algae and are visible in Mono Lake from April to October, peaking at an estimated population of four trillion. Though these animals do not survive the winter, their eggs do—in the lake-bottom mud—and hatch in spring.

The predators at the top of this simple food chain at Mono Lake consist of 80 species of migratory birds. Notable migrants are eared grebes, Wilson's and red-necked phalaropes, and two nesting species—California gulls and snowy plovers. In July and August, about 150,000 phalaropes catch brine flies at the lake before they leave to winter in South America. Even more eared grebes—about 800,000—arrive from August through October and dive for food in the lake. The 50,000 adult California gulls that come to nest in the spring produce 90 percent of the state's offspring of this species. A colony of 400 snowy plovers nests on the windswept alkali flats of the lake's eastern shore. Two bird nesting islands are visible from the shoreline—Negit Island and Paoha Island.

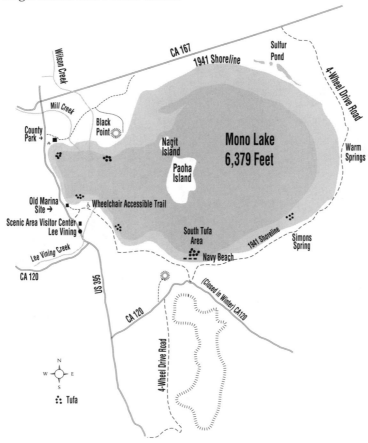

Mono Lake Tufa State Reserve

South Tufa Area

Activities A 1-mile self-guiding nature trail is a showcase for spectacular tufa formations along the south shore of Mono Lake. A nearby trail—back from the shore and accessed from CA 120—leads to the rim and dome of Panum Crater.

Mono Lake County Park

A boardwalk trail leads to striking tufa formations and engaging birdwatching at this unique park on the northwest shore of the lake.

Swimming and Paddling

Swimming in Mono Lake is a buoyant experience. See if you agree with Mark Twain, who thought the alkaline waters were incredibly cleansing. Do keep water from getting in your eyes, as it will sting sharply due to the high salt content. The closest parking area with water access for canoeists and kayakers is at Navy Beach. It is prudent to stay near the shore while paddling among the impressive tufa formations, since sudden high winds do occur.

Ecotouring and Safety Concerns Please do not damage or collect tufa. To protect nesting birds, stay at least one mile away from Paoha and Negit islands and the inlets between April 1 and August 1.

The Great Salt Plains of Oklahoma

Salt Plains National Wildlife Refuge
Refuge Manager
Route 1, Box 76
Jet, OK 73749
(405) 626-4794

Great Salt Plains State Park
Route 1, Box 28
Jet, OK 73749
405) 626-4731

Attractions: Digging for selenite crystals, bird watching, wildlife viewing, nature study, hiking, auto tour of refuge, fishing (handicap dock), water skiing, swimming
Hours/Season: Overnight; selenite crystal digging from April 1 to October 15,
Fees: Free for salt plains and wildlife refuge; fee for camping in state park
Picnicking: Sandy Beach in Great Salt Plains State Park
Camping: The state park has 155 campsites with restrooms and showers, with separate areas for RVs (with hookups) and tents both on the riverfront and by the reservoir; cabins may be reserved by phoning (800) 654-8240, Monday through Friday.

Access: The selenite crystal digging area is located 6 miles west of Jet on US 64, then north on a dirt road for 3 miles, then 1 mile east to the gate (some 40 miles northwest of Enid). Great Salt Plains State Park is 8 miles north of Jet on OK 38. The refuge headquarters is 1 mile west of OK 38 and 2 miles south of OK 11.

If salt plains sound boring, think again. Adults have as much fun as children digging holes in the wet, salty mud (not sticky like the usual mud) and leaving mounds scattered about on the flats. You'll need a shovel or some sort of scooping tool to dig for selenite crystals.

The salt flats are part of a 32,000-acre national wildlife refuge, with 12,000 acres of salt flats, 10,000 acres of impoundment, and 10,000 acres of upland. The refuge is an island that supports many special habitats surrounded by a sea of agricultural lands. During spring and fall migrations, some 24,000 geese and 25,000 ducks are attracted to the wetlands of this refuge. The wildlife refuge is a designated National Natural Landmark.

Though the salt plains were once in the midst of Cherokee Indian Territory, the United States treaty withheld the salt plains for the use of all Indian tribes, since the common salt obtained there was needed by all. The area also had great value for its rich hunting, as vast herds of animals were attracted to the salt supply.

Included within the refuge area are Great Salt Plains Reservoir, the Salt Fork of the Arkansas River, and Great Salt Plains State Park. The park is a perfect place to stay a few days and enjoy crystal digging, swimming, boating, hiking, and fishing in this vast recreational complex. As you sneak glances at the smooth perfection of the waterfall rolling over the dam, and white pelicans skimming across the water, pull out your brochure on the Selenite Crystal Area and prepare yourself for the next day.

Geology

The salt plains area consists of a deltaic river deposit of varied and mixed layers of clay, sand, and gravel measuring up to 27.5 feet deep, with a quite flat salt-encrusted surface that borders the Great Salt Plains Reservoir. Selenite is a crystalline form of the common mineral, gypsum (which is hydrous calcium sulphate and used to make plaster casts for broken bones). In these salt flats, gypsum forms selenite crystals just below the salt-encrusted surface in the wet soil. The chocolate brown color is due to the iron oxide. The finer the soil, the clearer the crystal. Sand and clay particles are incorporated within the crystals, often resulting in an "hourglass" shape only found here. Crystals occur as singles, penetration twins, and clusters. Individual crystals have measured up to seven inches, with complex combinations that can weigh as much as 38 pounds. To crystallize, the minerals in the soil must be present in a certain concentration. If rain dilutes the soil too much, the crystals will dissolve. The water level—nearly saturated with minerals—varies ranging from ground level to five feet below the surface. Common sodium chloride precipitates out onto the surface of the salt plains.

Plants and Wildlife

The salt plains themselves embody a vast unvegetated area. Pondweed, cattails, wild millet, smartweed and other wild plants combine with the 1,300 acres of planted wheat, maize, peas, and rye to feed the waterfowl. Cottonwood, red cedar, willow, and sandhill plum trees are found in certain habitat areas. Forbs and grasses provide wildlife food. Mulberry, hackberry, walnut, elm, and soapberry proliferate in the woodland habitat, which provides cover for deer and wild turkeys.

Snowy plover and the endangered least tern nest on the salt plains, often using the mounds left from crystal digging. In some winters more than 100,000 waterfowl are tallied in the refuge, with Canada geese most abundant, but white-fronted, blue, and snow geese are common. Frequently sighted ducks are mallard, pintail, green-winged teal, and 16 other duck species are recorded species. Sandhill crane and the endangered whooping crane stop during their migrations. Waterbirds include Franklin's gull, avocet, yellowlegs, sandpipers, dowitches, white-faced ibis, and godwits. Both bald and golden eagles winter here. Mississippi kites nest in the refuge yearly. Bobwhite and ring-necked pheasant are common. Look for the state bird—the scissor-tailed flycatcher—which nests in the refuge. In all, 296 species of birds are enough to thrill birders. Mammals of the refuge are white-tailed deer, raccoon, badger, opossum, squirrel, coyote, muskrat, beaver, and bobcat.

Activities

Selenite Crystal Digging

Digging areas are rotated annually. For the best techniques of finding crystals, read the brochure on the selenite crystal area before heading out. Remember that the crystals are fragile, so handle them gently. An observation tower with a 20X spotting scope has been placed at the entrance to the digging area. No permits are required. Cherokee celebrates a Crystal Festival in April, which includes both instructions and a contest for the best crystal specimens uncovered that day.

Eagle Roost Nature Trail

Accessed near the refuge headquarters, this hike is a 1.25-mile loop with numbered stops referenced in an accompanying brochure. The various habitats of marsh, woods, ponds, and Sand Creek lure wildlife. This is a good opportunity to practice your skills at animal track identification (the brochure has diagrams) and to look for evidence of beaver activity.

Harold F. Miller Auto Tour

This 2.5-mile drive will take you to other wildlife habitat areas in the refuge. Marshes, ponds, tree nesting sites, planted feeding fields for wildlife, high boxes for wood duck nesting, a tower for watching undisturbed wildlife, and short trails point out the diverse needs of individual wildlife species. Stops are numbered according to information in the tour brochure.

Ecotouring and Safety Concerns

Do not disturb nesting birds. Do drive only on prescribed routes in the salt plains, as quicksand is found in some areas.

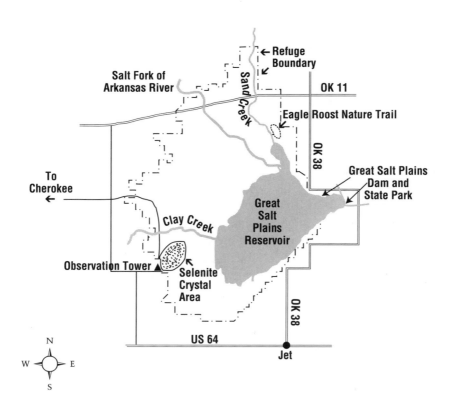

Great Salt Plains

15

FOSSILS AND PETRIFIED WOOD

West

A seashell found high in mountains, the imprint of a leaf in a high desert rock, a naturally preserved fish killed while swallowing a smaller fish, the hardened cast of a clam, a frozen woolly mammoth, a dinosaur footprint hardened in stone, a saber-toothed tiger preserved in tar. All of these are naturally preserved remains of prehistoric life called fossils.

Fossils are magic windows into the past. These clues once hidden and now uncovered inform us that dinosaurs once roamed Earth, provide knowledge about life-forms that support the theory of evolution, reveal how climates have changed, and even help fit together the enigmatic pieces of geological formations that existed long ago.

Only about 300 years old, the science of paleontology—the study of fossils—requires a knowledge of biology. Principles of nature do not change, only geological processes, so finding a certain type of plant or animal tells us about that place and what happened there in that long ago time.

Though fossils are found worldwide, their chancy preservation requires that they escape speedy decomposition. Rapid burial by sediments—or tar, ice, wind-blown sand, ash, or mudflows—is usually the first step. The Burgess Shale of British Columbia has yielded many soft-bodied fossils buried in mudflows on the Cambrian seabed more than 500 million years ago. Geologist Brian Anderson and his assistant Roger Wagerle made a rare fossil find in the Book Cliffs of Utah in 1992. They discovered a large piece of dinosaur skin fossil from a duck-billed hadrosaur, preserved because it was rapidly buried in the bed of a slow-moving river and identified from nearby bone fragments. But usually, various physical processes cause the soft parts of organisms to disintegrate. Sediments harden into rock, layers pile up, and minerals circulating in water impregnate the organisms, transforming them slowly to stony likenesses or perhaps just imprints of their former selves. Since sediments are carried by water, most fossils are found where water was once present—floodplains, seas, swamps, streams, or lakes.

Millions of years later, weathering—or human-related activities—exposes these fossils and paleontologists carefully complete their removal from the rocks, sometimes having to solve an intricate puzzle of bits and pieces in order to reassemble the organism. It is important to record the fossil's exact location in the geological terrain to determine information about climate and ecosystems of that time long ago when the plant or animal was alive. This science is now so advanced that subtle changes in habitats through time can be determined. With a time frame of millions of years, it is difficult to imagine that ancient soils have been preserved well enough to learn prior climatic conditions such as temperature. Even the orientation of fossil bones helps illuminate eddies, backwaters, and gravel bars of rivers that flowed millions of years ago.

Like bones that turn to stone, buried trees can also be petrified and then uncovered and strewn about the landscape. Water carrying mineral-laden silica deposits crystals of quartz throughout much of the tree's structure. When conditions are right, vast quantities of petrified wood are found in one area. To see huge chunks of once-living trees now glowing with colorful minerals, a collection of gems tossed about for viewing, is quite an enchanting sight.

Learning about fossils and petrified wood makes one ponder: What will the future reveal of life today?

John Day Fossil Beds National Monument
OREGON

John Day Fossil Beds
National Monument
420 West Main Street
John Day, OR 97845
(541) 575-0721

Attractions: Hiking, geology, fossils, badlands, photography, exhibits, history
Hours/Season: Day use; year-round
Fees: None
Visitor Center: Located off OR 19 in the Sheep Rock Unit with fossils, exhibits, and video; open daily March through October from 8:30 A.M. to 5:00 P.M., closed in winter on weekends and holidays
Picnicking: Cant Ranch Visitor Center and Foree Area in Sheep Rock Unit; Painted Hills Unit near information area; and at east entry to Clarno Unit
Camping: No campground in the monument

Access: The Sheep Rock Unit is 5 miles northwest of Dayville, off US 26 and OR 19. Painted Hills is 6 miles northwest of Mitchell, via US 26 and a signed county road. Clarno is 20 miles west of Fossil, off OR 218.

Three units make up the John Day Fossil Beds National Monument: Sheep Rock, Painted Hills, and Clarno. Together, these 14,000 acres have yielded diverse plant and animal fossils that span 40 million years. Paleontologist R.W. Chaney wrote that "... no region in the world shows more complete sequences of tertiary land populations ... than the John Day Basin."

An excellent entry location is via the 1,300-foot-deep Picture Gorge at the south boundary of the Sheep Rock Unit, where 17 layers of basalt from hot lava flows have been cut through by the John Day River. The scenery changes quickly here, though, as one passes Sheep Rock and arrives for a comprehensive orientation to the monument at the historic Cant Ranch Visitor Center. Do not miss the excellent, introductory video produced by students at small Dayville High School that won an award. Informative fossil and geology exhibits are offered at the center, and from July 1 through Labor Day, a ranger explains fossil preparation in a small rustic laboratory behind the center. Bring a picnic and enjoy the spacious grounds of this old ranch property. Past the center, at a bend in the John Day River, look for impressive Cathedral Rock, a huge block of John Day Formation that slid down a high bluff and caused the river to change its course.

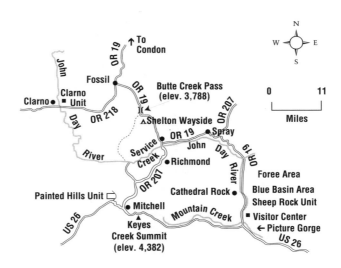

John Day Fossil Beds National Monument

Photographers are drawn to the Painted Hills Unit and you've probably seen the surrealistic colors captured by these professionals when the light is right, often with a bloom of spring flowers at the foot of these badlands. I still remember the emotional pull of this place shortly after sunrise when coyotes were howling in the distance.

A walk amongst the pinnacles at Clarno gives visitors a surprising look at how plants leave their imprints in rocks over the ages during geological events. The Clarno nutbeds are recognized as one of the finest fossil plant locations in the world.

Back in the 1860s, when paleontology was still a relatively new science, a young frontier minister named Thomas Condon recognized the potential of the John Day basin as an important site for finding fossils. He later became the first state geologist of Oregon. By the late 19th century, paleontologists had sent hundreds of specimens from this area to researchers at Yale, Princeton, and the Smithsonian.

Geology

The oldest geological records of the area are found in the Clarno Formation of 50 to 35 million years ago. Paleontologists have learned—from the splendid findings of fossil seeds, nuts, fruits, leaves, branches, and roots—that the terrain here at that time was a tropical to subtropical forest.

Many types of environments existed in this landscape 37 to 20 million years ago, which the John Day Formation spans. Deciduous forests grew then and there was great biological diversity, with more than a 100 groups of mammals that included dogs, cats, swine, oredonts, horses, camels, rhinoceroses, and rodents. It was a time of multiple volcanic events, with much deposition of volcanic ash, which allows accurate radiometric dating.

The Mascall Formation is between 15 and 12 million years old. Basalt was weathering into soil that nourished grasses and mixed hardwood forest in a moderate climate.

Sheep Rock and John Day River at John Day Fossil Beds National Monument.

Among these savannahs many animals roamed, with a resurgence of large mammals—camels, bears, rhinos, bear-dogs, and gomphotheres (early elephants).

Fewer fossils are found in the Rattlesnake Formation—8 to 6 million years old—but they still present an interesting assortment of fragment bones of peccaries, pronghorns, sloths, horses, and others that bridge the past and the present. The many grazing animals indicate a dryer and cooler climate and considerable grasslands. Erosion continues today.

Claystone is comprised of many colors because of the 12 elements, plus 17 trace ones, that mix in a variety of ways to produce these colorful badlands.

Plants and Wildlife

Plants do not vegetate the dense hills of claystone because they have a great thirst for water that is not available here. Bright yellow flowers of Chaenactis and bee-plant do grow, however, in the crevasses and gullies of the rusty-red hills. Mosses grow on the basalts. Deer and antelope create trails as they cross the land, and coyotes are heard and seen.

Activities

Sheep Rock Unit

Two trailheads are located in the Blue Basin area, 3 miles north of the Visitor Center. The 0.5-mile "Island in Time" interpretive trail takes the hiker into blue-green canyons. A more strenuous option is the 3-mile Overlook Trail that climbs to the rim of Blue Basin where one has a good view of the valley's badlands.

At the Foree area, 7.9 miles north of the center, two short trails wander about a geological landscape of sculpted John Day Formation sediments capped by huge flows of Picture Gorge basalt.

Painted Hills Unit

In this unit, stop at the Painted Hills Overlook to appreciated the panorama of colorful badlands. To the east is Sutton Mountain, where lava flows contain shades of red, pink, buff, gold, bronze, and black. A 0.5-mile trail edges along the ridgetop south from the overlook. For a higher viewpoint, hike the strenuous 0.75-mile Carrol Rim Trail originating across from where you entered the viewpoint road. Continue on the park road and turn right to hike the 0.25-mile Painted Cove Trail that circles a colorful hill. Two miles from the Painted Hills Overlook is an important scientific site, reached by hiking the 0.25-mile Leaf Hill Trail, where there is a small collection of fossils that were found in these hills of shale.

Clarno Unit

Two trails—Trail of the Fossils and the Clarno Arch Trail—begin at the base of the Clarno Palisades and head up through the lahars or ash-laden mudflows. This interpretive trail points out many plant fossils embedded in the rocks.

Visitor Center-Painted Hills Road Log

A handout is available at the Visitor Center that points out detailed geological and fossil highlights along the 75-mile drive to the Painted Hills Unit.

Ecotouring and Safety Concerns

Please remember that collecting in the monument is illegal. One must stay on the trails because of fragile, often unseen, fossils.

Badlands National Park
SOUTH DAKOTA

Badlands National Park
P.O. Box 6
Interior, SD 57750
(605) 433-5361

Attractions: Geology, fossils, hiking, backpacking, visitor centers, photography, interpretive programs and hikes, campground amphitheater, concessionaire with lodging, food, and gifts
Hours/Season: Overnight; year-round
Fees: Entry fee per vehicle and for camping
Picnicking: Ben Reifel Visitor Center, Journey to Wounded Knee Overlook, Conata
Camping: Cedar Pass Campground has sites and restrooms, primitive campground in Sage Creek Wilderness Area; contact a ranger before camping in the backcountry.
Access: From US 90, via Exit 131 or Exit 110 at Wall, via SD 44 from the south and east (78 miles from White River)

The name does not do justice to the beauty of these badlands striped with red clay-rich layers amidst the soft green of grasslands where bison roam and graze as in a forgotten era. In some areas, there are only rocks, starkly eroded in knobs, clastic dikes, armored mud balls, spires, and buttes—as if the landscape was on the moon. Yet, for the most part, the terrain has a long history of life. Humans have inhabited these badlands for more than 12,000 years; the earliest were mammoth hunters. Before that, the animal species were various and numerous, later buried, and now exposed and excavated to yield one of the country's richest fossil finds, with more than 300 fossil animal species identified. A recent dig uncovered an ancient pig-like animal with sturdy tusks, an *Archaeotherium.*

The park was established to preserve scenery, protect fossils and wildlife, and to conserve the mixed-grass prairie. Surrounding the parkland is the Buffalo Gap National Grassland. The elevation at the visitor center is 2,443 feet and the weather is very inconsistent, sometimes quite gusty, with hot, clear summer days.

Geology

The oldest rock in the park is the 65 million-year-old layer of black rock called Pierre Shale, which formed at the bottom of an ancient sea. At the close of the Eocene Epoch, 34 million years ago, the sea had retreated and the land here was a marshy plain with sluggish streams. Sediments were deposited during the Eocene and the following Oligocene Epoch. At the close of the Oligocene, volcanic eruptions to the west and southwest blew vast amounts of ash that became the whitish layer now visible near the top of the Badlands.

Periodic floods buried countless animals and they became fossilized in the red soil to form a fossil soil called a paeosol. These badlands are one of the richest fossil beds known, with the Oligocene layer so varied that it has earned the name, "Golden Age of Mammals."

Wind, rain, and frost have weathered the rock formations and produced a landscape of badlands as a wonderful array of fossil bones was uncovered. As time progressed, the climate changed, favoring the growth of grasslands and proliferation of different animals that thrived on the grasses.

Plants and Wildlife

The park, particularly in the wilderness area, contains remnants of once-great grasslands of mixed and short prairie grasses. Two wildflowers illustrate varied adaptations: Barr's milkvetch is a perennial living 40 or 50 years with a long root while Visher's buckwheat buries seeds that sprout in spring rains. Yucca is seen on barren slopes, while wetter areas nourish cottonwoods, wild roses, and skunkbush sumac. Of the 460 species of plants in the park, 68 are aliens.

The most notable wildlife are the 400 to 500 bison and bighorn sheep that were once exterminated from the area, but have been reintroduced. Bison are best seen in the Sage Creek area among the natural grasses that tie them together in the grassland ecosystem. Roberts Prairie Dog Town can be seen along the Sage Creek Road (unpaved). Pronghorns, mule deer, badgers, coyotes, jackrabbits, porcupines, chipmunks, mice, burrowing owls, and bats inhabit the park. Both desert and eastern chipmunks meet at this midway location. Snakes include prairie rattlesnakes, yellow-bellied racers, and bullsnakes. Bird watchers can scan for rock wrens nesting in crevices, white-throated swifts, cliff swallows, and an occasional golden eagle nesting on an inaccessible butte. Reintroduction of the endangered black-footed ferret into the park is being considered.

Activities

Stop at the many overlooks along Loop Road between the Ben Reifel Visitor Center and the exit road to the town of Wall reveal intriguing scenery.

Cliff Shelf Trail

With the trailhead for this 0.5-mile loop located just 0.5 mile northeast of the Visitor Center on Loop Road, it makes a nice excursion to walk up the road to do this hike through a wooded oasis in the midst of arid badlands.

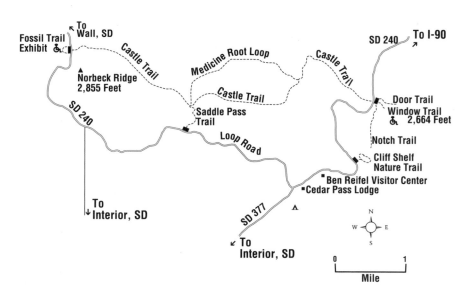

Badlands National Park

The Door Trail

This 0.75-mile-round-trip nature trail passes many fossil soils (87 fossil soils have been identified in the park). Notice the ash layer that caps the buttes, and the nodules of minerals. The trail ends where two canyons merge. This area is one of the most rugged in the park, amidst wildly eroded badlands. It is accessed 2 miles northeast of the Ben Reifel Visitor Center on the Loop Road.

Window Trail

This 0.25-mile-round-trip, wheelchair-accessible trail begins at the same area as the Door Trail and takes the walker to a natural "window" in a badlands wall where one can view an eroded canyon.

Castle Trail

Hikers desiring a longer hike should consider this 5-mile trail between the Door and Window parking area to the Fossil Exhibit Trail. It traverses fairly level grasslands backed by steep badlands. Spur trails connect to other access points.

Fossil Exhibit Trail

This trailhead is 5 miles west of the Visitor Center on Loop Road. When you walk this easy, wheelchair-accessible, 0.25-mile trail on an elevated boardwalk, let your mind envision a time 70 million years ago when huge flying reptiles (pteradons) swooped low to catch fish while swimming plesiosaurs sought the same meal. One might see sea turtles (archelons), coiled shelled ammonitids, and straight shelled baculites as they ejected water to propel their movement. Large pearly clams lived in the mud bottom.

Real fossils are not exhibited along this trail of Oligocene fossils. Vandals have necessitated the use of painted plaster fossil casts, which are housed in con-

Fossil museums feature dinosaur replicas; these are tyrannosaurs.

crete boxes with strong plastic domes (since even these casts of less value

233

still entice vandals). *Merycoidodon,* a member of the oreodont family (close relatives of the camels) and the small Oligocene horse, *Mesohippus,* are on exhibit, as are an Oligocene rhinoceros and an ancestor to the modern rhinoceros. A bizarre addition is the ball-shaped fossil boluses (dung worked and buried by dung beetles). Exhibited with a hyena-like mammal are fossil seeds of hackberry, so rich in calcium that they fossilized, plants that are still widespread today. Fossils of land turtles and snails reveal creatures common on the Oligocene landscape.

Sage Creek Wilderness Area

Though there are no maintained trails, backpackers can orienteer through this area. Bison trails do exist.

Ecotouring and Safety Concerns

It is dangerous to climb badlands as they are steep and give way under your weight. Weather changes quickly here and may bring lightning and high winds. Keep a safe distance from the bison.

Escalante State Park
UTAH

Escalante State Park
P.O. Box 350
Escalante, UT 84726-0350
(801) 826-4466

Attractions: Hiking, petrified wood, photography, wildlife viewing, boating, fishing (ice fishing in winter), swimming, visitor center
Hours/Season: Overnight; year-round
Fees: Day-use or campground fee
Picnicking: One picnic area is near the Petrified Forest Trailhead and other picnic tables edge Wide Hollow Reservoir.
Camping: The park has 22 campsites, restrooms with showers, and group camping is available.
Access: Travel 1 mile west of the town of Escalante on UT Scenic Byway 12; then take signed Wide Hollow Road 1 mile north to park.

Many people visit Petrified Forest National Park, but few know about the enchantment of a quiet walk on the Summerville Cliffs of Escalante State Park. Frequently, one is alone on this trail, and it offers chance to let the mind wander and fill with contemplative thoughts of how so much petrified wood came to be scattered here, some 5.5 million tons.

If exploring such a place—where one can see how the petrified wood naturally collected—is new to you, you may be surprised at the richness of the colors. No longer do the wood colors predominate, rather any spaces that could collect minerals are filled with a marvelous variety of colored crystals—rosy red, amethyst, gold, purple, amber, silver, and orange. Adding to the intrigue is the weaving of these colors, the patterning of cracks, the veins of variation, and the overlays of contrasting lichens. One tends to walk slowly amidst this outdoor art gallery and think back to a time when the Fremont and Anasazi Indians used these lovely pieces in tool making.

Although the park name honors Father Escalante because of his expedition to Utah, he was not actually in this area. The meaning of the word "escalante"—to escalate upward, like stairsteps—very aptly applies to this region of plateaus.

Start your visit with a trip to the Visitor Center to see the display of petrified wood, petrified dinosaur bones, ammonite fossils, and shell fossils, as well as information about the slow process of forming petrified wood. And for those who are not up to hiking, the park offers easy access to the Petrified Wood Cove, adjacent to the campground.

Wide Hollow Reservoir at Escalante State Park, seen from the nature trail.

Geology

If you look north from the Petrified Forest Trail, the Morrison Badlands can be seen from your location atop the Summerville Cliffs. These badlands, long called the "Painted Desert," are rich in the minerals that infuse petrified wood with rich insertions of crystalline colors. Erosion loosened these jeweled rocks from their previously buried positions and washed them down to this location.

This strata was once a shallow lake bed, streambed, or floodplain rich in nutrients where plants proliferated and dinosaurs gathered. Tall conifers and cycads (ancestors of palm trees and some ferns) grew in the area. At that time, towering volcanos were seen to the northwest and a large mountain range rose to the east, the ancestral Rockies.

Black boulders visible along the beginning of the Petrified Forest Trail are the remains of lava flows that occurred less than 50 million years ago when Boulder Mountain erupted, long before the uplifting of the Colorado Plateau that began 10 million years ago and raised the region 5,000 feet. The park is now at 5,800 feet elevation.

Plants and Wildlife

The desert terrain to the north of the campsites nutures prickly pear, Engelmann's hedgehog, and colorful wildflowers in season. A "pygmy forest" of pinyon pine and Utah juniper is traversed on the Petrified Forest Trail. Though small, these trees are hundreds of years old. Cottonwood trees thrive along the wet shores of Wide Hollow Reservoir. It is difficult for scientists to find petrified wood specimens in which the trees are preserved enough to be recognized, but several conifers have been identified.

The park's wetland bird watching is good enough to get it listed in the Utah Wildlife Viewing Guide, one of only a few such areas in the harsh rocky land of southern Utah. In late summer, I sighted several immature white-faced ibis on the reservoir, as well as geese and coots. Boat-tailed grackles are frequent visitors to the campground area and chukars hang out there on the ground, tame enough to eat out of one's hand. Other wildlife in the area are deer, coyote, small rodents, and lizards. Anglers can find bluegill and rainbow trout in Wide Hollow Reservoir.

Petrified Forest Nature Trail

Activities

Pick up a brochure for this 1-mile, self-guiding trail. The trail initially climbs considerably, past lava rocks and precariously balanced boulders colored with lichens, but then levels out for most of the hike through a pygmy forest. Notice the glaze of desert varnish, shiny black or rusty oxidation products of iron and manganese, that has baked on some rocks during thousands of years of sun, heat, and moisture. As pieces of petrified wood begin to appear along the trail, slow down, and soon the deposits become more frequent, particularly in washes. Near trail's end, a 5-foot section of a fossilized log comes into view and one can discern the color changes from the center to the outside rings of the tree. The trail also provides vistas of the surrounding geology and the town of Escalante in the distance.

Sleeping Rainbows Trail

This 0.75-mile trail branches off from the Petrified Forest Trail and accesses vast deposits of petrified wood, but it is a strenuous, scrambling over rocks affair that descends sharply and then reclimbs to return to the nature trail.

Large chunks of petrified wood seen along the Petrifed Forest Trail at Escalante State Park.

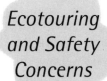

Ecotouring and Safety Concerns

It is very tempting to pick up an exquisite piece of petrified wood for a souvenir when walking along the petrified wood trails. It is *strictly forbidden!*

Petrified Forest National Park

ARIZONA

Petrified Forest
National Park
Superintendent
AZ 86028
(520) 524-6228

Attractions: Geology, petrified logs, hiking, backpacking, scenic drive, photography, petroglyphs, scenic drive, visitor center, museum, prehistory
Hours/Season: Day use (except for backcountry camping); year-round
Fees: Entry fee per vehicle
Picnicking: Chinde Point, Rainbow Forest
Camping: Wilderness camping only (with a permit) in Painted Desert Wilderness with entry at Kahina Point, or Rainbow Forest with entry point at Flattops and camping 0.5 mile from the road
Access: From the west, take US 180 from Holbrook to south entrance, drive north through park, and exit at Interstate 40. From the east, leave I-40 at the north entrance, exit at south entrance and take US 180 to I-40 at Holbrook.

Surprises await travelers who find the approaching views to the park rather ordinary desert. Along the park drive are many wonders in a landscape that urges close inspection. One must get out and walk to individually inspect the petrified wood and its spectacular variations. And though the vision of badlands is quite mystical as a vast landscape, one should gaze silently at the shapes and colorful striations of the eroding badlands that surround you on the Blue Mesa Trail, where they are within touching distance and the distant countryside is blocked from your view.

Fossils found in the park since 1981 include those of the earliest dinosaurs, strange giant reptiles, weird-looking plants, and unusual fish. Ongoing fossil research in the park continues to reveal the life of the Triassic forests 225 million years ago. In 1984, fossil remains of a dinosaur named "Gertie" was discovered and her place in the dinosaur family history remains enigmatic. Nearly 200 species of fossil plants have been identified through ancient pollen and leaf impressions analyzed with a variety of micro-paleontology techniques. Clam beds, shark teeth, and fish scales hint at the ancient presence of ponds and lakes. Each rainstorm reshapes the land and exposes more fossil discoveries.

The more recent past is that of the Indians in this area and the rock art they left behind, which always intrigues with the motivations that spawned it. Be especially alert for petroglyphs at stops along the scenic drive.

Rainbow Forest Museum has exhibits, history, an interpretive trail, fossil casts and bones, and a wonderful petroglyph of a huge cougar.

Look for petroglyphs in red rock country.

Geology

What is now high, dry tableland in the area of the park was once a tropical floodplain crossed by streams 225 million years ago, with tall pine-like trees along the headwaters to the south and a variety of ferns and other plants. Giant fish-eating amphibians, crocodile-like reptiles, and small dinosaurs roamed the area. When fallen trees and other organisms were covered by silt, mud, and volcanic ash, the slow process of fossilization occurred as ground waters carrying silica seeped into logs and dead species of plants and animals. The region then flooded and was covered with freshwater sediments. Uplift pushed and cracked underground logs and raised the land onto the Colorado Plateau.

The badlands of the park are part of the Chinle Formation, once a relatively flat series of sedimentary layers. The rounded hills that form the Painted Desert were once capped with harder materials of sandstone, limestone, and lava, but these substances eroded away, exposing the softer porous clays underneath which eroded faster. Today, during a rain, these bentonitic clays absorb huge amounts of water. The sun then bakes them and they crack and crumble. The next rain easily carries pieces down gullies, and thus the badlands undergo continual sculpting, slowed somewhat by the scarcity of rain.

Erosion and weathering continue as time passes and some of the fossil-bearing material that resides as deep as 300 feet below the surface is slowly exposed.

Plants and Wildlife

Petrified Forest National Park is mostly badlands with little vegetation, though splashes of color arise in some areas from the prickly pear, cholla cactus, desert primrose, asters, mariposa lily, and Indian paintbrush. With only 9 inches of annual rainfall, one immediately thinks desert, but there are plant communities and ecosystems of the shortgrass prairie, though these are marginal and found on the loamier soils of the higher mesas. Blue gramma is the dominant grass species. Four-wing saltbush and black greasewood—both called halophytes or salt lovers—and Mormon tea have adapted to this terrain.

The large conifers that became petrified logs are of the genus *Araucarioxylon,* now extinct but related to today's subtropical Norfolk Island Pine and the monkey puzzle tree.

More than 60 species of mammals, 20 species of reptiles, a few amphibians, and at least 203 bird species have been identified within the park. The most frequent animal sighting in the park is the pronghorn, North America's fastest land mammal. A few mule deer wander about, and coyote, jackrabbit, cottontail, fox, porcupine, prairie dog, collared lizard, kangaroo rat, raven, and golden eagle are in the area. In the daylight, look for tracks.

Activities

Scenic Drive Points

The 27-mile drive through the park has frequent pull-outs and overlooks (some with trailheads; see individual descriptions)—all very worthwhile—so plan for a leisurely day. The Flattops are remnants of a continuous layer of sandstone capping parts of the area. At the Jasper Forest Overlook, look over a terrain with petrified logs strewn about. The Navajos thought these logs were the bones of Yietso, an ancient monster. Agate Bridge is a huge petrified log that spans an open space to form a bridge. One cowboy dared to cross this bridge successfully (the park forbids even standing on it now). The Tepees are aptly named badlands formations. The fine collection of rock art on Newspaper Rock can be viewed from an overlook or by descending 120 steps down a steep cliff face. Chinde Point and several other nearby overlooks provide varied perspectives of the wonder of the Painted Desert. The Painted Desert Inn at Kachina Point was once a waystop for travelers on famed Route 66. The Painted Desert Visitor Center, at the north end of the drive, has a 17-minute film on the formation of petrified wood.

Giant Logs Self-Guiding Trail

Accessed from the Rainbow Forest Museum, take a brochure and explore this relatively easy 0.5-mile trail with intermittent stops. It is a fine introduction to the geology of the area, with petrified wood logs that looked sawed but were really cracked by nature's forces during periods of uplift when they were buried. One log weighs 44 tons and is 35 feet long. Notice the various colors, with yellow, orange, rust, and red—the result of iron compounds—and manganese and carbon producing the blue, black, and purple hues.

Long Logs Trail

A short path cuts through a concentration of particularly big logs, some over 100 feet long. Near the end of the trail is Agate House, a pretty structure built some 700 years ago of agatized wood thought to be a traveler's stop of perhaps seven rooms. It was partially rebuilt by the park service.

Crystal Forest Nature Trail

Discovered by Army mappers and surveyors in the mid–1880s, the amount of petrified wood collected in this area was so great that concerns arose and President Theodore Roosevelt established the area as a national monument in 1906. If you look carefully, you will see cracks and hollows in logs that once held quartz and amethyst crystals removed by souvenir and gem collectors. The trail is an 0.8 mile paved loop.

Blue Mesa Loop Trail

A 3-mile spur road leads to this 1-mile-loop hike that descends to the bottom of badlands, revealing interesting striations of color and petrified wood on the slopes—a pretty walk that focuses your attention on your surroundings from this low perspective. Pedestal logs are visible atop soft clays that eventually erode, the log falls, and the cycle begins anew.

Puerco Indian Ruin Trail

Anasazi Indians left these ruins that once numbered as many as 75 rooms, occupied from 1100 to 1200 and from 1300 to 1400, but vacant when Spanish explorers arrived in 1540. Exciting petroglyphs can be seen on a nearby jumble of boulders; one looks like a turtle, several are bighorn sheep, and one is possibly a great blue heron (or another wading bird) with a frog in its bill.

Backpacking or Horseback Riding

To camp in either of the two units of the wilderness, obtain a permit at the visitor center or at the museum and depart from either the Flattops or Kachina Point trailheads. There are no established trails but they are not needed so much in open spaces. A topographical map and compass, however, are essential. No grazing is allowed for horses.

Ecotouring and Safety Concerns

Do not climb on logs as they are sharp and dangerous. Violators who remove petrified wood can be fined ($250 minimum), imprisoned, or both. Petrified wood in shops is obtained from collections on private land. Avoid close contact with wildlife (which is always a good idea for both the animal and you); the presence of bubonic plague has been detected in this area.

Trip Tips

Information on fossils is included in the section on Mariscal Canyon area of Big Bend National Park, listed in Chapter 1.

16

GLACIAL LAKES

West

Why is it that some of the most startlingly beautiful landscapes are the most difficult to describe? The emotions are there but the words are not up to the task of describing what the eyes can see, let alone the sum total of the experience. Glacial lakes nestled in snow-peaked mountains can have this effect.

The majestic Rocky Mountains of today rose from the plains in a long series of events that astound geologists with their complexity. This massive collection of ranges stretches from the Brooks Range in Alaska south through Canada, the United States, and into Mexico. The spine of these mountains, though not sharply defined, forms the erratic course of the Continental Divide, and sends waters east and west.

When Pacific plates slid under the West Coast and ocean islands crashed into it, forces rippled on land and the early Rockies rose. They continued to buckle and uplift, to fold and fault, thrusting and mashing from vast underground temperature interactions, building and eroding over and over.

The surface of these mountains was gouged and chiseled by Pleistocene glaciers, which advanced upon the land four times between two million and 10,000 years ago. We know most about the Wisconsin glaciation, the most recent Ice Age, which capped one-third of the continent, though earlier glaciers probably covered even more territory. Glaciers are defined as masses of ice that move slowly due to gravity. We are talking about Antarctic-sized icefields that moved south from the Arctic, the result of lower temperatures and more snowfall. In the mountains, these powerful glaciers whittled and picked up rocks and debris as they moved, scooping out depressions to produce sheer cirque walls and rugged ridges, leaving hanging valleys and cutting cliffs.

V-shaped gorges earlier carved by cascading water were widened into U-shaped canyons as the glaciers plucked their way downward, loosening and moving rocks ranging from chips to house-sized ones. Simulating a giant sanding machine, rocks riding on the bottom of glaciers sculpted the landscape, grinding and polishing. Striations in rocks caused by abrading glaciers reveal the direction of glacial movement. Pressure on the underside of glaciers caused ice to melt and fill cracks, where it refroze and caused more fractures as it expanded, a cycle much repeated.

As the glaciers receded and melted backward, they left piles of unsorted rocks that formed natural dams that soon enclosed glacial lakes. Each deathsite lull of the ice left such a collection of boulders, cobbles, gravel, and sand called end moraines. The farthest point of advance formed a terminal moraine, with rock debris left along the sides of a glacial named lateral moraines. Plants seeded themselves in the glacier debris and wildlife arrived as the land became less harsh around these lovely lakes that sat at the bottom of splendid canyons.

Lake Louise
ALBERTA

Banff National Park
P.O. Box 900
Banff, Alberta TOL 0C0
Canada
(403) 522-3833

Attractions: History, geology, nature study, fishing, paddling (rental canoes available), backpacking, skiing, photography, interpretive programs
Hours/Season: Overnight; year-round
Fees: Entry charge and fee for campground
Lake Louise Information Centre: Information, exhibits, multimedia show on how the Rocky Mountains came to be, publications; open daily in summer from 8:00 A.M. to 10:00 P.M. in the Lake Louise Village, 10:00 A.M. to 6:00 P.M. the rest of the year
Picnicking: Off Lake Louise Drive
Camping: Year-round campground at Lake Louise; backcountry camping with a permit
Access: Lake Louise Information Centre at Lake Louise Village is 58 kilometers (35 miles) northwest of the town of Banff via the Trans-Canada Hwy 1 or the slower, scenic Bow Valley Parkway 1A on the opposite side of the Bow River. Lake Louise is 4.5 kilometers (2.7 miles) west of the village, via Lake Louise Drive.

A red canoe glides across the blue-green water of Lake Louise against an awesome backdrop of glaciers called "The Plain of the Six Glaciers" that hang high above, so obviously an integral link to this glacier-formed lake that seems to disappear into a circle of high peaks. Rising in the center, high above the forested lower slopes, is Mount Victoria, a challenge to mountaineers. In contrast to the alpine terrain, the near end of the lake fronts Chateau Lake Louise, sitting amidst manicured green lawns and flower gardens. A paved walkway rims part of the lake, with trails winding into the mountains, some to rustic teahouses in hanging valleys.

The lake was named after one of the five daughters of England's Queen Victoria. Part of Banff National Park, this great wilderness area was protected in 1885, Canada's first such park, a wonder of early conservation achievement.

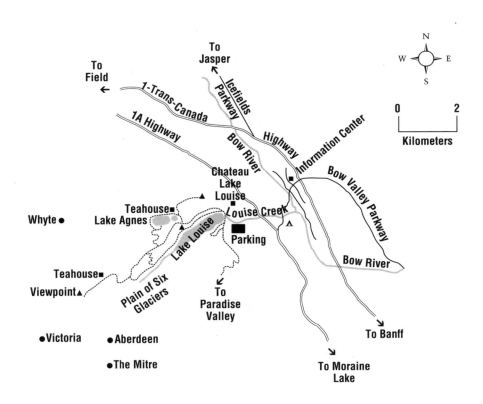

Lake Louise

Geology

The peaks and valleys of this incredible segment of the Rocky Mountains formed many million years ago during a time of complex and violent geologic upheaval. The glaciers and icefields that covered the land between 2 million and 10,000 years ago were enormous and instrumental in shaping the magnificence we view today. Lake Louise was birthed from springs and movement of the Victoria Glacier, which is visible today directly above the lake. Silt and rock dust give the lake its subtle color. The Continental Divide runs along the top of the jagged peaks behind Lake Louise.

Plants and Wildlife

Alpine wildflowers bloom in the short summer as they hug the ground—mountain avens, moss campion, alpine forget-me-not, and purple saxifrage, which contain pigments to screen out the sun's damaging ultraviolet rays. Evergreens line much of the trail to Lake Agnes. Autumn is a time to see golden larch trees.

This is wildlife country with large mammals well represented—mules, white-tailed deer, moose, elk, caribou, cougar, coyote, and wolves—though you will have to do some backcountry trekking to find most of these. Both black bears and grizzly bears inhabit the park, with fewer black bears that mostly stay in the valleys. The number of grizzly bears is larger, but they tend to stay in the higher alpine country. Rocky Mountain bighorn sheep, with their pale brown fur and dull brown horns, can be distinguished from the mountain goats, with their white coats and black horns. Of these mammals, elk and bighorn sheep are found in the highest numbers. Birds include raven, black-billed magpie, Clark's nutcracker, and black swift, a bird that summers in Banff and winters in Costa Rica.

Activities

Connecting Trails

Two paths connect Lake Louise Village and Lake Louise. The 2.7-kilometer Louise Creek Trail (1.6 miles) begins on the downstream side of the Bow River (with a connecting spur soon entering from nearby Lake Louise Campground) and follows a wild mountain stream to Lake Louise. At the intersection with the Tramline Trail, cross the bridge and continue on the Louise Creek Trail to Lake Louise.

The 4.5-kilometer Tramline Trail (2.7 miles) was once the bed of a narrow gauge railway. It begins at the Lake Louise train station, crosses Louise Creek, and rambles to the south before joining the Louise Creek Trail shortly before reaching Lake Louise. The two trails can be combined to form a loop hike.

Lake Louise Lakeshore Stroll

Starting in front of the Chateau, a level trail follows the northwest shore of the lake for 3 kilometers (1.8 miles) and goes beneath the high cliffs (popular with rock climbers) at the far end of the lake before it ends at a flat, muddy plain just past the cliffs. Try this walk on a summer moonlit evening.

Lake Agnes Trail

This trail, paved at first, climbs in 3.6 kilometers (2.1 miles) to Lake Agnes, where a rustic teahouse is located. Situated in a hanging valley 360 meters (1,182 feet) above Lake Louise, Lake Agnes has beehive-shaped mini-mountains on both sides of it that can be climbed on strenuous trails. Most hikers opt for a walk to the other end of the small lake for a snowball fight followed by some delicious refreshments at the teahouse.

Plain of Six Glaciers Trail

This 13-kilometer-round-trip hike (8 miles) begins by taking the Lake Louise Lakeshore Trail and continuing up the valley above a turbulent creek, moraines left by glaciers, and finally reaching the crevassed Victoria Glacier. Look for mountain goats on the slopes of the surrounding glaciated peaks. The Highline Trail joins this trail at 4.1 kilometers (2.5 miles) and a teahouse is reached at 5.5 kilometers (3.3 miles). A viewpoint of Abbot Pass and the glacier-filled gorge called the Death Trap is reached in another 1.3 kilometers (0.8 mile), with the return via the same route. The elevation gain is 360 meters (1,182 feet) to the teahouse and 405 meters (1,330 feet) to the viewpoint.

Ecotouring and Safety Concerns

Prevent human-bear conflicts by keeping your distance and never giving them human food or garbage as as substitute for their natural diet of dandelions, horsetails, ants, and berries. Though there are wildlife walkways under highways that the animals have learned to use, caution is still required for drivers to avoid hitting animals that cross roads.

Trip Tips

Hiking opportunities are many and varied in this large wilderness park. Stop at the visitor center for information on other choices, including a number of hikes led by park interpreters.

Grand Tetons
National Park
WYOMING

Grand Tetons National Park
Superintendent
P.O. Drawer 170
Moose, WY 83012
(307) 739-3600

Attractions: Hiking, backpacking, mountaineering, bicycling, horseback riding, paddling, fishing, geology, photography, wildlife viewing, boating, windsurfing, waterskiing, river float trips, skiing, snowshoeing, interpretive programs

Visitor Centers: Moose Visitor Center is at the south end of Teton Park Road (open daily year-round with reduced schedule in winter; contact point at this time of year); Jenny Lake Visitor Center is 8 miles north of Moose off Teton Park Road (open daily June 5 to September 5); and Colter Bay Visitor Center is at the north end of park off the highway (open daily mid-May through September).

Hours/Season: Overnight (campgrounds open late May through early September); year-round

Fees: Entry fee per vehicle and for campgrounds

Picnicking: Areas near lakes are Cottonwood Creek, String Lake, Colter Bay, and north along Jackson Lake.

Camping: Campgrounds near lakes are at Jenny Lake (tents only and very popular), and a large campground at Colter Bay with nearby showers and a concessionaire trailer village with hookups.

Access: Via US 89/191/26, 4 miles north of Jackson, WY, then northwest on Teton Park Road to access the glacial lakes

I go to this park for a close encounter with its awesome mountain range, its fantastic wildlife encounters, and a series of enchanting glacial lakes. The glacier-carved peaks rise abruptly above the sparkling waters, with no foothills to obscure views. At 13,770 feet, Grand Teton is the highest mountain, but 12 peaks soar above 12,000 feet. The waterfront at Jackson Lake at sunrise is magical as the first warm rays of light enhance the rugged ridges, cirque walls, and jagged peaks that shimmer on the water.

The wildlife is incredible: a beaver swims across a pond carrying a lily pad to its lodge, a moose may be just around the next bend in the trail, Canada geese honk overhead, and white pelicans return to land at dusk in a V-formation.

Geology

The Teton Range began rising nine million years ago with jolting movements along the Teton Fault Zone—accompanied by thrusting within the range along other faults—followed by massive, sporadic earthquakes. The mountain block was uplifted on the west side of the major fault, while the valley dropped to the east to form Jackson Hole. Numerous small glaciers did the final awesome carving of this range, gouged U-shaped canyons between peaks, and formed basins today occupied by glacial lakes—Leigh, Jenny, Bradley, Taggart, and Phelps—which are surrounded by glacial debris called moraines. Jackson Lake was formed by an enormous glacier that flowed south from what is now Yellowstone National Park. In the past 10,000 years, the Snake River cut through moraines and flowed south out of Jackson Lake. The Teton Range is the youngest of the Rocky Mountain systems, but with some of the oldest rocks now visible. At high elevations, a dozen smaller glaciers are remnants of the giant ice-age ones.

Plants and Wildlife

Moraines left by glaciers support forests of lodgepole pine and other conifers where elk and black bear find refuge today after grazing in nearby meadows. These meadows are ablaze with color in early summer with the blooms of yellow columbine, bluebells, red paintbrush, pink daisies, and lavender asters. Dazzling flower displays edge canyon streams; Open, Cascade, and Paintbrush canyons are rewarding destinations. The balsamroot flowering at the edge of Jackson Lake, near the Colter Bay Campground, enhances the photogenic landscape.

String Lake is one of the glacial lakes at Grand Tetons.

Most of the bears are black bears, though one should not eliminate the possibility of seeing a grizzly. Look for large animals where there is natural food; beaver and moose eat willows found in wetlands. At higher elevations during the summer, the country's largest elk herd winter feeds in the valley. Snowshoe hare, golden-mantled squirrel, pikas, coyote, mule deer, pronghorn, bighorn sheep, and bison find habitat in the park. Trumpeter swans often choose the vegetation in Christian Pond for nesting. Osprey, great blue heron, bald eagle, Canada geese, mallard, white pelican, and cinnamon teal are other birds to spot.

Grand Tetons National Park is part of the larger Greater Yellowstone Ecosystem, a great intact natural area that wildlife needs to maintain integrity.

Early morning reflections of the Grand Tetons at Colter Bay.

Paddling and Boating

Activities

With motorboats allowed only on Jackson, Jenny (7.5-horsepower maximum), and Phelps lakes, String and Leigh lakes are good choices for canoes and kayaks and are easily accessible. Sailboats, water skis, windsurfers, and jet skis are permitted only on Jackson Lake. Boating permits for all craft are required. A 1.5-hour interpretive Jackson Lake cruise is led by a ranger (call (307) 543-2811 for fare information).

Hermitage Point Trailhead

A vast system of interconnecting short trails begins a short distance southeast of the Colter Bay Visitor Center, where you can obtain a trail map and make your own choices. A 1.8-mile loop past Swan Lake and Heron Pond is interesting. Some years ago I was fascinated for an afternoon watching beaver activities (and listening to the young inside the beaver lodge) at the latter pond (where the mountain view is inspiring). I almost bumped into the papa beaver before he dove into the pond and slapped his tail loudly to warn the others of my presence. Other larger wildlife and birds are seen in the area.

Cascade Canyon Trail

A scenic trail begins at the east shore boat dock on Jenny Lake and follows the lake for 2 miles before it turns west and climbs 0.5 mile to Hidden Falls. Hike another 0.4 mile to Inspiration Point at 7,200 feet elevation for a total round-trip of 5.8 miles (2 miles via shuttle boat to west side of lake). On the early part of the trail, paths lead off to Moose Ponds, a possible place to spot these large animals.

Taggart Lake Trail

Hike to another glacial lake in 3.2 miles round-trip from the parking area, 3 miles northwest of Moose. This path traverses the Beaver Creek Fire area.

String Lake Loop

From the String Lake picnic area and trailhead, follow the lakeshore north for 0.9 mile to the water crossing near Leigh Lake and climb for 0.8 mile to intersect the Paintbrush Canyon Trail. Turn left and south to return in 1.3 miles to String Lake, a stretch of high openness with views of Jenny Lake. A spur trail of 0.3 mile crosses the light green waters of String Lake; walk back to the trailhead along the entry road (3.3-mile loop).

Death Canyon Trail

Phelps Lake can be viewed on a scenic part of this trail by hiking 0.9 mile to an overlook. Backpackers can continue on the Death Canyon Trail as it climbs into the mountains, but sample this a short distance to feel some good mountain vibes.

Ecotouring and Safety Concerns

Remember that "a fed bear is a dead bear" and that the park is the bears' home; we are visitors. Be alert to avoid sudden encounters with bears; singing or clapping your hands is good, bells do not carry well. NEVER RUN. Photographers are asked to maintain a safe distance of at least 300 feet from large animals, so bring a good telephoto lens. Nesting birds want to raise their young in privacy; it is often essential to their survival.

Trip Tips

For other glacial lakes to visit in the Uinta Mountains of Utah, see the Mirror Lake Scenic Byway in Chapter 6.

APPENDIX

West

Additional Information Sources

National Outdoor Leadership School
288 Main Street
Lander, WY 82520
800-332-4100

National Speleological Society
Cave Avenue
Huntsville, AL 35810
(205) 852-1300

Reading Resources

Abbey, Edward. *Desert Solitaire.* New York: Ballantine Books, 1968.

Abbey, Edward. *Down the River.* New York: E.P. Dutton, 1982.

Allen, John Eliot. *The Magnificent Gateway.* Portland, Oregon: Timber Press, 1979.

Atkinson, Richard. *White Sands, Wind, Sand and Time.* Tuscon, AZ: Southwest Parks and Monuments Association, 1987.

Bannan, Jan Gumprecht. *Sand Dunes.* Minneapolis, MN: CarolRhoda Books, 1989.

Bass, Rick. *The Ninemile Wolves.* New York: Ballantine, 1993.

Bates, Marston. *The Forest and the Sea.* Alexandria, VA: Time-Life Books, 1960.

Berger, Bruce. *The Telling Distance.* Portland, OR: Breitenbush Books, 1989.

Blanchet, M. Wylie. *The Curve of Time.* Seattle, WA: Seal Press, 1993.

Bowden, Charles. *Blue Desert.* Tuscon, AZ: University of Arizona Press, 1986.

Cadieux, Charles. *Wildlife Extinction.* Washington, D.C.: Stone Wall Press, 1991.

Carefoot, Thomas. *Pacific Seashores.* Vancouver, B.C.: J.J. Douglas Ltd., 1977.

Carrighar, Sally. *One Day at Teton Marsh.* New York: Ballantine Books, 1947.

Cummings, Joe. *Baja Handbook.* Chico, CA: Moon Publications, 1994.

Davis, Mary Dymond. *Going Off the Beaten Track.* Chicago, IL: Noble Press, 1992.

Dietrich, William. *The Final Forest.* New York: Simon & Schuster, 1992.

Egan, Timothy. *The Good Rain.* New York: Alfred A. Knopf, Inc., 1990.

Eiseley, Loren. *The Star Thrower.* New York: Harcourt Brace Jovanovich, 1978.

Elias, Thomas S. *Trees of North America.* New York: Van Nostrand Reinhold Company, 1980.

Foreman, Dave and Wolke, Howle. *The Big Outside.* New York: Harmony Books, 1992.

Harris, Stephen L. *Fire & Ice.* Seattle, WA: The Mountaineers, 1980.

Kappel-Smith, Diana. *Desert Time.* Tuson, AZ: University of Arizona Press, 1992.

Kirk, Ruth. *Exploring the Olympic Peninsula* (3rd Ed.). Seattle, WA: University of Washington Press, 1980.

Kozloff, Eugene. *Plants and Animals of the Pacific Northwest.* Seattle, WA: University of Washington Press, 1978.

Kricher, John C., and Morrison, Gordon. *Ecology of Western Forests.* Boston, MA: Houghton Mifflin, 1993.

Lopez, Barry Holstun. *River Notes.* New York: Avon Books, 1979.

Lopez, Barry Holstun. *Desert Notes.* New York: Avon Books, 1976.

Matthiessen, Peter. *Wildlife in America.* New York: Viking, 1987.

McCall, Karen and Dutcher, Jim. *Cougar.* San Francisco, CA: Sierra Club Books, 1992.

McKenny, Margaret. *The Savory Wild Mushroom.* Seattle, WA: University of Washington Press, 1971.

McPhee, John. *Rising From the Plains.* New York: Farrar, Straus & Giroux, 1986.

Meloy, Ellen. *Raven's Exile.* New York: Henry Holt, 1994.

Naar, Jon, and Naar, Alex. *This Land is Your Land.* New York: HarperCollins, 1993.

Nabhan, Gary Paul. *The Desert Smells Like Rain.* San Francisco: North Point Press, 1987.

Peacock, Doug. *Grizzly Years.* New York: Henry Holt, 1990.

Peterson, Roger Tory. *A Field Guide to Western Birds.* Boston, MA: Houghton Mifflin, 1961.

Powell, John Wesley, *Exploration of the Colorado River of the West.* New York: Dover, 1961.

Rawlins, C. L. *Sky's Witness.* New York: Henry Holt, 1992.

Redfern, Ron. *The Making of a Continent.* New York: Times Books, 1983.

Reisner, Marc. *Cadillac Desert.* New York: Viking Penquin, 1986.

Ricketts, Edward F., and Calvin, Jack. *Between Pacific Tides* (4th Ed.). Palo Alto, CA: Stanford University Press, 1968.

Riley, Laura and William. *Guide to the National Refuges.* New York: MacMillan, 1993.

Ross, Cindy and Gladfelter, Todd. *A Hiker's Companion.* Seattle, WA: The Mountaineers Books, 1993.

Ryden, Hope. *Lily Pond.* William New York: William Morrow, 1989.

Savage, Candace, *Peregrine Falcons.* San Francisco, CA: Sierra Club Books, 1992.

Schullery, Paul. *Mountain Time.* New York: Simon & Schuster, 1984.

Sierra Club Guides to the National Parks: The Desert Southwest. New York: Stewart, Tabori & Chang, 1984.

Snyder, Gary. *The Practice of the Wild.* San Francisco: North Point Press, 1990.

Stokes, Lee Stokes. *Geology of Utah.* Salt Lake City: Utah Museum of Natural History and Utah Geological and Mineral Survey, 1988.

Storer, John H. *The Web of Life*. Dubuque, IA: Times Mirror, 1956.

Teale, Edwin Way. *Autumn Across America*. New York: Dodd, Mead & Company, 1956.

Tilden, Freeman. *The National Parks*. New York: Alfred A. Knopf, 1976.

Wiedemann, Alfred M., Dennis, La Rea J., and Smith, Frank H. *Plants of the Oregon Coastal Dunes*. Corvallis, OR: Oregon State University, 1982.

Williams, Terry Tempest. *Refuge*. New York: Pantheon Books, 1991.

Wood, Wendell. *A Walking Guide to Oregon's Ancient Forests*. Portland, OR: Oregon Natural Resources Council, 1991.

Zwinger, Ann Haymond. *The Mysterious Lands*. New York: Truman Talley Books/Plume, 1989.

Zwinger, Ann Haymond. *Run, River, Run: A Naturalist's Journey Down One of the Great Rivers of the American West*. Tuscon, AZ: University of Arizona, 1975.

INDEX

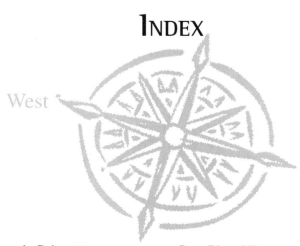

West

ABOUT THE AUTHOR

After working as a research biochemist, Jan Bannan became a freelance writer and photographer so that she could be in the outdoors learning more about natural history and science. Jan specializes in outdoor photography and travel writing that focuses on exploring wild places. She has written and illustrated many magazine and newspaper articles and is the author of *Sand Dunes, Oregon State Parks,* and *Utah State Parks.* Jan lives near the beach in Newport, Oregon.